"This book, which tells the highly interesting story behind two Supreme Court precedents, has it all: heinous crimes, protective judges, dogged journalists, skilled local lawyers, captious Supreme Court justices, and a very fortunate public that, thanks to the *Press-Enterprise*, secured a First Amendment right to attend jury selection and preliminary hearings."

—JAMES T. HAMILTON, Hearst Professor of Communication at Stanford University

"Dan Bernstein has written a wonderful account of two landmark Supreme Court cases that established the right of the press and the public to attend key phases of criminal court proceedings. Meticulously researched and beautifully written, Bernstein's book tells the fascinating story behind these key First Amendment decisions."

—ERWIN CHEMERINSKY, dean and Jesse H. Choper Distinguished Professor of Law at the University of California, Berkeley School of Law

"During the 1970s and 1980s, the U.S. Supreme Court made public access to criminal court proceedings a constitutional right. . . . *Justice in Plain Sight* documents the struggle to achieve those rights and adds to the public's understanding of what makes the American justice system the most transparent and trusted system in the world."

—LUCY DALGLISH, dean of Phillip Merrill College of Journalism at the University of Maryland

"It is hard to believe that thirty years ago, courts closed their doors to the press in criminal court proceedings. Dan Bernstein, armed with local knowledge and extensive research, weaves a gripping narrative of how that changed. His story is filled with high constitutional principles, colorful characters, and frequent peeks behind the scenes at the Supreme Court of the United States, where the legal landscape changed thanks to the determination of a small local newspaper publisher."

—DENNIS J. HUTCHINSON, William Rainey Harper Professor in the College and senior lecturer in law at the University of Chicago and author of *The Man Who Once Was Whizzer White*

"It is meticulously researched, engagingly written, and tells an extraordinarily important and relevant story."

—KATHLEEN CAIRNS, former reporter and editor for Knight-Ridder and author of *The Case of Rose Bird: Gender, Politics, and the California Courts*

"Dan Bernstein's new book disproves two stereotypes about history: first, that it's made only by the famous, and second, that it's boring. This is a tale of small-town heroes, newspaper professionals, and lawyers who (with one possible exception) would have insisted that there was absolutely nothing special about them. That they were just doing their jobs. And yet, purely in the public interest, they fought and won a years-long battle to keep trials open to the public. The tale of that legal struggle touches on California history, newspaper culture, crime and criminal law, legal tactics, Supreme Court politics, and the oddities of human nature. In Dan's capable hands, it's smart, funny, and above all enlightening."

—GEORGE RODRIGUE, two-time winner of the Pulitzer Prize and president and editor of the *Cleveland Plain Dealer*

"I simply loved *Justice in Plain Sight*. It is like a fairy tale with a landscape populated by now-extinct beasts: A local newspaper using its own money to take on prosecutors and judges on behalf of the public interest. A wise and aggressive newspaper editor, Norman Cherniss, who wanted to open up court proceedings. And a newspaper owner, wonderful Tim Hays, who fought all the way to the Supreme Court and won twice but deflected any credit and avoided the spotlight, as was his way. . . . For those who want to understand what journalism can mean to a community, here's a well-told story of a very good newspaper."

—DONALD E. GRAHAM, former publisher of the *Washington Post*

"With meticulous reporting and a compelling narrative, Dan Bernstein brings alive the newsroom, courtrooms, and internal deliberations of U.S. Supreme Court justices in this story of a tenacious newspaper's fight more than thirty years ago to open up jury selection and preliminary hearings in criminal cases. As courts and the media today face political criticism and threats, Bernstein's story of the paper's landmark victories is a timely reminder of how crucial public access is to the integrity of our judicial system."

—MARCIA COYLE, chief Washington correspondent of the *National Law Journal* and author of *The Roberts Court: The Struggle for the Constitution*

"A suspenseful, true-life legal page-turner about honest men and women standing up for freedom. A thoroughly compelling and engaging read."

—JONATHAN EIG, *New York Times* best-selling author of *Ali: A Life*

"The doors of America's courtrooms are open today because one small newspaper in California refused to let justice take place in secret. *Justice in Plain Sight* is a long-overdue look at the legal fight that changed the history of the First Amendment."

—DAVID E. MCCRAW, vice president and deputy general counsel, the New York Times Company

JUSTICE IN PLAIN SIGHT

JUSTICE
IN PLAIN
SIGHT

How a Small-Town Newspaper

and Its Unlikely Lawyer

Opened America's Courtrooms

DAN BERNSTEIN

University of Nebraska Press | Lincoln and London

Library of Congress Cataloging-in-Publication Data

Names: Bernstein, Dan, author.

Title: Justice in plain sight: how a small-town newspaper
and its unlikely lawyer opened America's courtrooms /
Dan Bernstein.

Description: Lincoln: University of Nebraska Press,
[2019] | Includes bibliographical references and index.

Identifiers: LCCN 2018003950

ISBN 9781496202017 (cloth: alk. paper)

ISBN 9781496211989 (epub)

ISBN 9781496211996 (mobi)

ISBN 9781496212009 (pdf)

Subjects: LCSH: Newspaper court reporting—United
States. | Press-Enterprise (Riverside, Calif.) | Conduct of
court proceedings—United States. | Free press and fair
trial—United States. | Journalism, Legal—United States. |
United States. Constitution. 1st Amendment.

Classification: LCC KF9223.5 .B47 2019 | DDC
070.4/49347731—dc23

LC record available at https://lccn.loc.gov/2018003950

Set in Minion Pro by Mikala R. Kolander.

*To the memories of Tim Hays and
Norman Cherniss and for
my patient, plain-speaking, and
long-suffering wife, Candia.*

CONTENTS

ILLUSTRATIONS

JUSTICE IN PLAIN SIGHT

Prologue

This is the story of a rather staid, some might say excruciatingly thorough, family-owned newspaper that set out to do its job: tell readers about shocking crimes in their own backyard. A deadly bank robbery, the brutal rape and murder of a high school girl, and a sinister series of at least a dozen drug-induced murders of elderly hospital patients. All three crimes occurred in Riverside County in less than a year. All three resulted in death penalty trials. But as judges kept slamming courtroom doors on the public and the press, it became impossible to tell the whole story. So the paper fought back. Led by a wealthy, self-effacing publisher who cared deeply about his readers and his community and a short, pipe-smoking executive editor with a stiletto eye for news and the intellect of a constitutional lawyer, the newspaper took two cases to the U.S. Supreme Court in the 1980s. These cases have been cited thousands of times, including in court proceedings stemming from some of the most notorious crimes in recent American history, such as the Aurora theater shooting, the Boston Marathon bombing, and the September 11 terrorist attack of 2001.

The *Press-Enterprise* could not be accused of setting modest goals. It sought nothing less than First Amendment rights for the public and press to attend jury selection and preliminary hearings. By the time the first *Press-Enterprise* case was argued in 1983, the Burger court had spent years wrestling with First Amendment issues affecting the public and the press. This wrestling and jousting played out amid powerful social and political crosscurrents. By 1980 Richard Nixon, the disgraced law-and-order president who appointed the conservative Warren Burger as chief justice, had been gone from

Washington for six years; five years had passed since the last American troops fled Vietnam. The bitter aftertaste of that war, of Watergate, of inner-city riots, George Wallace's "segregation forever," and Bull Connor's fire hoses and attack dogs had cultivated a palpable uneasiness about the people and institutions that ran the cities and counties, the states and the country. Put bluntly, the public—and the press—didn't necessarily trust these entrenched caretakers. Not even the U.S. Supreme Court was immune. On April 21, 1971, more than 150 Vietnam vets locked arms on the courthouse steps, singing, chanting, and imploring the justices to rule on the constitutionality of the war.[1] Two months later a deadlocked Supreme Court artfully dodged a chance to send Muhammad Ali to jail with a unanimous ruling that the Justice Department had committed a technical error, enabling the draft-evading boxer to go free.[2]

By 1980, with the country having sailed past its two hundredth birthday and with the same milestone in sight for its Constitution, defendants in criminal proceedings had been guaranteed a Sixth Amendment right to a "speedy and public" trial for 189 years.[3] But Americans had no constitutional right to witness these trials. They had no constitutional right to determine for themselves, or through firsthand accounts by reporters, whether their criminal justice system was really just and fair. These often mundane proceedings, from preliminary hearings to jury selection to full-blown trials, had long been presumed to be open—until the moment they were closed. Then the public was shut out, and the proceedings were conducted behind closed doors. When, in July 1980, the Supreme Court finally recognized a First Amendment right of access to criminal trials, the public and the press still had no constitutional right to attend jury selection, even in death penalty cases where jurors could be, and were, chosen in secret and later decided whether a defendant was guilty or innocent and whether that defendant should live or die. The public and press had no constitutional right to attend preliminary hearings even though up to 90 percent of all criminal cases never went to trial. These hearings included a judge, prosecutor, defense attorney, the accused, evidence, and testimony. They were very much like a trial and often the only forum where citizens could sit in a courtroom and pass judgment on the fairness of their criminal justice system. But in Riverside County and across the nation, judges weren't allowing the citizens to come in.

In Riverside, California, a city of 170,000 situated squarely between Los Angeles and Palm Springs, Tim Hays, the editor of the hometown paper, was convinced that the public and the press *should* have these constitutional rights. And Norman Cherniss, the paper's executive editor, played no small role in convincing Hays that these rights were an essential antidote to the government's penchant for secrecy. The *Press-Enterprise* didn't crack the top one hundred of the nation's largest dailies; it didn't even crack the top ten of California's largest dailies. But that didn't matter. The paper covered the news. With California's 1978 reinstatement of capital punishment, death penalty trials were increasingly part of the news. Yet judges up and down the state were preventing the public from bearing witness to what was going on in their courtrooms. Over one seven-month span, five Riverside County judges closed their courtrooms to jury selection in death penalty trials.

This story transports readers back to a pre-internet Golden Age when newspapers enjoyed handsome profits and were *the* major provider of in-depth news. It takes readers inside the Supreme Court and even into the exclusive, ornate conference room where only the nine justices meet to state their views and cast their votes. It explains how it came to pass that a skilled, affable Riverside business lawyer with no experience in constitutional law argued two First Amendment cases before the highest court in the land.

This was a time when newspaper owners could afford to wage battles based purely on principle, knowing they were unlikely to boost circulation or ad revenue. Tim Hays and Norman Cherniss believed that a public left in the dark about their government—especially about their justice system—was a public left to speculate about what went on behind closed doors. They believed such speculation eroded the public's confidence in democracy. And, with the help of James David Ward, a lawyer in his late forties whose last brush with constitutional law occurred in law school, they were determined to pound on those doors until they opened.

"They Can't Do That, Can They?"

They had it all planned out: Detonate a diversionary bomb at a nearby office building. When every cop, deputy sheriff, firefighter, and anyone else worthy of the title *first responder* rushed to the scene, the robbers, armed to their eyeballs, would waltz into Security Pacific Bank, take the money, and run. But there is the plan and there is the execution. In this case never the twain did meet.[1]

They picked a bank in Norco, a small Southern California city known for the equestrian trails and public hitching posts that would later inspire its official nickname: "Horsetown USA." They rolled into town on Friday afternoon, May 9, 1980, and made their first mistake. The bomb, placed beneath the building's gas meters, turned out to be such a colossal dud that office workers, noticing a column of black smoke, snuffed the blaze before firefighters arrived. The five robbers, outfitted in fatigue jackets, ponchos, and the obligatory ski masks, stormed the bank, terrorized employees and customers alike, and, of course, demanded money. They couldn't have known that their diversionary explosion had diverted no one. Or that a teller in a bank across the street had spotted the suspicious quintet entering Security Pacific and called the Riverside County Sheriff's Department. They certainly hadn't bargained on encountering Glyn Bolasky, the twenty-four-year-old deputy sheriff who responded to that call in less than sixty seconds, greeting the robbers in the bank parking lot. The unraveling had begun.

One gunman, the driver, died right there in the lot as the robbers and Bolasky traded fire. Bolasky, hit four times, lived. The four surviving suspects, two of them wounded, ditched their disabled van and hijacked a yellow pickup, leaving their dead comrade and the $20,000 behind. With deputies in pursuit—the twenty-five-mile chase reached speeds of ninety miles per hour—the robbers cracked open their arsenal, spraying bullets and hurling homemade bombs that struck patrol cars and injured officers. The worst was yet to come.

Their plan in shambles, the robbers headed north on Interstate 15, the artery that shuttles Southern Californians to Las Vegas and beyond. But the fugitives soon exited the freeway and headed toward the Lytle Creek area, an unforgiving, storm-savaged camping ground in the foothills of the San Gabriel Mountains. They might have figured they'd have clear sailing all the way up to Mt. Baldy Village. But a dirt road had washed out. Soon they had nowhere to go but out the truck and up the mountain, where they had no trouble spotting the lead patrol car rounding a blind curve.

When Riverside County Sheriff's deputy James Evans abruptly came upon the abandoned pickup, he hit the brakes and, taking fire, got out of his car. He fired back until his gun was empty, managing to reload before he was shot in his right eye. A husband and father, James B. Evans was only thirty-nine.

By nightfall, more than two hundred officers, including some who poured in from Los Angeles, some fifty miles to the west, had joined the hunt. By 1:40 p.m. Saturday, three suspects—brothers Christopher and Russell Harven and George Smith—were in custody. The fourth was shot dead by the posse. Smith and the Harven brothers were charged with, among other things, first-degree murder. The Riverside County District Attorney's office announced it would seek the death penalty. The *Press-Enterprise*, a morning and afternoon daily whose circulation hovered around one hundred thousand and served much of Riverside County, including the tiny horse town sixteen miles west of Riverside, would cover the trial. All of it. Including jury selection. That was the plan.

But on August 28, a little more than three months after the Norco bank robbery, the California Supreme Court handed down what a *Press-Enterprise* editorial later called a "rambling" ruling that many California trial court judges would interpret as a green light to close their courtrooms during jury selection in death penalty cases. It became known as the *Hovey* ruling, authored by Chief Justice Rose Bird, who had been appointed to the bench by Governor Jerry Brown. A fierce opponent of capital punishment, Bird voted to overturn every death penalty case that came before her.[2] The *Hovey* ruling came down just two years after Californians reinstated the death penalty and stemmed from an appeal by Richard Adams Hovey, who was sentenced to die for the kidnap and murder of an eight-year-old girl in Northern California.[3] Hovey challenged the fairness of the jury selection in his trial, contending that the "death qualifying" process, during which prospective jurors were probed about their views on capital punishment, resulted in an "unbalanced jury" that favored the prosecution.[4] After discussing an experiment by a University of California psychology professor that strongly suggested that prospective jurors could be prejudiced by fellow jurors' answers to death-qualifying questions,[5] Chief Justice Bird wrote: "In order to minimize the potentially prejudicial effects identified by the Haney study, this court declares . . . that in future capital cases that portion of the *voir dire* of each prospective juror which deals with issues which involve death-qualifying the jury should be done individually and in sequestration."[6] The very next sentence said, "This rule will not in any way affect the open nature of a trial." But that wasn't the line everyone remembered.[7]

What did "in sequestration" mean? It appeared to mean whatever a trial judge wanted it to mean. Following *Hovey*, some judges continued to keep their courtrooms open. Others, from San Diego to Shasta and other sprawling counties in between, opted for secrecy. At least twenty-five judges banned the public and press from some or all of jury selection, or voir dire, in death penalty cases.[8]

More than three decades of deaths, faded memories, and discarded files have made it impossible to pinpoint the exact case that prompted Norman Cherniss, the executive editor of the *Press-Enterprise*, to pick up the phone and call a business lawyer named Jim Ward. When he got Ward on the line, Cherniss told him, "They just kicked my reporter out of a courtroom. They can't do that, can they?"[9] Some who knew Cherniss surmise that he was actually *telling* Ward, not asking him. Decades earlier, Cherniss won a prestigious journalism fellowship and immersed himself in constitutional law at Harvard. He was, as he might have put it, not entirely sympathetic to government secrecy, and the paper had a distinguished history of afflicting Riverside County's corrupt legal establishment. It was easy to picture Cherniss puffing away on his ubiquitous pipe and growling to Ward, "They can't do that, *can* they?"

Ward didn't have a clue. He was bright; there was no doubt about that. And conversant in a kaleidoscope of subjects. He was also an ambitious networker well before the word ever networked its way into the lexicon. He made it a point to meet Howard H "Tim" Hays, the *Press-Enterprise*'s editor and publisher, and the acquaintance resulted in occasional lunches, tennis invitations, and "penny ante" business work for Ward and his law firm. His link to Hays eventually led him to bachelor Cherniss, who asked Ward to write his will and be the executor of his estate. Both were well within Ward's expertise. But closed courtrooms? Constitutional law? "Everybody thinks that attorneys have all this mystical knowledge from law school," said Ward. "But what we really know is how to look things up." So when Cherniss called that day, Ward said he'd look it up.[10]

While he and his young associate, John Boyd, dug into the law books, the phone kept ringing. When a *Press-Enterprise* reporter got kicked out of a courtroom, Cherniss would call, and off Ward would go, to one courtroom or another to protest the closure.[11] The lawyer who jousted in civil court became such a familiar presence in the county's criminal courts that bailiffs began to recognize him. Saw him coming. And no matter how often he showed up, the result was always the same. The judges refused to budge. Between June 1981 and January 1982 alone, five Riverside County judges banned the public and the press from all or part of voir dire in death penalty trials, denying the pleas of *Press-Enterprise* lawyers to keep their courtrooms open.[12]

The Norco bank robbery was a big story for *Press-Enterprise* readers, and the trial was already going to be difficult to cover. The sheer mayhem and bloodiness of it all—thirty-three patrol cars damaged or destroyed, one sheriff's helicopter shot down, eight wounded deputies, two dead robbers, and one dead deputy—helped convince the judge to move the trial out of Riverside because of the pretrial publicity.[13] Not just out of the city, where the courthouse was a leisurely four-block walk from the newspaper. But out of Riverside County, which was roughly the size and shape of Massachusetts and stretched across the vast desert to the Arizona border. Only neighboring San Bernardino surpassed Riverside as the largest county in the United States. But neither county, it seemed, was large enough to host the Norco bank robbery trial, which was headed south to the city of Vista in adjacent San Diego County.

Riverside County Superior Court judge J. David Hennigan would preside over the trial, and the judge and the *Press-Enterprise* had a history. In 1977 four armed men invaded Hennigan's Riverside home and sexually assaulted his wife and daughter. After heated internal debate, the newspaper named Hennigan's wife and adult daughter in the story.[14] Hennigan was an attorney at the time. Now he was on the bench in a death penalty trial in a distant city, and there were concerns that this history might influence the judge's decisions.[15] One of the first decisions Hennigan would have to make was whether jury selection would be open to the public.

The newspaper didn't just take this case seriously; it took it personally. Mel Opotowsky, a senior editor who argued that Hennigan's wife and daughter should be named in the paper's assault story, was also a friend of Jim Evans, the sheriff's deputy killed during the Norco bank robbery chase. When Mary Evans drove her kids to school, the Opotowsky kids rode along.[16] When Evans was killed, Opotowsky did something he had never done before: wrote a lengthy, un-bylined tribute that the executive editor regarded as inappropriate. "Norman objected to it," saying Opotowsky should keep his "opinions out of the news.[17] Now, Evans's alleged killers were about to stand trial in another county.

The newspaper rarely covered jury selection. Veteran court reporter James Richardson could not recall ever sitting through an entire voir dire, let alone writing daily stories about it.[18] But now there was a principle at stake. California voters had reinstated the death penalty. Capital cases were piling up, and the California Supreme Court said jurors should be picked "individually and in sequestration." To some judges, that only meant prospective jurors had to be separated from *each other* so their views on capital punishment would not be influenced by others' answers. But that's not how Judge Hennigan interpreted it. In June 1981, weeks before voir dire was to begin and despite pleas from *Press-Enterprise* lawyer Jim Ward, Hennigan announced that his courtroom would be closed during jury selection to protect the defendants' right to a fair trial. Jury selection would last an astonishing six months.

To Tim Hays, the newspaper's editor and publisher, this was unacceptable. He believed readers had a right to know what their government was doing, especially in cases like this. Norman Cherniss was especially distrustful of this bent toward secrecy. If judges closed jury selection, what would they close next? Mel Opotowsky was on board with both concerns, but there was something he wanted even more: the names of the jurors. Who were these people and how could they be contacted once the trial ended so a reporter could talk to them about the verdict? If a judge closed his courtroom to voir dire, Opotowsky feared it would be more difficult to get those names. And if that happened, *Press-Enterprise* readers wouldn't get the full story.[19]

So the *Press-Enterprise* and Copley Press, publisher of the *San Diego Union-Tribune*, which was covering the trial that had been moved to its county, appealed Hennigan's closure to the state Court of Appeal. This wasn't the first time the two news organizations had teamed up. When a U-T reporter got kicked out of a courtroom, San Diego lawyer Ed McIntyre would appeal, and Jim Ward would support him with a brief. When a *Press-Enterprise* reporter got booted and Ward appealed, McIntyre would return the favor.[20] This time, both papers appealed, and the result was the same: the Court of Appeal backed Hennigan but ordered the voir dire transcript be made public before the first witness was sworn. That wasn't good enough. The newspapers appealed to the California Supreme Court, which refused to hear the case.

That left just one more court that could tell Judge Hennigan and all the other judges that they had been wrong to close their courtrooms for jury selection. In December 1981, with the secret Norco jury selection in its sixth month, the newspapers appealed Hennigan's ruling to the United States Supreme Court.[21] The newspapers' petition for a writ of certiorari—a brief urging the court to hear the case—arrived at a fortuitous, or at least a fluid, time. Just weeks after the Norco bank robbery the U.S. Supreme Court ruled in *Richmond Newspapers, Inc. v. Virginia* that the public finally had a First Amendment right to attend criminal trials. Closure might be permissible, said the court, but only if the judge made specific findings that there was "overriding interest" in keeping the public out. And only if the judge determined that there were no other alternatives to protect a defendant's Sixth Amendment right to a fair trial.[22] Hennigan had not done this. He simply closed the doors for a jury selection that would last half a year. With the Richmond case, it looked like the momentum was swinging the other way. But was jury selection actually part of the trial? If jury selection was conducted in secret, but the transcript was made public before the first witness took the stand, wasn't that enough openness? If the Supreme Court agreed to hear the newspapers' case, these questions might be resolved. But at least four justices would have to vote to hear it, and it would be months before the justices took that vote.

As the Norco closed-jury case wended its way through the courts, Jim Ward found himself in yet another Riverside County courtroom, asking yet another judge to allow the public and the press to witness jury selection. The death penalty defendant was an African American male who had been charged with raping and killing Susan Louise Jordan, a white Riverside high school sophomore. The district attorney and the defendant's lawyer were determined to conduct the voir dire behind closed doors.

2

"You'll Never See Your Daughter Again"

Susan Jordan didn't like walking to school, even though it was just a four-block trek, barely a mile, along Victoria Avenue, Riverside's historic two-lane thoroughfare framed by feathery palm trees and stout eucalyptus. Aside from the traffic, it seemed like a perfectly safe excursion. Susan and her family had lived on Victoria for nine years and never once felt uneasy or threatened.[1] Joggers loped along the scenic avenue's bike path. Cyclists cruised past acres of orange trees. Equestrians occasionally clip-clopped along the landscaped median.

Once the city's economic engine, Victoria Avenue's dense, leafy citrus groves now framed a tranquil corridor a few miles and a century away from the serpentine slab known as California Highway 91. The high school's assistant principal noted that only "a small number of students" walked the avenue to Arlington High simply because not many families lived in the area. But Stanley Connerley added, "You don't see many kids walking Victoria because orange groves are kind of spooky."

It was three days before Halloween, October 28, 1980. A week later, Ronald Reagan would be elected president of the United States. Susan, a sophomore, wouldn't have minded the weather on that Tuesday morning, a day when Riverside's high reached a balmy 78 degrees. With a summer of smog behind it, this was the time of year when Riverside could be breathtakingly beautiful. It was not unheard of for an early storm to rinse the city with a cleansing rain even as it dusted the nearby San Bernardino and San Gabriel mountains with a blanket of snow. Against this glistening backdrop, Riverside's blue skies and swaying palm trees put the city on postcard-perfect display.

Many residents commuted to work in Los Angeles, Orange, and San Bernardino Counties. But every night, they came home to Riverside, a distinctive Southern California city that, despite its 170,000-plus population, had the feel of a small town. Unlike many of its neighbors, whose boundaries bled into one another, Riverside stood alone, with its four colleges, including a University of California campus, and a downtown mountain with a 360-degree view that stretched for miles. Downtown Riverside was hardly vibrant. Many retailers had either folded or bolted to nearby malls, leaving empty buildings and a quiet pedestrian mall behind. Even so, downtown Riverside was a mosaic of eye-catching, architecturally important churches, museums, and office buildings. And then there was the Mission Inn hotel, the majestic national treasure that took root in 1876 and expanded in an eclectic array of architectural styles. Even during its bleakest days—in 1980 it was a city-owned fixer-upper—the inn could still make Riverside residents and tourists feel as if they'd been transported to a European city. Riverside's neighborhoods were a patchwork of old and new, affluent and modest: old-money estates tucked into or near the citrus groves; the "Wood Streets" (Larchwood, Elmwood, Beechwood, etc.) dotted with early twentieth-century stucco homes with clay tile roofs and Craftsman bungalows with shaded verandas—all dwarfed by the cypress and palm trees that lined the parkways. There were the ranch-style Cowboy Streets—Laramie, Shenandoah, Cheyenne—as well as the lower-income Eastside and Casa Blanca neighborhoods, populated mainly by African Americans and Latinos. And there was the inevitable tension between developers of new subdivisions and residents who jealously guarded the city's citrus greenbelt and hillsides. Riverside, like all of Southern California, was growing.

Though well-paying jobs were not as plentiful as those that drew Riversiders to LA and Orange Counties, many locals found work with the government (Riverside was the county seat), the local newspaper, hospitals, school districts and universities, and factories that rolled out precision electronic components, aluminum sheeting, recreational vehicles, and parts for military aircraft. And once Riverside's children had worked their way through elementary and middle school, they could finish up at one of six high schools, including Arlington High, Susan Jordan's school.

The only thing Susan didn't like about the walk to Arlington was carrying all those school books. They were so heavy and ungainly that she usually hitched a ride with her dad. It was no big deal for James Jordan to drop off his daughter before easing onto the 91 for his daily commute to LA. But on this day, October 28, 1980, he had an early appointment in faraway El Segundo, where he worked at the Hughes Aircraft plant. So, on the last day of her life, fifteen-year-old Susan Louise Jordan, a shy, introverted brunette who had been visibly happy days earlier when she completed a business class assignment, scooped up her bundle of books and set out for school. First, though, she escorted her little sister and brother to Harrison Elementary School, something she always did when she walked because the heavy Victoria Avenue traffic worried her. Once she had safely deposited Karen and James, Susan continued on her way.

By 5 p.m. that evening, Susan hadn't come home. James and Angelina Jordan had no idea where their daughter was. "She was quiet, conservative and punctual," Angelina told a *Press-Enterprise* reporter. "I thought maybe she stayed after school to make up some work." But Susan hadn't called. It wasn't like her, not at all. The Jordans called the Riverside police.

James Jordan and neighbors fanned out to search for Susan while Angelina stayed home, hoping and worrying. When the telephone rang, she picked up. It was a chilling conversation, one that she would recite word for word fourteen months later, in court.

"Hello, Mrs. Jordan. Susan isn't home from school yet, is she?"

"No," Mrs. Jordan answered.

"You'll never see your daughter again. You'll find her body on the corner of Victoria and Gibson." Susan Jordan's mother could not believe what she was hearing and asked the caller to repeat what he had just said. "He did, and then hung up."² The second call, this one recorded by police, came later that night. The caller said they could find Susan's identification in a gas station telephone booth several miles away from the Jordan home.

Shortly after 9 p.m., a police dog that had sniffed one of Susan's socks led police to her body in an orange grove near the high school. She was naked from the waist down. She had been strangled with one of her shoelaces. There were leaves and debris in her mouth and nostrils. Her clothes were scattered about. A state criminologist later determined that she had been raped. It was what Deputy District Attorney Robert Spitzer called a "serious case." When there was a serious case, police summoned a deputy DA, and Spitzer happened to be on call that night. As Sergeant Mario Canale drove him to the scene, he said, "Bob, you're never going to look at those orange groves in the same way again."[3]

Albert Greenwood Brown Jr. had raped before. In 1977 he left a bowling alley and slipped through the open window of a Riverside home and hid out until morning. When the parents left for work, leaving two sisters behind, Brown continued to wait. After one sister ran along to school, Brown moved in on the other. He pulled a jacket over the teen's head, grabbed her around the throat and, despite her protestations—"God doesn't want you to do this!"—proceeded to assault her.[4] But he didn't kill her.

Now, the twenty-six-year-old Brown, paroled as a "model prisoner," was back in Riverside. Police were looking for him, though they didn't yet know it. They were looking for a late-model bronze or metallic brown Pontiac Trans Am that had been spotted in the area about the time Susan Jordan was walking to school. They were looking for an African American male in jogging attire who, rather than loping along Victoria Avenue, had bolted out of an orange grove, his sweats covered with dirt. After the *Press-Enterprise* published a description of the car, with its "Made in America" paper license plate, witnesses began to come forward: one of Brown's neighbors recognized the car; several witnesses had seen the Trans Am parked on Victoria; various students and joggers noticed a black man walking, not jogging, behind Susan Jordan. He acted "somewhat strangely," trying to cover his face as students walked by. When police set up a morning roadblock on Victoria Avenue, hoping to snare more witnesses, a brown Trans Am almost drove right into it before pulling to the shoulder.

Albert Brown later told the cops he regularly drove this route to his work at a car dealership. The car dealer told police that Brown always punched in right on time, except for the morning of October 28, when he was a half hour late. Three witnesses identified Brown in a photo lineup. Police put Brown under surveillance and, fearful that he might be destroying evidence, arrested him ten days after Susan Jordan was murdered. When they searched Brown's home, police found Susan Jordan's Spanish textbook and *The Citadel*, a book she had checked out of the Arlington High School library, a book she had lugged to school the morning her dad had a meeting in El Segundo. In a two-minute court hearing, Albert Greenwood Brown Jr. was formally charged with first-degree murder and rape. The Riverside County district attorney's office announced it would seek the death penalty. The *Press-Enterprise* intended to cover the trial.

Jury selection in the death penalty trial of Albert Greenwood Brown Jr. would not begin until October 1981. In March 1981 John Hinckley Jr. attempted to assassinate President Reagan in Washington DC. The same month, Robert Rubane Diaz, a nurse, started working the graveyard shift in the intensive care unit at a small hospital near Riverside. Soon, elderly patients began to die.

3

Slamming the Door

Soon after Riverside Superior Court judge William Mortland issued the call, the first wave of prospective jurors filed into the courtroom where Albert Greenwood Brown Jr. would stand trial for first-degree murder. It was Thursday, August 27, 1981. A certified Riverside scorcher, the temperature would soar well north of 100 degrees. It was good day to be indoors, even for jury duty. Even for unwitting guinea pigs.[1]

Brown's lawyer, Joseph Peter Myers, quickly asked that the proceedings be closed to the public, including the press, arguing that media presence would make jurors reluctant "to give answers from their heart."[2] The bright, affable, though at times thin-skinned Mortland denied the motion. He wanted these prospective jurors to be questioned in full public view. But there was a catch: this was not the actual jury selection for the trial of Susan Louise Jordan's alleged murderer. It was a fake voir dire. An experiment. The "prospective jurors" would not be told they were guinea pigs. They would not serve on the real jury, either.

The rape and murder of Susan Jordan had received so much press coverage, thought Myers, that his client's odds of getting a fair trial in Riverside County, let alone Riverside itself, had diminished to nil. Nine months of stories had created "a lasting impression on the public that Brown is guilty."[3] Though the jury pool would extend well beyond the city limits, the "public" included just under 171,000 Riverside residents, of whom 137,500 were white. There were just 11,776 African Americans, and Albert Greenwood Brown Jr. was one of them.[4] Myers backed up his claim by presenting to the court the results of a publicly funded door-to-door survey of 400 Riverside County residents. It showed such an unusually high awareness of the case that Myers wanted a change of venue. But Judge Mortland wasn't buying it, at least not yet. Instead, he decided to put Myers's contention to the test. He would stage a phony voir dire during which he, Myers, and Deputy Riverside County DA Robert Spitzer would interview fifty "prospective jurors." Spitzer, the prosecutor who hoped to convince a real jury to convict Albert Brown and send him to the gas chamber, said the mock jury selection would shed light on "whether actual jurors in the community can put aside preconceptions about the case." Myers said this testing-the-waters tactic would make it less likely that a higher court would reverse Mortland if the judge denied a change of venue. "He's conscientiously trying to avoid making an error."[5]

Four days later, Mortland stopped the charade. He and the lawyers had questioned just twenty-five prospective jurors, but that was enough to convince the judge that Albert Brown could get a fair trial in the city of Riverside, where Susan Jordan was raped and murdered. It would be several weeks before Mortland summoned the next wave of jurors—the *real* prospective jurors. Would they, like the dress-rehearsal cast, be questioned in public? The Riverside County district attorney's office didn't want this to happen.[6] Neither did Joe Myers. But the *Press-Enterprise* very much wanted the Albert Brown voir dire open to the public and the press. The judge would have to decide.

J. William Mortland had been on the bench for twelve years when the Albert Brown murder trial made its way to his courtroom. Governor Reagan, a Republican, appointed him to the Riverside County Municipal Court in 1969, and Governor Jerry Brown, a Democrat, elevated Mortland to the superior court seven years later. The native Pennsylvanian joined the U.S. Navy in 1951 and graduated second in his class from the University of Southern California Law School in 1957.[7] Regarded as intelligent and always ready with a joke, Mortland's admirers viewed him as a "very careful practitioner" who "made courageous decisions in high-profile matters."[8] But the bright and bald Mortland also struck some as a high-strung sort who "could explode very quickly."[9] Several months before the Albert Brown trial began,

Mortland became so angered at how the press was treating him in unrelated cases that he briefly stopped taking criminal matters all together.[10] Now the *Press-Enterprise* was asking the judge to keep his courtroom open during jury selection. Jim Ward, the newspaper's lawyer, knew it would be an uphill battle. The California Supreme Court had already refused to give the *Press-Enterprise* the time of day when it appealed closed voir dire in the Norco bank robbery death penalty case.

On October 19, 1981, Judge Mortland called Department 5 of the Riverside County Superior Court to order and instructed Ward to make his pitch for public jury selection. The newspaper's lawyer opened with a flourish that was by turns lofty and rigid. "[W]e don't stand here simply as the representative of the Press or a single newspaper, but we stand here representing the right of the public to attend all phases of the trial." The public, he continued, has an "absolute right to attend the trial," asserting that the trial begins with jury selection. "We believe, in many ways, that the selection of the jury is perhaps the most critical portion of the trial" because the jury is "the ultimate decision-making body that will determine the fate of the action."[11]

Ward's oral and written arguments took an everything-but-the-kitchen-sink approach. He invoked the landmark 1980 *Richmond Newspapers* ruling, in which U.S. Supreme Court Chief Justice Warren E. Burger wrote, "without the freedom to attend [criminal] trials . . . important aspects of freedom of speech and of the press could be eviscerated."[12] He noted the Sixth Amendment guaranteed defendants a right to a public trial, but that didn't mean "the defendant has the right to a private trial."[13] And he urged Judge Mortland to accept a particular logic of the First Amendment. "Unless the media is [able] to gather the information, its right to disseminate it is meaningless."[14]

Ward conceded what many reporters on the courts beat knew firsthand: jury selection is "a long and frankly dull process." But the decision to watch it or cover it was the public's and the media's to make. "If you . . . say that . . . prospective jurors have the right *not* to have their views and their feelings aired in public, the same argument could be made regarding witnesses and regarding defendants. You either believe in the right of the public to attend trials and the free and open process of the search for the truth, or you don't believe in it. And the minute you start making exceptions . . . you break down the entire process."[15] Fully expecting the jury to be picked in secret no matter what he said, Ward criticized Mortland for embracing a broad interpretation of the California Supreme Court's 1980 *Hovey* ruling. While it was all right to sequester potential jurors from each other, it was "far too drastic and far too violative of the basic rights to a public trial" to sequester prospective jurors from the press and the public.[16]

When Ward finished, Joseph Peter Myers rose to respond. He was among a dozen or two Riverside private defense lawyers in the rotation to take court-appointed cases. *The People v. Albert Greenwood Brown Jr.* was that kind of case, but at first Myers wasn't sure he wanted any part of it. His daughter was almost the same age as Susan Jordan. Myers even thought she looked a little like Jordan. "But it was a murder case and they're truly interesting."[17] If there was one thing that defined Joseph Peter Myers, it was the broad range of subjects he found interesting.

Born in Hollywood in 1940, he majored in zoology at Pomona College and attended Stanford University Med School until he realized he was in over his head. He eventually received a law degree from USC and, much later while serving on the Riverside school board, earned a master's degree in education from the University of California, Riverside. He played banjo, joined the dinner theater cast at Riverside's Mission Inn hotel, and employed his deft, mischievous wit to file a lawsuit in rhyming verse on behalf of a client who alleged the presence of mouse parts in his fast-food burger. Though this would be his first death penalty case, Myers had an affinity for clients accused of murder. "They're much easier to deal with than almost any other client. It's extremely high stakes. They understand you're there to protect them as best you can."[18] Myers believed he had two winning arguments that, at least in the jury-selection phase, would give his client all the protection he needed. He began by challenging a fundamental premise to the *Press-Enterprise*'s case. Jury selection, Myers insisted, was not part of the trial.

"The trial does not, in fact, commence until the jury has been sworn and generally a witness has been sworn," Myers told Judge Mortland. "[O]n that technical ground alone, the Court can refuse to grant the petition of the *Press-Enterprise*."[19] Myers's second argument, linked to his client's Sixth Amendment right to a fair trial, could be summed up in two words that would dog Jim Ward for the duration of the case: *juror privacy*. The way to protect that Sixth Amendment right, said Myers, was by protecting prospective jurors who would be forced "to have an extra shell about themselves . . . knowing a reporter is present in the room." If Mortland let them in the room, answers to questions designed to reveal jurors' "most personal and private feelings" would not be totally candid. That would "prevent us from having a fair trial."[20] And give the defense grounds for appeal. Myers didn't say that. He didn't have to.

Myers argued that if the judge allowed the "openness" that Jim Ward sought, potential jurors might think but would never be able to say, "I don't want to admit to a newspaper reporter that I have feelings of racial prejudice that I can't put out of my mind . . . I don't want the newspaper to know that I don't think that this is the kind of crime that justifies the imposition of the death penalty when I have been through two wars and have seen so many more people killed under so many different circumstances." Those feelings, said Myers, "are private, they only become . . . relevant when a person, by mere chance, is brought before this Court with the possibility of serving as a prospective juror."[21]

Deputy DA Robert Spitzer, who spoke next, said he had no objection to having the public and press on hand for "general *voir dire*," during which questions regarding the "presumption of innocence" and "burden of proof" and "their ability to be fair and impartial" could be posed to jurors as a group. But questioning jurors individually about such matters as the death penalty should be handled "as suggested in the *Hovey* decision."[22] The DA's office wasn't interested in a wide-open voir dire, and Spitzer was even less interested in becoming a cheerleader for the *Press-Enterprise*. Two days earlier, Saturday, October 17, the newspaper published a story by court reporter Chris

Bowman headlined, "Ex-ACLU Leader Has No Qualms in Asking for Penalty of Death." Bowman's story noted that the thirty-two-year-old Spitzer had been president of Riverside's three-hundred-member chapter of the American Civil Liberties Union but had decided not to seek reelection because "it would be embarrassing to the ACLU" to have a chapter president arguing for the death penalty. The ACLU historically opposed capital punishment.

Bowman's profile portrayed Spitzer as a young man who came of age in Southern California, where he spearheaded a voluntary integration program between his affluent, mostly white La Jolla High School and the mostly black Lincoln High in San Diego. He went door-to-door registering voters in San Diego's minority communities and, in 1966, "joined a busload of 'white liberals' from his church" and rode to the South to register black voters. He joined the ACLU in 1975, when he was in law school at USC. Two years later, when he hired on with the Riverside County district attorney's office, Spitzer was assured he would never be asked to try a case "that I had a moral or professional objection to."[23] Now, two days before jury selection was to begin, *Press-Enterprise* readers were learning that Spitzer, the "white liberal" ACLU president, felt the death penalty was "appropriate" for Albert Brown because "[t]he kind of experience she [Susan Jordan] felt and that her friends and family continue to feel is abhorrent in a civilized society."[24]

Spitzer hated the story. "Robert Spitzer opposes the death penalty, but in this case he favors it, so the crime must be so heinous," is how he scornfully summarized it.[25] That message would make it extremely difficult to assemble a jury that was even close to being free of preconceived notions. But what rankled Spitzer even more was that he considered it old news that was being dredged up for an "untimely article." Spitzer had announced he would not seek reelection as the ACLU chapter president ten months earlier. "It created an issue that hadn't existed before." Joe Myers pounced on that issue, demanding that Judge Mortland kick Spitzer off the case for tainting the views of prospective jurors. Mortland refused.[26]

Though Spitzer didn't say much during the courtroom debate about whether jury selection should be open or closed, the little he did say resembled a template for balance, or compromise, that had been used in the past and could be used again. "There is a very common question asked of jurors, whether or not they or any member of their family has ever been charged with a serious offense such as the defendant is currently charged with . . . or if they have ever been a victim of a violent or serious crime. And I know a number of judges [who] . . . have insisted that the continuation of that line of questioning, after there is an affirmative response, be conducted in private, wherein people can explain in detail what their own personal lives have taught them about the case."[27]

Judge Mortland kept jury selection open for three days, or long enough to assemble a pool of potential jurors whose jobs, family duties, and vacation schedules would still allow them to serve. Then, interpreting *Hovey* to mean prospective death penalty jurors should be questioned in secret, he shut his courtroom to the public and the press for the next six weeks.

Tom Hunter was a thirty-three-year-old telephone company supervisor when he received his summons for jury duty. He and his wife lived just outside of Riverside. Decades later, memories of the death-qualifying process still seemed fresh and vivid. "It was kind of strange.[28] It was just me sitting in the jury box. Somebody [one of the lawyers] asked me how I voted on the death penalty.[29] I said I voted for it. It didn't bother me that they asked me. It didn't bother me that I answered it."

"At one point [Joe] Myers handed me two pictures. They were upside down. 'I want you to look at these and when you get done looking at them, I want you to look at me and tell me what you saw.'" Myers showed prospective jurors color photographs of Jordan's half-naked body lying in the orange groves.[30] "They were two photographs of the Susan Jordan crime scene. One with a shoelace tied around her neck. I don't recall the other one. I looked at Myers and I said they're pretty ghastly photos. It's not like I hadn't seen anything like this before. As a kid, I worked part time in a mortuary and saw people who had blown their brains out."

Hunter's individual voir dire didn't last long. Not even a half hour. He said he wasn't asked about his "opinion of rape" or "racial" questions even though the defendant was black and Susan Jordan was white. Though he doesn't recall being assured that his responses would remain confidential, "I must have known at that time it was going to be sealed. You were going to be interviewed by yourself and they produced that atmosphere for the most candid responses. So I must have known that it was going to be sealed." Hunter recalled that one potential juror, a woman, "told a couple of us that her daughter had been raped." Tom Hunter became Juror No. 6.

In late December 1981, following six weeks of secret questioning of one hundred and one prospective jurors, an all-white jury was finally selected.[31] The *Press-Enterprise* returned to court and asked Mortland to release the voir dire transcript. He refused. In early February 1982 the jurors found Albert Greenwood Brown Jr. guilty of first-degree murder. On February 22, the United States Supreme Court refused to hear the *Press-Enterprise* and Copley Press appeal of the closed voir dire in the Norco bank robbery case. At least four Supreme Court justices must vote to hear a case, but the newspapers only got three: William Brennan, Thurgood Marshall, and Sandra Day O'Connor. The next day, Jim Ward went back to Judge Mortland's courtroom. By then, Albert Brown had been sentenced to die in San Quentin's gas chamber. Once again Ward asked the judge to release the voir dire transcript. Once again, Mortland refused. Instead, he ordered it sealed. Permanently.

Like the famous California song, the *Press-Enterprise* was right back where it started from. In a matter of days it had been shot down by the highest court in the land and rejected yet again by Judge Mortland. As the newspaper pondered its next move, another case was picking up steam.

4

The "Thrill-Killer" Nurse

On Tuesday, April 21, 1981, at 12:17 p.m., Mickey Worthington, an investigator for the Riverside County coroner's office, received an anonymous tip: during a two-week period, nineteen "sudden and mysterious deaths" had occurred at Community Hospital of the Valleys, a thirty-six-bed hospital in Perris, a small city less than twenty miles south of Riverside. The next day the caller phoned again, this time ticking off names of the dead and their medical chart numbers. The caller described the similar, chilling "symptoms" of the patients' last minutes of life: seizures, convulsions, turning blue from the waist up.[1]

County coroner's officials began to dig up bodies. The county pathologist conducted autopsies, seizing the remains of one woman whose body had been loaded into a station wagon about to travel from a Riverside mortuary to a crematorium. Another woman's remains rested in a viewing room at a funeral home. Investigators asked that the viewing room be closed early.[2] Meanwhile, other law enforcement officials searched for common denominators among the dead: What time of day did they die? Which nurses were on duty? *How* did they die? A nursing registry had sent Robert Diaz to Community Hospital of the Valleys the previous month. He worked there for just twelve days. But during ten of his shifts, patients died of overdoses of lidocaine—a muscle-relaxing drug that could actually save lives by calming severely distressed hearts. Irene Annie Graham, an eighty-nine-year-old grandmother, was the first to die. She received a lidocaine overdose on March 30, 1981, Robert Diaz's very first shift. On two of the days Diaz worked, *two* patients died during each of his shifts.[3]

Diaz, forty-three, had come to California via Gary, Indiana, where he was raised by his maternal grandmother. He was the seventh of sixteen children, a brood that included eleven stepbrothers and stepsisters. Diaz claimed that one of his great, great, great grandfathers was the Spanish national hero El Cid, born in 1040. One of Diaz's idols was Albert Einstein. "I knew the Theory of Relativity backwards and forwards by the time I was in eighth grade," he said in a newspaper interview. Much of what Diaz told the reporter either could not be confirmed or was disputed.[4]

Diaz dropped out of high school in tenth grade and joined the U.S. Marines. Though he said he was discharged as a corporal, records show he never rose above private first class. He graduated from the Purdue School of Nursing in Hammond, Indiana, in 1977 and, boosted by high test scores, became a registered nurse a year later. Though he studied to be an emergency room technician, he gave it up, concluding that ER techs "are very limited" because they don't make decisions and only act under guidance and supervision. The best nurses, he thought, worked the hospital graveyard shift because they have such little contact with physicians.[5] In 1978 Diaz spotted an ad in the Gary newspaper. There was an opening for a nursing job in Torrance, California. Diaz and his new wife, Martha, headed west, where he worked as an ICU nurse for several hospitals in Los Angeles County. He moved to Apple Valley in San Bernardino County in December 1980, and in March 1981 the nurse registry sent Robert Diaz to the Community Hospital of the Valleys in Perris.

Patrick Magers, the son of an auto mechanic with an eighth-grade education, had a paycheck-to-paycheck childhood. A bright kid and a curious student who loved science, math, and the simple elegance of logic, he also had rock-solid test scores and graduated at the top of his class at Whittier High in Los Angeles County.[6] His dad couldn't afford to put him through college but said the kid could still have his bedroom. So every school day Magers left his home in Whittier and drove thirty miles south to the University of California, Irvine, where he spent four hours in class. Then he drove back up north to work his eight-hour shift as a retail clerk in a food market. It was a grueling routine. Many of his classmates weren't just smart; they grew up in Newport Beach and other nearby cradles of privilege. Magers might have been more competitive if he'd been able to devote full time to his courses—or take less than a full load, which was out of the question because he would lose his draft deferment. So after two years and a 2.5 GPA, Magers chucked the hard sciences and switched to psychology. He graduated with a bachelor's degree and a low (35) draft lottery number. Certain he was destined for Vietnam, he enrolled in night law school and waited for Uncle Sam's letter. When he finally heard from the military, he learned he had gotten lost in the system and was no longer subject to the draft. Magers finished putting himself through Western State Law School by working as a graveyard-shift janitor at the Anaheim Convention Center.

He began his legal career as a criminal defense lawyer in Orange County, where he rather quickly tried six murder cases. Then he moved east to San Bernardino County for a dream job: a county public defender in the mountain resort town of Big Bear. Life was great for a while, but "major crime" consisted of disturbing the peace and being drunk in public. The restless Magers shipped his résumé to Riverside County, where the public defender asked if he wanted to handle homicides and other serious cases. For the next eighteen months Magers did the "heavy stuff"—all part of his grand scheme to work his way back to Orange County. Then one day he received a telephone call from the enemy. The assistant district attorney of Riverside County wanted to talk to him. In confidence.

"I want you to come and work for me," Thomas Hollenhorst told Magers. This was almost unheard of: a public defender going over to the dark side. But in March 1981, the same month Robert Diaz went to work in small hospital near Riverside, Patrick Magers went to work for the DA. The moment he arrived, Magers was put on ice, in effect, until all the cases he'd handled as a public defender had been wrapped up.[7] Off to juvenile court he went, trying cases, though not the "heavy stuff," and loving every minute of it. The minutes piled up for days and weeks, and it was several months before Tom Hollenhorst called.

Magers's cases were finally finished, and Hollenhorst had another assignment for the young prosecutor. "You've probably heard about it," Hollenhorst told him. "It's been in the papers. They've exhumed some bodies. You're going to do it. Investigate this case. Tell me where it leads. Do what you need to do. When you're done, let me know what your conclusion is." Patrick Magers was going to "do" the Diaz case.

"It was not," Magers observed, "your typical murder case where you have a family member killing another family member in the heat of passion." By the time Magers got involved, the DA's office and the coroner had exhumed thirty-eight bodies. Magers would have to decide how many, if any, were homicides. If any were, he would have to zero in on a suspect. Then he would have to prove beyond a reasonable doubt that homicides were "a result of direct intervention by a third person." Tissue samples had already been shipped to the Center for Human Toxicology at the University of Utah. One of the first things Magers did was travel to Utah.

"They [Center for Human Toxicology] basically shut down their lab for our use because we had so many samples. Going over all the results, we were able to isolate twelve individuals who clearly, from a toxicological standpoint, died from a result of massive dosages of lidocaine. All died within about a three-week period." Eleven died at Community Hospital of the Valleys, the twelfth at San Gorgonio Hospital in the Riverside County city of Banning, where Diaz went after authorities were tipped off to the deaths in Perris.

From a scientific standpoint, investigators had to solve a three-piece puzzle: The Utah toxicologists concluded the patients had died after being injected with lethal doses of lidocaine. Riverside County's pathologist could find no other cause of death besides massive doses of lidocaine. Cardiologists at nearby Loma Linda Medical Center, relying in part on Perris hospital nurses who had witnessed patients "actually flopping up and down on the bed" in their final, agonizing throes, came up with what Magers called a "fingerprint."

"Generally, in the hospital," said Magers, "you see seizures because of respiratory arrest. The seizure would be a product of oxygen deprivation because of respiratory arrest. In our case, the cart was before the horse in each death. The cardiologists said this was a classical picture of a lidocaine overdose causing a seizure, then going into respiratory arrest and cardiac failure. It was a fingerprint."

Once Magers concluded that the patients, ranging in age from fifty-two to ninety-five, had been murdered, he and his investigators turned their attention to the murderer. Diaz was already a suspect, but Magers wasn't going to start there. "I wanted a clean slate. I said I was going to contact everybody involved in this case, and I did." He interviewed nurses and other witnesses, frequently more than once. Diaz not only remained a suspect; he emerged as the common denominator. Who was present at all the deaths in the six-bed intensive care unit at Community Hospital of the Valleys? Diaz. Who was the "charge nurse"—the person chiefly responsible for the patients? Diaz. Who only worked the graveyard shift? Diaz. True, other nurses worked graveyard, too. But they answered to Diaz. When did the patients die? During the graveyard shift.

Then there was Diaz's "very unusual behavior." Magers explained: "Initially, he would make his rounds with his nursing assistant, who was also an RN, and he would predict deaths. And interviewing the other nurses, they were shocked. These patients were not expected to die, they were not terminal. But Diaz would actually predict the death of a patient that night on his shift. And they did die."

But if Diaz did it, how did he do it? An expert from the Utah toxicology center, testifying at Diaz's trial, said the normal intravenous dose of lidocaine ranged from fifty to one hundred milligrams. But the patients who died on Diaz's watch received at least a thousand and sometimes two thousand milligrams. Magers faced an obvious challenge: "I had to prove how Diaz could do that. He couldn't stand there and inject ten to twenty boluses [syringes] of lidocaine into a patient. He'd be caught. It would be obvious. Plus, he'd have all these empty syringes."

When authorities searched Diaz's Apple Valley house in May 1981, they found lidocaine. It wasn't a controlled substance. You couldn't get high on the stuff. It had no street value. It didn't have to be locked up or checked out. But to Magers, the discovery of lidocaine at Diaz's residence solved the how-did-he-do-it mystery. "What he did at home, he would take a bolus of lidocaine, squirt it out, stick the syringe portion of the bolus into the two-gram bottle of lidocaine and pull up a concentrated amount. Now he would have a bolus that he fixed himself with two grams of lidocaine, which would be a fatal dosage. He'd put it in his pocket, go to the ICU and at the appropriate time, he would walk over to a patient with his 'gun,' inject it into the port of the IV drip, and it would immediately go into the patient causing a grand mal seizure."

Magers was convinced that these patients had been murdered and that Robert Diaz was the murderer. "From my standpoint, they were thrill killings. This was not a situation where these patients were euthanized. They were not terminally ill. So he violated that position of trust. [For him, it was] a thrill. Control. I can kill you and I will kill you."

Another theory, not raised by Magers, is that Diaz "had a pathological need to prove he knew the practice of cardiac emergency medicine better than the doctors who bossed him around." So he'd inject them with lidocaine and then swing "into action, directing what for him were exhilarating life-saving efforts." Sometimes it worked; often it didn't. But when he "saved" a life, Diaz, not the "dumb" doctors, was a hero.[8]

Several months after Magers was ordered to investigate the case, he went to see the man who had told him, "Do what you need to do. Let me know what your conclusion is." Magers had reached a conclusion. "Diaz did it," he told the assistant DA Hollenhorst. "I'm convinced he's guilty."

"Are you sure you can prove it?"

"I said yes. He said, 'Do it.'"

On November 23, 1981, as secret jury selection proceeded in the death penalty case of Albert Greenwood Brown Jr., Riverside County authorities arrested Robert Rubane Diaz and charged him with murdering twelve patients: eleven at Community Hospital of the Valleys and one at San Gorgonio Pass Hospital in Banning. Both hospitals were in Riverside County. The next day, prosecutors announced they would try to have Diaz put to death.

On July 6, 1982, Riverside County Municipal Court judge Howard Dabney, once the number two man in the DA's office, opened the preliminary hearing to determine whether Diaz would stand trial for murder. Diaz, through his lawyer, asked that the hearing be closed to the public and the press. Magers, who wanted to minimize pre-trial publicity and avoid a change of venue, did not object.[9] Dabney, citing California law and a U.S. Supreme Court ruling,[10] explained it was his "obligation" and "constitutional duty" to protect Diaz's right to a fair trial—a duty that included taking steps to avoid prejudicing potential jurors. "I feel in this particular case . . . there has been national publicity. I feel that because of the preliminary hearing in which many times the defenses are not presented to show the defendant's side of the issue, that only one side may get reported in the media. . . . Therefore, the media cannot be present, nor can the public. . . . [L]adies and gentlemen . . . you will have to remove yourselves from the courtroom."[11]

When Diaz's lawyer asked to close the July 6 hearing, the *Press-Enterprise* was silent. It is possible that the paper was still coming to grips with the California Supreme Court's refusal, just seven days earlier, to hear the Albert Brown closed–voir dire case. Some have also speculated that the paper had been counting on the district attorney to step in and object to Dabney's closure. But there was just an acting DA at the time and no policy calling for open courtroom proceedings. It is likely that the *Press-Enterprise* did not object simply because closed preliminary hearings had become routine. The paper needed a wake-up call, and it would come from an unlikely source.

5

The Hays-Cherniss Newspaper

Tim Hays and Norman Cherniss couldn't have been shocked or even surprised that day in late February 1982 when Judge William Mortland ruled on yet another *Press-Enterprise* request to release the voir dire transcript of Albert Greenwood Brown Jr. The murder trial was over. Mortland had sentenced Susan Jordan's killer to die in San Quentin's gas chamber. But in Mortland's eyes that had nothing to do with making the transcript public. "While most of the information is dull and boring," he explained from the bench, "some of the jurors had special experiences in sensitive areas that do not appear to be appropriate for public discussion." With that assertion of juror privacy and a nod to *Hovey*, Mortland sealed the transcript. Permanently.

The newspaper sent Jim Ward up the next rung of the legal ladder, and the state Court of Appeal replied with a "crummy postcard" informing the newspaper, "The petition for a writ of mandate is DENIED."[1] The paper then appealed to the California Supreme Court, which made the Court of Appeal seem positively verbose: "HEARING DENIED," replied the state's highest court.[2] That June 30, 1982, rebuff came less than a week after secretly selected jurors in Washington DC found John W. Hinckley Jr. not guilty by reason of insanity in the attempted assassination of President Ronald Reagan. The verdict sparked public outrage, and a *Washington Post* story fueled it further. Five days of jury selection had taken place behind closed doors, and the *Post*'s story, based on the newly released transcript of that voir dire, reported: "At least three jurors had relatives who were once confined to a mental hospital." A fourth juror's sister had been treated for a nervous breakdown. And a fifth juror had received brief psychiatric treatment following a decades-old car accident.[3]

For Hays and Cherniss, it was déjà-vu and Groundhog Day all over again. The paper could either accept defeat or try to persuade the U.S. Supreme Court to do what it had refused to do in the Norco bank robbery case—decide whether jury selection should be open to the public. Only Tim Hays could make the call. But if he had any doubts about what that call should be, Norman Cherniss would be there to sweep them aside. The Hays-Cherniss tandem that shaped the character and content of the *Press-Enterprise* had been operating and evolving for nearly thirty years.

When they returned from lunch that day in the late 1960s, *Press-Enterprise* reporters Marcia McQuern and Ben Shore grabbed a copy of the afternoon paper, anxious to savor the first installment of their two-parter on Riverside's deteriorating downtown. The story wasn't there. The full-page spread had been replaced by canned filler. The managing editor and city editor were reportedly off getting drunk. McQuern and Shore, who had reported and written the stories, were furious. They were also being summoned by Tim Hays, editor and copublisher of the *Press-Enterprise*. Had the man who seemed so committed to the highest journalistic values spiked their story without even consulting them? As they walked to "The Corner," McQuern and Shore decided to resign.[4] "Are you sure we are right?" That's what Tim Hays always asked his reporters and editors before signing off on a sensitive or tough story. "There's no doubt, is there?" he'd press.[5] If the reporters and editors were sure, without doubt, Hays okayed the story. But on that afternoon he had already approved the story. Now, recalled McQuern, Tim Hays was "clearly distressed."[6]

"You are owed an explanation," he told the reporters. "I made a mistake."[7] Hays was so proud of their stories he had shown the first installment to copublisher Art Culver, who ran the paper's business operations. When Culver read the account of a dying downtown, not unlike many downtowns across the United States, he went ballistic. This piece would anger advertisers and cost the paper money, he fumed. Worse, this story would infuriate the people Culver cared about most: his friends who ran the town. Tim Hays's father, Howard H Hays Sr., was all but retired by then. But he happened to be in his office that day, and Culver paid him a visit. The senior Hays was as appalled as Culver when he saw what was about to be printed that afternoon. He would be shamed, shunned, and run out of town. He demanded the story be killed. Father and son fought; the senior Hays prevailed, and the junior Hays called in the reporters to explain. "I can't send my father out of town," he told Shore and McQuern. "However, if it ever happens again, I'll be leaving town." Instead of resigning, the reporters found themselves consoling their editor, who stuck around for three more decades. Because it never happened again.[8]

If there was such a thing as the Hays empire, it began with Howard H Hays Sr., born in 1883 in the southern Illinois town of Metropolis. Raised by a grandmother, he became a high school debater and journalist. He attended the University of Illinois but fell ill and dropped out. In 1905 Hays came west to recover and went to work on a sheep ranch in Montana. A year later, instead of returning to college, he spent the summer driving a surrey at a new park. Soon Hays was climbing the management ladder at Yellowstone National Park, organizing coast-to-coast promotional railroad tours.[9] He invested in and became operator of the Yellowstone Park Camps Company, which lured tourists traveling by stage coach and train to spend weeks amid spectacular surroundings. He was also president of the Sequoia and Kings National Park Co. and the Glacier Park and Transportation Co.[10] He met Margaret Amanda Mauger at a 1914 Santa Barbara convention of the Railroad Traveling Passenger Agents Association. They married two years later. Their first of three sons, Howard H (Tim) Hays Jr., was born on June 2, 1917.

In 1924, following a bout of tuberculosis, Hays moved the family to Riverside, where he had once drummed up business for Yellowstone. In 1930, tapping into a substantial nest egg, he had no trouble buying his first stake in the afternoon *Riverside Press*: forty shares for $12,000. The *Press* and the morning *Daily Enterprise* became The Press-Enterprise Co. a year later.[11] Likely influenced by the national park culture of conservation and stewardship, the senior Hays ran a paper to serve what he regarded as the best interests of his employees and the community.[12] When an employee got sick and missed months of work, he still got paid. When a subscriber phoned to say he didn't get his paper, the old man hopped in his car and personally delivered it.[13] But it was a community paper that didn't dig too deep and didn't ruffle too many feathers.

Then, in 1949, the old man's son, Tim, became the editor. "I don't know," mused Joel Blain, the newspaper's editorial page editor from 1984 to 2002. "Maybe when he was seven years old he sat down with his crayons and yellow pad and wrote that he wanted to produce a newspaper of note. I rather doubt it. He stumbled into it. He inherited a newspaper and had this sense of noblesse oblige. And he took the oblige seriously when it came to being the custodian of the newspaper."[14]

Tim Hays was in his early thirties when he became editor of the *Press-Enterprise*. He didn't earn the title by virtue of his journalistic résumé. True, he had edited the Riverside Poly High School paper. At Stanford, he worked on the *Daily*. But then it was on to Harvard Law, and when he got out, in the thick of World War II, he spent three years as a special agent for the FBI. By 1946 Hays was back in Riverside. He passed the California bar but wanted no part of practicing law and was especially proud that he never did. But there was something Tim Hays very much wanted to try: newspapering.[15]

Trim and courtly, a handsome man with an open if sometimes distant smile, Hays was "enormously private," recalled Charlie Field, a longtime friend, ex-Riverside County Superior Court judge, and former *Press-Enterprise* board member.[16] "His knowledge of how the other half lived was minimal," wrote George Ringwald, the former *Press-Enterprise* reporter Hays commissioned to write a history of the paper, which was never published. Tony Perry, a reporter for the newspaper in the 1970s, told Ringwald that Hays "didn't really understand the common man. But he had a vision."

Hays, who, with his wife Helen, had two sons, cared deeply about his community, his employees, his newspaper, and journalism writ large. Like his father, Tim Hays befriended people who interested him: college professors and highway builders, judges and lawyers and connoisseurs of the arts. He sought out people who might help him improve the *Press-Enterprise* and reinforce the highest values of journalism as he saw them. He counted Katharine Graham, who ran the *Washington Post*, as a friend. He knew the key newspaper publishers of his time and corresponded with an ex-newspaper boy, future newspaper owner, and legendary investor named Warren Buffet.[17] In 1966 he launched the Press-Enterprise Lecture, an annual event that brought the Who's Who of American journalism to Riverside.[18] "The important thing to know about Tim," a fellow editor once said, "is that wherever he is, he is about to be somewhere else."[19] So it was that the "enormously private" editor gravitated to the epicenter of American journalism, even if it sometimes made him uncomfortable.

As president of the American Society of Newspaper Editors, he traveled to Washington for the 1974 annual convention. At a White House reception, Jean Wingard, Hays's secretary, simmered with frustration as her self-effacing boss stood back while other editors clambered to meet President Gerald Ford. (ASNE presidents customarily brought their secretaries to the convention.) She finally button-holed a uniformed guard and asked, "Could we arrange to let Mr. Hays, who is president of this organization, meet the president?" The two chief executives finally shook hands at an elevator as Ford was preparing to leave.[20]

But if he was remote and reserved—except when he demonstrated the authentic, ear-splitting Blackfoot war whoops he learned as a youth in Montana[21]—Hays was also steely and decisive, an insightful judge of talent and character, and, as the business lawyer Jim Ward would learn, steadfastly loyal. Soon after he became editor, Hays promoted a reporter to city editor only to learn that he had once been a member of the Communist Party. Tom Patterson had disclosed this when he was hired, but the word never went up the chain of command.[22] Despite an ensuing spate of red-baiting, ranging from small-town gossip to attacks by a state senator, the new city editor kept his job.[23] Tim Hays had "a pretty good sense of what was right and what was wrong," said James Bettinger, the paper's city editor in the 1970s and 1980s and the longtime director of Stanford's John S. Knight Journalism Fellowship program.[24] If that pretty good sense rattled the local business, political, and social big shots, that was too bad. By the time Judge William Mortland closed his courtroom to jury selection in the 1981 murder trial of Albert Greenwood Brown Jr., Hays had spent decades charting the course of the *Press-Enterprise*, grappling with such volatile issues as school desegregation in Riverside and the plight of Mexican Americans in Riverside County. When the paper learned of a Riverside real estate clique's secret agreement to keep blacks out of all-white neighborhoods, readers learned about it, too.[25] When he greenlighted a story exposing crooked auto mechanics, Hays knew auto dealers would yank their ads, but he predicted they'd come back. Sure enough, in this pre-internet, one-newspaper-town era, they came back.[26] When the flamboyant San Francisco lawyer Melvin Belli strode into the newsroom to inform the "hick-town" editor that a story about Belli's crooked client "was not going to run, the editor's door closed for what seemed a long time [and] the lawyer exited as dramatically as he entered. . . . Not only did the story appear, but a detailed description of the dissuasion effort was published as well."[27] When the paper published a 1964 series about the "'Santa Claus' of the federal court"—a judge who meted out astonishingly lenient sentences—Tim Hays received a complimentary note from a man who requested that his letter not be published "because I have no supervision over the district judges." The letter, written by Earl Warren, the former governor of California and then-current chief justice of the United States Supreme Court, did not see print.[28]

In 1966 *Newsweek* magazine published a brief feature in its "Press" section headlined "Digging by the Riverside": "The *Press-Enterprise* honors a simple but rare formula: in-depth reporting by staffers free of pressure from politicians, publishers or advertisers. The result is some of the most energetic local coverage in America—and, inevitably, some ruffled feelings in Riverside."[29] Two years later, more than feelings would be ruffled.

It was Tim Hays who first suggested that reporter George Ringwald look into a federal program, administered by the Riverside County Superior Court, that placed the Agua Caliente Band of Cahuilla Indians under the supervision of local judges, lawyers, insurance and real estate agents, and even the Palm Springs mayor and police chief. The one-hundred-member band owned roughly twenty-seven thousand acres of Palm Springs–area land, valued at $50 million. There were growing suspicions that the judges and other conservators were stealing from the Indians by collecting exorbitant fees from their bank accounts. As Ringwald began to dig and write, the conservators tried to derail his investigation. One of the judges sought to have Tim Hays arrested in order to grill him about *Press-Enterprise* editorials that were highly critical of how the court was handling Indian assets. County officials declined to issue a warrant. "I think if I were doing it over again," Hays said years later, "I'd have put myself in the hands of the fellows who were going to arrest me. It would have made a more interesting story."[30]

The efforts to suppress and intimidate the newspaper were understandable. Ringwald's year-long series uncovered such an astounding pattern of abuse that all three judges involved in the guardianship program were forced to either retire or resign. In 1968 the *Press-Enterprise* received the most prestigious of journalism's Pulitzer prizes: the gold medal for Meritorious Public Service.

The editorials that inspired the attempted arrest of Tim Hays were not written by Hays himself, who long ago had concluded this area of journalism was not exactly his strong suit. In his first years as editor, Hays often ran canned editorials provided by the Newspaper Enterprise Association. In 1952, when Hays advertised for a full-time editorial writer, a young man in his mid-twenties responded. The two met in Chicago, at the Republican National Convention. Soon afterward Tim Hays offered the job to Norman A. Cherniss, who had been working for an Indiana paper. Nearly twenty years and several promotions later, Hays appointed Cherniss the paper's first executive editor, a position he held from 1971 until his death in 1984.[31] Cherniss provided the journalistic and intellectual wattage that jolted the *Press-Enterprise* from a "good middle-sized newspaper to a newspaper of middle-size but of national standing. The best choice he [Tim Hays] ever made as editor was choosing Norman," said Joel Blain, the paper's longtime editorial page editor. "He told me that."[32]

Norman Arnold Cherniss was no Tim Hays, not by any stretch of imagination, bank account, or wardrobe. "My daddy never owned a newspaper," he periodically grumbled. Cherniss was born into a Jewish family in Council Bluffs, Iowa, on July 26, 1926, and his daddy was a furniture salesman. The *Crimson & Blue*, Abraham Lincoln High School's yearbook, lists Norman Cherniss as president of the June 1944 graduating class. He was also "Band lieutenant," a member of the National Honor Society, and the sports editor of *Echoes*, the school newspaper. At fifteen he was a sportswriter for the Council Bluffs paper, the *Daily Nonpareil*. While attending the State University of Iowa (now Iowa State University), he wrote editorials for the *Des Moines Register*; after he graduated in 1950, his editorials appeared in the *Evansville (IN) Courier*. Cherniss signed on as an editor of the *Press-Enterprise* editorial page in 1953. Asked for his typing speed on the employment form, Cherniss wrote "Lightening." Asked for his reason for leaving Evansville, he wrote, "hatred."

Though he went to work for a Harvard Law grad, Cherniss seemed even more intrigued by the law than Tim Hays. "When I was covering courts," recalled James Bettinger, who later became city editor, "he was always interested in legal proceedings. When somebody was arrested, there would be a story about a prelim [preliminary hearing] and a superior court arraignment. We covered the shit out of it." When Cherniss won a prestigious Nieman journalism fellowship in 1958, he spent much of his time at Harvard studying constitutional law.[33] Blain, who worked directly for Cherniss, stopped short of calling him a frustrated lawyer. But, he stated, "I think for sure that if he had been a kid of privileged upbringing and not the barefoot boy out of Iowa, he would have gotten himself a law degree and then probably gone into journalism."[34]

Not much more than five feet tall and a tad roly-poly, Cherniss had an aversion to dieting and a habit of banging his pipe on his resonant desktop ashtray. He was a jigsaw puzzle of a man. He could be devastatingly witty, once imploring a Jewish reporter to give more than twenty-four hours notice before taking the next Yom Kippur off, reminding him that the holiday had been planned for five thousand years. He was urbane, bookish, and sentimentally patriotic. An original Picasso hung in his condo bathroom. A bare living room wall, transformed into white floor-to-ceiling bookshelves, required a ladder to retrieve the highest of the high-brow material. A confirmed bachelor, Cherniss was an elegant dresser and a lady's man, a gourmet cook and a habitué of the newspaper's junk food vending machines.

He presided over a second-floor newsroom carpeted in "turquoise Brillo"; the lone window was in a door that led to the roof.[35] He believed local stories belonged in the local section. Period. Riverside County stories rarely found a home on page one. Cherniss's micromanagement style was legendary. He didn't just write memos. He preserved copies of them in three-ring binders. One memo critiqued newsroom manners. "There is too much variety in the way news/editorial people answer the telephone. It seems to range from just plain grunts up." Despite his short stature, Cherniss could be intimidating to the reporters and editors who towered above him. "My door is always open," he assured the newsroom staff. But Cherniss was not given to debate, disagreement, or challenge. He had a vision, said James Bettinger, "of what the paper should be, and he was the opposite of collaborative when it came to that vision."[36] But there were times when he truly needed someone to walk through that door. "He would call me into his office," recalled Yolanda DeLeon, a longtime newsroom administrator. "He always kept a bottle of some kind of alcohol in a desk drawer. It was brown, that I know. He would have two glasses. 'I know you don't drink,' he'd say, 'but I need a drink right now, and you sit here and listen to me.' And he would drink both glasses. He wanted to vent."[37] "He was a bundle of contradictions," said Joel Blain. "He could be the most generous person in the world and the meanest too. He had an amazing sense of when he had gone too far." (A former secretary said he once dispatched her to buy one pair of briefs he needed for tennis; she finally found a three-pack that had been ripped open at J.C. Penney.)[38] "And he could do incredibly generous and nice things." (DeLeon recalled that when burglars broke into her car in the company lot, Cherniss decided the paper would pay for repairs and her stolen community college textbooks.)[39]

Cherniss was the newspaper's house intellect, but also a journalist to his core, insisting on thorough, responsible coverage as firmly as he insisted on public and press access to public proceedings. "I think," he wrote in a memo to the managing editor a day after the June 17, 1972, Watergate break-in, "the unusual invasion, for whatever reason, of the Democratic national headquarters is an unusually interesting story and it seems to me our six-inch story on A-4 today badly downplays it." The day after Cherniss died of heart attack in 1984, Riverside lawyer Barton Gaut told the paper, "He and I have gone over some real tough stories. He was interested that people should get the news they should have," not sensational stories that Cherniss dismissed as "lip-smackers."[40]

"Norman wasn't the easiest guy to work for," noted Blain. "And Tim wasn't the easiest guy to work for. Norman would come fuming back into his office and would announce to me, 'You are so far down [my] list of irritating people!' And I knew immediately what happened was that Tim had refused to give Norman something that Norman wanted, which probably would have been for the betterment of the newspaper, or was it for the betterment of Norman? I don't know, and I'm sure the two were confused at the time."[41]

But when it came to the big things, the important things, the *Press-Enterprise* became the Hays-Cherniss newspaper. When the U.S. Supreme Court refused to hear the closed voir dire appeal in the Norco bank robbery case and, the very next day, Judge Mortland *permanently* sealed the jury selection transcript in the Albert Brown death penalty case, outsiders might have assumed, even expected, that the paper would just pack it in and stop fighting. "No one was taking bets on the *Press-Enterprise*," wrote Jack Landau, executive director of the Reporters Committee for Freedom of the Press.[42]

But the assumptions and expectations inside the *Press-Enterprise* were quite different.

"It's not surprising that [Tim] hired someone like Norman," said Jane Carney, a well-regarded Riverside lawyer, community leader, and friend of both men. "He really wanted to do those Supreme Court cases because he cared about doing something real as he built the newspaper. This was an opportunity to do something real."[43] But he could not do it alone.

"Without Tim, it couldn't have happened," said Blain. "Without Norman, it wouldn't have happened."

6

"They Won't Laugh at You Now"

"In recent years, U.S Supreme Court has received roughly 8,000 petitions each term [first Monday in October through the end of June] and voted to hear oral arguments for about 70 cases. The Burger Court received about 5,000 such petitions per term and heard about 150 cases."[1]

Encouraged that it had fallen just one justice short in the Norco voir dire case, the *Press-Enterprise* decided to take another crack at the U.S. Supreme Court. At first it appeared to have the makings of a lonely battle. Judith Epstein, a Northern California lawyer whose firm represented Gannett Newspapers, warned Jim Ward that the paper's case would "go down in flames" on the issue of juror privacy alone.[2] "My law partners," wrote Ward, "were glumly negative about our prospects."[3] But their glumly negative view didn't deter Ward, who, as a Thompson & Colegate partner, enjoyed a certain amount of autonomy. He told *Press-Enterprise* editors that the Supreme Court battle would cost $25,000—a "cut-rate" price the firm used in its high-volume insurance practice. This was hardly a high-volume-type case. But as Don Grant, one of Ward's partners at the time noted, "Jim didn't know anything about constitutional law."[4]

By September 1982 Ward and his young associate, John Boyd, both ex-newspaper boys, had submitted an eighteen-page Petition for Writ of Certiorari, urging the U.S. Supreme Court to hear the Albert Brown secret voir dire case. The petition framed the issue as a "conflict" between a defendant's Sixth Amendment right to a fair trial and the public's First Amendment right to attend criminal proceedings.[5] The paper argued that jury selection was "an integral portion" of those proceedings and therefore was covered by the court's 1980 *Richmond* decision, which granted the public and press First Amendment access to criminal trials. But the petition backed away from Ward's courtroom assertion to Judge Mortland that the public had an "absolute right to attend a trial." The toned-down version read: "While it is clear that the rights of the accused must be protected in capital cases, the protections afforded, especially to exclusion of the constitutional rights of others, must have a firm and reasonable basis."[6]

The First Amendment didn't just protect speech and a free press, the newspaper argued, but included "the right to receive information." Picking a jury behind closed doors amounted to an unconstitutional prior restraint of the newspaper's First Amendment rights. And the *Hovey* requirement was so vague that picking jurors "in sequestration" had resulted in no less than six different interpretations among Riverside County judges alone. Then there was the transcript. Judge J. David Hennigan closed his Norco bank robbery courtroom for *six months*, but released the voir dire transcript before trial testimony began. The U.S. Supreme Court refused to hear the Norco case by the narrowest margin. The newspaper hoped the permanently sealed Albert Brown voir dire transcript would flip that vote. The petition urged the court to "clarify the rights of the public to attend criminal trials, specifically the *voir dire* proceeding, not only in capital cases, but all cases in which sensitive areas of *voir dire* examination may arise."

Despite what Ward called "negative remarks" up and down the state, the California Newspaper Publishers Association (CNPA) weighed in with a friend-of-the-court (or amicus curiae) brief in support of the *Press-Enterprise*. It argued that while recent U.S. Supreme Court decisions had actually opened criminal trials to the public, California courts were lagging behind and threatened to lag even further behind because of the latest state supreme court rejection of a *Press-Enterprise* challenge to closed jury selection. "In California, as in the rest of the nation," wrote the CNPA lawyers, "the courts are increasingly under attack. The people's concern about the increase of crime in their lives has caused them to focus on the courts as they look for someone to blame for society's problems. The CNPA is concerned that the apparent increase in denial of access to the courts . . . will exacerbate the problem."[7]

The CNPA brief showed solidarity on the issue of open jury selection *and* signaled to the U.S. Supreme Court that the *Press-Enterprise* wasn't some rogue outlier. It was speaking for many, if not all, California papers.

By October 1982 the paper's petition and the amicus brief had reached the Supreme Court. Among the first to look them over were laser-sharp lawyers with a minimum-wage title: clerk. Most clerks are not more than a year or two out of the nation's biggest-name law schools. Each justice is allowed four clerks per term, except for the chief justice, who may hire up to five. Clerks research cases, read briefs, write memorandums, critique drafts of Supreme Court opinions, and recommend how their bosses should handle cases like *Press-Enterprise Co. v. Superior Court*. Much like human resource officers sifting through mountains of résumés, the young clerks examine thousands of petitions for certiorari. They're looking for good cases, of course, but they're also looking for reasons to say no. Explained Alan Madans, the Duke University law school grad who clerked for Justice Harry Blackmun in 1982–83: "If you're a clerk, the last thing you want to do is suggest the court hear a case that turns out to have some problem where the court will not be able to decide the case. . . . It would be a waste of the court's time."[8] The views of some clerks, as well as those of the justices, can be mined from the papers of the Supreme Court justices themselves. Some justices donate their papers to the Library of Congress, others to colleges and universities. Some papers are open to the public, whereas others remain off limits until a time designated by the individual justice.[9]

Some clerks thought justices should steer clear of the latest *Press-Enterprise* case. In a late-November 1982 memorandum, M. Kathleen Smalley, a clerk for Justice Sandra Day O'Connor, observed that the court had already denied the *Press-Enterprise*'s appeal in the Norco bank robbery case. Norco's closed voir dire had been "correct" because it was in line with *Gannett v. DePasquale*, a 1979 Supreme Court ruling that upheld a secret pretrial hearing to avoid "a reasonable probability of prejudice" to the accused.[10] But the trial judge in that case released a transcript of the hearing. Smalley was not bothered that various Riverside County judges were offering various interpretations of *Hovey*'s "individually and in sequestration" requirement. That didn't make it "constitutionally vague," as the *Press-Enterprise* contended; the "individualized application" showed *Hovey* was not "a prior restraint"—red-flag language that First Amendment rights were in peril if not already violated. But Smalley *was* troubled by Judge Mortland's refusal to release the voir dire transcript. She called it "problematic" and "wrong." Still, the *Press-Enterprise* "has not given any indication that the practice of denying transcripts is a frequent occurrence." Wrote Smalley: "I recommend a denial here."[11] A clerk with the initials "M.N."—most likely Mark Newell, who clerked for Justice Powell—agreed that the sealed transcript "arguably violates" *Gannett* because the sealing "effectively is a permanent—or at least indefinite—refusal to disclose." Still, added Newell in a handwritten note on Smalley's memo, "I don't think it is so clear as to warrant a summary reversal." M.N.'s recommendation: Deny.[12]

Justice Harry Blackmun's clerk, Alan Madans, recommended a CFR: a "call for response" from the Riverside County Superior Court. He noted that three justices had voted to hear the Norco bank robbery case "and this [Albert Brown case] does contain an additional troublesome feature": the sealed transcript. Perhaps a Riverside County response "would help clean up" that issue "or indicate that it is a problem."[13] The justices did call for a response, and the county lawyers obliged. The Riverside County counsel, representing the Superior Court, reminded the justices that they had already rejected the *Press-Enterprise* in the Norco case, and there was nothing new in this one.[14] Yes, they said, Judge Mortland had closed his court to the public and press, but it hadn't been "automatic." He had applied the "three-pronged standard" the high court had set in *Richmond Newspapers*.[15] The county said *Hovey* safeguarded "the neutrality, diversity and integrity of the jury," which helped protect the defendant's right to a fair trial. Prospective jurors are just doing their civic duty when they swear to answer voir dire questions "truthfully." But that doesn't mean "they are forced to leave their rights at the door of the courthouse." There it was: juror privacy. The issue some feared would ruin the *Press-Enterprise* case even if the justices decided to hear it. Finally, the county addressed what some clerks had found so "problematic" and "wrong": "Although [the *Press-Enterprise*] contends that the *voir dire* transcript was sealed 'permanently' there is no evidence that the transcript could not or will not be released at a later, appropriate time."

Madans, the Blackmun clerk who recommended the CFR, continued to have qualms. He still thought the "lower courts may have violated *Gannett* on the transcript issue," but he questioned whether Judge Mortland's "permanent" sealing was "symptomatic of a trend. . . . I would wait for a later case to see if the transcript issue remains a problem." As for the closure of jury selection itself? Madans thought it "did comply . . . with Gannett." The problem with this case, noted Madans, was that there was no state supreme court opinion (just "HEARING DENIED"), making "the standards applied by the higher court . . . uncertain." Madans's handwritten notes concluded, "[I] recommend that you not provide a fourth vote to Grant [certiorari]." But above his initials he wrote, "X?" which meant "deny, but it's a close call."[16]

Jim Ward had been "thrilled" to learn that the Supreme Court asked Riverside County to respond to the newspaper's petition. "This meant they were considering our case for cert."[17] But he would have been less than thrilled if he'd been privy to what happened on January 14, 1983. Roughly four months after the *Press-Enterprise* submitted its petition, the justices finally cast their ballots, and only the two most liberal, Thurgood Marshall and William Brennan, voted to hear the case. The paper had gotten three votes in the Norco case; now it seemed to be going backward. But the first vote was not the final tally. Justice Sandra Day O'Connor had not voted on the first go-around. She wanted to think it over, so she "passed" and asked her colleagues to "relist" the case—set it for reconsideration. Four days later, she wrote to her colleagues: "This case was relisted for me. I now vote to grant certiorari. Sincerely, Sandra."[18] When the second vote was taken on January 21, Brennan, Marshall, and O'Connor voted to hear the case. But the newspaper still needed a fourth vote, and this time it got one. Justice Harry Blackmun had not voted to grant or deny on the first ballot. He had written "Join 3," meaning if three justices wanted to hear the case, he would provide the fourth, deciding vote.[19] And he did.

Jim Ward was eating breakfast in his Riverside home on January 24, 1983, when his phone rang. It was 7:30, which meant it was 10:30 in Washington DC, where the *Press-Enterprise* had a one-man bureau. Martin Salditch had likely just called his boss. Now, Norman Cherniss was calling Ward. Cherniss's tone, wrote Ward, was "controlled but obviously pleased."

"Remember all those people who laughed at you when you petitioned?" asked the executive editor. "They will not laugh now."[20]

7

"Mr. Everything"

"Once cert was granted," recalled Jim Ward, "things changed dramatically. People began to call from all over the country. Local lawyers paid attention to us."[1]

People began to call, all right. But Ward wouldn't know the half of it until later, when Tim Hays finally told him that he had been lobbied to replace the business lawyer with a veteran First Amendment attorney. "Clearly what happened," Ward surmised, "is that some of the big shots said, 'We've been handling these First Amendment cases. We've been to the Supreme Court.'"[2] Bruce Sanford, the Washington DC attorney who represented the Society of Professional Journalists and would be the lead writer of the national amicus brief on behalf of the *Press-Enterprise*, said it "was not too surprising that when a case was granted cert that the New York people would swoop in and try to get the case." Some lawyers may have "stealthily put out publishers to call Tim and lobby him. It's the New York view of the world: Nobody is as smart and great as we are. That old New Yorker cover."[3]

While some might have frowned on this form of poaching, others understood the rationale even if they didn't agree with it. Edward J. McIntyre, a San Diego lawyer who represented the Copley Press, viewed Jim Ward as a valued ally in numerous court access battles. But McIntyre sensed "a slight unease" among First Amendment experts about "a lawyer from a small firm in Riverside coming back to argue an issue involving the First Amendment. "I'm sure the powers that be would have loved to have someone . . . out of the Supreme Court elite."[4] This case, won or lost, would affect *all* media and the public, not just a Riverside daily. The stakes were high, and Ward was a constitutional law neophyte. Still, McIntyre believed he was the right man for the job. The elite lawyers "would not have had the same passion for the First Amendment that Jim had or the battle scars of the experience. Jim had been fighting this fight. This was not a one-off case. It was a long-standing effort on the part of Copley and the *Press-Enterprise*."[5] Even Jane Carney, the Riverside lawyer and community leader who knew Tim Hays and Jim Ward well and thought highly of both, probably would have understood the sentiment behind a dump-Ward campaign. "Tim was involved in the world of publishing. He could have found a First Amendment lawyer who had done a number of cases before the Supreme Court. But he believed in promoting people that he thought were talented. And I think that's part of what was at work here, though it's kind of shocking. If you're going to all the expense of arguing before the Supreme Court and you let somebody argue for you who's never been there before?"[6] Certainly this must have occurred to the editor of the *Press-Enterprise*. But Tim Hays saw something in Jim Ward. Something that he liked—and trusted.

James David Ward was born on a Sunday, September 8, 1935, in Sioux Falls, South Dakota. Juanita Marion Ward had given birth to a daughter five years earlier and desperately wanted a son. "It was made clear to me that I was a spoiled child," Ward wrote in "Not a Memoir," a 330-page, three-ring binder account of his first twenty-five years. When Jim was just two, his father fretted in a 1937 diary entry that his son might become a "sissy."[7]

Charles David Ward Jr., Jim's father, was one of three sons. C. D. Ward Sr. started out as a railroad worker, became a salesman for Marshall Fields department store in Chicago, and eventually "scrounged up enough money to start a little lumber yard that also sold hardware, coal, ice and cement blocks." The lumber business turned out to be so successful that C.D. decided to open two more yards so that each son would have one. By the time he died, there were two Ward lumber companies in Illinois and one in Sioux Falls.[8] "This was back in the day when the lumber business was a significant business in the community," said Jim Ward. "That's the business I was going to go into. I was going to be a lumber man like my dad. I was totally enamored of my dad."[9]

But one Sunday morning, after Jim had finished delivering the *Des Moines Sunday Register* and had gone out to the backyard to read, a family friend suddenly "emerged from our backdoor" and told him "something bad" had happened. "I won't tell you now, but I came to be with you." Ward soon learned that his father, who had taken up flying—and who had sometimes taken Jim up with him and flown over the Ward home where Juanita stood in the backyard, waving a white dish towel—had crashed his plane. He was forty-one. Jim was just eleven.[10] Everything changed. "My mom was a high school graduate, a bright lady, a very, very pretty lady with a lot of social graces. But she didn't know the ways of the world. She was ill-prepared to be a widow and take care of two kids. Because my dad died, I had no direction. I had to make it all up. It made me stronger."[11] His father's brothers stepped up. One of them, "Uncle T" or "Toad," became a surrogate dad who was "always there." But something else was always there, too. It was something Ward could identify but not readily explain, especially after losing his father at such a young age. "I've always had confidence in myself. I can handle it. I can do it."[12]

By the time he was a senior at Washington High School, Jim Ward was doing it, or had already done it, in a big way. The 1953 edition of the *Warrior*, the high school yearbook, features what today might be regarded as a nerdy photograph that shows Jim Ward wearing a jacket, tie, and crew cut. His large glasses cast dark shadows over his eyes, but his smile is as radiant as his dimples are deep. The photo contrasts starkly with the serious-to-sour high school pictures of the native Iowan Ward met decades later: Norman Cherniss. Ward was one of twenty "senior representatives" the *Warrior* variously described as energetic, artistic, enthusiastic, scientific. Ward's label: Vigilant. "Jim Ward, always on the lookout for another job to help. What would WHS have done without him this past year? First semester co-editor of the Orange and Black [newspaper] and President of Student Council." An inch-deep caption lists no less than eighteen activities, organizations, and titles. "I was Mr. Big Shot in high school. I was Mr. Everything.

I joined every organization, gave speeches, served as master of cere-monies. If I was in an organization, I wanted to be president of it."[13]

Mr. Everything was part of a "feared" debating team that won a South Dakota championship. And he may have been an even better seat-of-the-pants orator. At the 1953 National Forensic League speech tournament in Denver, Ward placed third in the nation in extem-poraneous speaking.[14] A natural-born speaker, even something of a showman, Ward was "willing to get up and speak anywhere, anytime to anybody."[15] Not just in high school, but well beyond. "He was a very good trial lawyer," said Don Grant, one of his long-time partners at Thompson & Colegate. "He had a good presence in the courtroom, a good ego. He was very verbose. He could laugh and make jokes [and] he came in with big verdicts."[16]

Ward's mother, Juanita, gave him a trip to Europe when he gradu-ated from high school in 1953. It was the first zig in a series of post–high school zags. That fall he enrolled at the University of Colorado and dropped out after his freshman year. In 1954 he went back to Europe with his mom, though he soon went off on his own. He spent a year touring and taking courses at the universities of Oslo and Vienna. Not yet twenty, he fell in love with Paris, where he met and eventually fell in love with a Long Beach, California, student named Carole June Sander. They married in 1956.[17]

Ward returned from Europe with what he considered to be a man-of-the-world Van Dyke moustache and beard and a spotty academic record. But he also returned with a plan. He reluctantly shaved the foliage and enrolled in the University of South Dakota. In a two-year stretch that included summer and night school, Ward completed his undergraduate work and squeezed in a year of law school. Then he headed to California, where he graduated from the University of San Francisco Law School in 1959, only a few months after his mother, who was just fifty, died of cancer. Ward was in the U.S. Army when he learned he passed the California bar exam.[18] Once he had obtained the necessary papers from the State Bar of California and explained certain procedures to a base officer, Jim Ward raised his right hand in a "sparsely furnished office in a wooden building at Ford Ord" and on January 19, 1960, got himself sworn in as a lawyer.[19]

Three months later, in search of a small Southern California city and a job with a district attorney, the Wards found their way to Riverside, where the newly minted lawyer went to work for the Riverside County DA. Four years later, he joined Thompson & Colegate. In decades that followed, Ward became the Mr. Everything of Riverside: president of the county bar association, vice president of the Board of Governors of the State Bar of California, chairman of the state Judicial Nominees Evaluation Commission, president of the Riverside Opera Association, and on and on. "I jumped into the community. I got to know a lot of people."[20] Including the editor of the local paper.

They weren't "bosom buddies," Tim Hays and Jim Ward. But they socialized, had dinner together, played tennis. Hays had his own court and a regular doubles foursome. Charlie Field, a very good tennis player, a judge, and Tim Hays's longtime friend, belonged to that foursome. "Tim wasn't terribly good at tennis, but that's not the point. The point is, it's an interesting way to analyze people. Your character comes out—if they're cheaters, if their morality is a little weak, just about anything along those lines. Character is revealed by tennis."[21] Though Ward wasn't part of that foursome, he was a frequent sub, and it's safe to say that he revealed his character, and Hays found it to his liking. He even threw a little *Press-Enterprise* business to Mr. Everything well before Ward became Riverside's Mr. Everything.

Jim Ward launched his new life in Riverside with Carole, their new baby girl, Kelly, and that trademark self-confidence. While in law school, Ward had become a fan of Don Sherwood, a San Francisco radio deejay who billed himself as "the world's greatest disc jockey." Ward loved it, thought it was funny, and stole it.[22] As the new Riversider introduced himself around town, making the connections an ambitious lawyer makes, he would add, always with a grin, "I'm commonly known as the world's greatest attorney." When California began issuing vanity license plates, James David Ward, who customarily drove a Cadillac, ordered JDWWGA. If Ward had fun with it ("I milked it for years "), others did, too. Once, as Ward prepared to speak before a Riverside gathering, the man who introduced him told the audience WGA stood for "Won't Go Away."[23]

That was certainly the case in 1983: Jim Ward wasn't going away. Tim Hays proved "impervious" to overtures on behalf of big shot First Amendment lawyers. "He's not a follower," Charlie Field said of Hays. "Don't try to lead him. Dump Jim Ward? It wouldn't occur to him. Jim sold himself. Jim seriously believed his firm could handle the case very well. It's true there were other firms far more experienced, but a lack of experience never slowed down some people."[24]

No, JDWWGA wasn't going away. He was going to the United States Supreme Court.

8

The Battleground

FIRST AMENDMENT: Congress shall make no law . . . abridging the freedom of speech, or of the press, or the right of the people peaceably to assemble.

SIXTH AMENDMENT: In all criminal prosecutions, the accused shall enjoy the right to a speedy and public trial, by an impartial jury.[1]

FOURTEENTH AMENDMENT: No state shall make or enforce any law which shall abridge the privileges or immunities of citizens of the United States; nor shall any state deprive any person of life, liberty, or property, without due process of law; nor deny to any person within its jurisdiction the equal protection of the laws.[2]

When the U.S. Supreme Court agrees to hear a case, it doesn't explain why. But the *Press-Enterprise* was hopeful: if the four justices had been happy with the California Supreme Court's curt disposal of closed voir dire—"HEARING DENIED"—why did they vote to take the case?

Press-Enterprise Co. v. Superior Court arrived at a time when the Burger court, much like California newspapers and courts, was being confronted by First Amendment issues. In some key cases the Burger court was putting the squeeze on the press. True, it had ruled in 1971 that the Nixon administration could not stop the *New York Times* from publishing the Pentagon Papers, a secret report ordered by the Defense Department that documented decades of government lies about the Vietnam War. The court ruled that prior restraint—*preventing* the publication of information except when, for example, it could compromise national security—violated the First Amendment.

But decisions that followed were distinctly unfavorable to the press. In *Branzburg v. Hayes* (1972) and two companion cases, three reporters from separate news organizations had been subpoenaed by separate grand juries. All based their refusal to testify on protections guaranteed by the First Amendment. Justice Byron White, writing for the court's 5-4 majority, said reporters wanted the court "to grant newsmen a testimonial privilege that other citizens do not enjoy. This we decline to do."[3] In *Zurcher v. Stanford Daily* (1978), with Justice White again writing for the majority, the court ruled that a Palo Alto Police Department's search of the college newspaper's office did not violate the Fourth Amendment, since the department obtained a legitimate warrant, or the First Amendment, since the press was not exempt from search warrants. Again, no special privileges.[4] In *Herbert v. Lando* (1979), the court had to decide whether Colonel Anthony Herbert, who had exposed what he claimed to be atrocities by U.S. troops in Vietnam, could probe the state of mind of CBS's *60 Minutes* staffers, including Mike Wallace, the pull-no-punches interviewer whose investigative report suggested Herbert had invented some of these claims to make himself look better. The court sided with Herbert, ruling that the First Amendment did not grant the media a privilege to *not* answer questions about thoughts, opinions, and conclusions.[5] It was against this backdrop that the *Press-Enterprise* appeal narrowly reached a Supreme Court populated by a quartet of Richard Nixon appointees: Burger, Harry Blackmun, Lewis Powell, and William Rehnquist. "'Oh my goodness!'" exclaimed Jim Ward as he mockingly reprised one of the "negative" rants he heard from other lawyers before the court took the case. "'You've got to wait for a court that's more disposed to rule in our favor!'"[6] But while the court seemed to be putting the squeeze on the press, it was also undergoing a gradual, at times herky-jerky, transformation when it came to balancing a defendant's Sixth Amendment right to a fair and public trial with a *constitutional* right that did not yet exist: public and press access to courtrooms. It was an evolutionary process that began at a time when the press and judges were behaving so badly that the Supreme Court had to step in. The following eat-your-spinach primer tracks this evolution starting with the out-of-control trial of a Cleveland doctor that resulted in *Sheppard v. Maxwell*. Next came the media-gagging judge whose excessive control led to *Nebraska Press Association v. Stuart*. The closure of a pretrial hearing produced the controversial and sloppy, yet pioneering and pivotal, *Gannett v. DePasquale*. The closure of an *entire* trial resulted in *Richmond Newspapers v. Virginia*, a genuine landmark case granting a *constitutional* right of public access to criminal trials. And, finally, *Globe Newspapers v. Superior Court*, which solidified *Richmond* but did not address whether the public and press had a First Amendment right to attend jury selection and preliminary hearings.

Sheppard v. Maxwell (1966)

Before dawn on July 4, 1954, Marilyn Sheppard, the pregnant, thirty-one-year-old wife of Dr. Sam Sheppard, was bludgeoned to death in her Bay Village home near Cleveland. Sam Sheppard, a prominent osteopath, told authorities he had tangled with a "bushy haired" man—presumably the killer—only to pass out on the Lake Erie beach after taking a hit to the head. Investigators didn't believe him. On July 30, Bay Village police arrested Sheppard, also thirty-one, for murder. But the arrest came much too late for "Mr. Cleveland"—Louis Benson Seltzer, editor of the *Cleveland Press*.[7]

That summer the Sheppard story went low-tech viral. British and French newspapers ran with it. So did *Stars and Stripes*, a newspaper with worldwide reach serving the U.S. military community. Louis Seltzer's *Cleveland Press* and its afternoon rival, the *News*, flooded the city with numerous editions throughout the long summer afternoons. Readers ate it up, and circulation climbed.[8] And "Mr. Cleveland," a short, bald, sixth-grade dropout with a thirst for exposing wrongdoing and a deep resentment of the upper crust, whipped up a public frenzy.[9]

"SOMEBODY IS GETTING AWAY WITH MURDER," read the July 20 headline on Seltzer's front-page editorial. "If ever a murder case was studded with fumbling, halting, stupid, uncooperative bumbling-politeness to people . . . the Sheppard case has them all."[10] The next day, another front-pager: "Why No Inquest, Do It Now, Dr. Gerber." Coroner Gerber agreed to hold an inquest the very next day.[11] As July slogged through its final week, the *Cleveland Press* flogged the story. "You can bet your last dollar the Sheppard murder would have been cleaned up long ago if it had involved 'average people,'" sneered another front-page editorial.[12] On July 30, the *Press* demanded, "Why Isn't Sam Sheppard in Jail?" Later editions shrieked: "Quit Stalling and Bring Him In!" That night, police brought him in.[13]

When the trial began on October 18, 1954, the press corps numbered roughly sixty reporters, including the *New York Daily News*, which boasted the largest daily circulation in the nation.[14] Television, the up-and-coming new medium, rolled its cameras on the courthouse steps. Dorothy Kilgallen, the popular TV quiz show panelist who banged out her syndicated Hearst column on a pink electric typewriter, yearned to be viewed as a serious reporter. But when the star-struck trial judge, Edward Blythin, invited her into his chambers and told her, "It's an open-and-shut case. He's guilty as hell," Kilgallen didn't write a word.[15]

Jury selection in this "Trial of the Century" was open to the public and press.[16] Wide open. Nearly a month before they even showed up for jury duty, seventy-five prospective jurors' names and addresses appeared in all three Cleveland dailies.[17] Once voir dire began, "reporters and photographers . . . interviewed potential jurors, took photos and ran articles."[18] The jurors "received mail from people, telling them to convict Sheppard."[19] When the trial got underway, photographers stood on tables or perched on the judge's bench as jurors posed for pictures. Sheppard's lawyer objected; the judge ignored him.[20] On December 21, 1954, the jury convicted Sheppard of second-degree murder, and Judge Blythin sentenced him to life. When, after years of trying to get a new trial, Sheppard's aging lawyer died in 1961, a new young lawyer stepped in. F. Lee Bailey persuaded federal judge Carl A. Weinman to rule that Sheppard's trial had been "a mockery of justice. . . . If there ever was a trial by newspaper, this is a perfect example."[21] But a federal appeals court reversed Weinman, so Bailey appealed to the *highest* court. On June 6, 1966, the U.S. Supreme

Court, ruling in *Sheppard v. Maxwell*, voted 8–1 that Sam Sheppard had been deprived of his constitutional rights and deserved a new trial. He got one and was acquitted.[22]

The opening passages of the Supreme Court's opinion were blistering and damning: "Newsmen were allowed to take over almost the entire small courtroom, hounding [Sheppard] and most of the participants. Twenty reporters were assigned seats by the court . . . in close proximity to the jury and counsel, precluding privacy between [Sheppard] and his counsel. The movement of the reporters in the courtroom caused frequent confusion and disrupted the trial. . . . Before the jurors began deliberations they . . . had access to all news media, though the court made 'suggestions' and 'requests' that the jurors not expose themselves to comment about the case. Pervasive publicity was given to the case throughout the trial, much of it involving incriminating matter not introduced at the trial, and the jurors were thrust into the role of celebrities."

Though the Supreme Court recognized for the first time that prejudicial press coverage could lead to an unfair (and unconstitutional) trial,[23] Justice Tom Clark, who wrote the opinion, treated the media gingerly: "A responsible press has always been regarded as the handmaiden of effective judicial administration. . . . The Court has, therefore, been unwilling to place any direct limitations on the freedom traditionally exercised by the news media for what transpires in the courtroom is public property."

But in this case, where there was scant evidence of a "responsible press," where "bedlam reigned at the courthouse during the trial," where a "carnival atmosphere could easily have been avoided," somebody had to take the fall.[24] That somebody was Judge Blythin. He could have done more to shield jurors from the press. He could have done the same for witnesses. He could have ordered lawyers, witnesses, and law enforcement not to talk to the press. Instead, he lost control of his courtroom.[25]

In ruling that Sam Sheppard had been deprived of his constitutional rights, the court found that the press had gone too far and the judge had not gone far enough. The case moved state bar associations and the media to adopt voluntary guidelines to balance the interests of fair trial and free press.[26] It also encouraged judges to tighten control over their courtrooms. But some judges tightened it into a stranglehold.

Nebraska Press Association v. Stuart (1976)

The name Erwin Charles Simants still sends shudders through Sutherland, a small town in western Nebraska.[27] On Saturday evening, October 18, 1975, the rifle-toting Simants entered the home of his next-door neighbors, Henry and Audrey Marie Kellie. Their ten-year-old granddaughter, Florence, was home alone. Simants, twenty-nine, sexually assaulted her, then shot her to death. As other family members arrived, Simants shot and killed them: Henry, sixty-six, and Audrey, fifty-seven, whom he sexually assaulted after he killed her; then Henry and Audrey's son, David, thirty-two, and David's children, Deanna, six, and Daniel, five. Simants was arrested the next day.[28]

The murders stirred a national wave of newspaper, radio, and television coverage. Three days after the crime, Simants's lawyer and the Lincoln County prosecutor asked the county judge to muzzle everyone, including the press, because of "the reasonable likelihood" that "prejudicial news" would make it impossible for Simants to get a fair trial.[29] The judge issued a "restrictive order" prohibiting *everyone*, media included, from "releas[ing] or authoriz[ing] the release for public dissemination . . . any testimony given or evidence." That same day the court held a preliminary hearing, which was open to the public. Simants was ordered to stand trial for murder and sexual assault.[30] The day after being gagged at the preliminary hearing, various media organizations and reporters tried to have the gag lifted. But Lincoln County District Court judge Hugh Stuart imposed a new order that barred the press from reporting "the existence or contents" of a confession Simants made to law enforcement officers. The confession had been introduced in open court.[31]

The press appealed to the Nebraska Supreme Court, which loosened the gag a little but still prevented the reporters from writing about any confessions or admissions unless Simants confessed directly to them. On June 30, 1976, ruling in *Nebraska Press Association v. Stu-*

art, the U.S. Supreme Court unanimously reversed the Nebraska Supreme Court.

Chief Justice Warren Burger, who wrote the majority opinion, said the trial judge had been "justified" in concluding the case would generate "intense and pervasive pretrial publicity." But, he added, "Pretrial publicity, even if pervasive and concentrated, cannot be regarded as leading automatically and in every kind of criminal case to an unfair trial." Prior restraint that stopped the press from publishing evidence presented in open court "violated the settled principle that there is nothing that proscribes the press from reporting events that transpire in the courtroom." The Supreme Court's ruling warned that muzzling the media could backfire. Because the murders occurred in a community of 850 people, "it is reasonable to assume that, without any news accounts being printed or broadcast, rumors would travel swiftly by word of mouth." Those rumors could be "far more damaging than reasonably accurate news accounts."

Burger reached back a few centuries, citing the "historic episode in which John Adams defended British soldiers charged with homicide for firing into a crowd of Boston demonstrators." He noted that lawyers who helped draft the Constitution and Bill of Rights were well aware of "the part that passions of the populace sometimes play in influencing potential jurors." He recalled the "acute problems" Chief Justice Marshall faced in "selecting an unbiased jury" in the 1807 Aaron Burr treason trial. He cited the "carnival atmosphere" surrounding the 1935 trial of Bruno Hauptmann, accused and later convicted of kidnapping and killing aviator Charles Lindbergh's baby. Pretrial publicity could create real problems, and an irresponsible press could compound them. "Freedom of the press," said the majority opinion, "is not an absolute right." But immediately resorting to prior restraint was absolutely wrong.

In the eyes of the Supreme Court the Nebraska judge failed to consider alternatives the Supreme Court laid out in *Sheppard v. Maxwell*: change of venue, postponing the trial, close questioning to weed out prospective jurors who had made up their minds, clear instructions that jurors weigh nothing but evidence presented in court. These were the remedies that should have been considered and tried first, because "prior restraints on speech and publication are the most serious and the least tolerable infringement on First Amendment rights."

In a concurring opinion Justice William Brennan, perhaps the court's fiercest defender of the First Amendment, raised another alternative to the gag: "closing pretrial proceedings." But he quickly added, "We are not now confronted with such issues." Brennan may not have intended this as an invitation, but some trial court judges, viewing this as another way to control their courtrooms, would take him up on it.

Gannett v. DePasquale (1979)

The Supreme Court's stance on public access to courtrooms was beginning to evolve. But it was still very much in its adolescence: gangly, sloppy and, perhaps unwittingly, pioneering. All in one case.

The story began on July 19, 1976, when Wayne Clapp, a former city police officer near Rochester in upstate New York, disappeared while fishing on nearby Seneca Lake. Clapp and two youths had been seen at a marina, but when his bullet-riddled boat returned later in the day, Clapp was missing. So were his truck, his .357 magnum, and the two young men. Divers searched the lake, but Clapp's body was never found. Following a nationwide dragnet that deployed helicopters and tracking dogs, Michigan police arrested Kyle Greathouse, sixteen, and David Jones, twenty-one. According to press accounts, the pair confessed and returned to New York, where a Seneca County grand jury indicted them for second-degree murder and robbery.[32] At a pretrial hearing to suppress confessions that they claimed were coerced, the defendants asked Judge Daniel DePasquale to evict the public and press. Their lawyers claimed the "unabated build-up of adverse publicity" had already compromised the chances of a fair trial. The prosecutor didn't object to closing the courtroom. Neither did Carol Ritter, the reporter covering the hearing for the *Rochester Times-Union* and *Rochester Democrat & Chronicle*, both Gannett newspapers.[33] Ritter, thirty-five, sat in her regular courtroom seat that day: right up front, the first seat next to the clerk. Though she faced the jury box, Ritter had a bird's-eye view of her friend, "Danny"

DePasquale. Sometimes the judge came to the Ritters' home, where he "stood around our piano until three or four in the morning. . . . He knew the words to every song written between 1910 and 1970. Everybody loved Danny."[34] When the judge booted her out of the courtroom (he told her it was nothing personal), it wasn't exactly a stunner. "A lot of courtrooms were being closed. I had been kicked out of a couple of courtrooms for various reasons. Even though I had reported it to my bosses, they didn't take particular interest in it. But this was a very gory, disgusting murder case."[35]

Ritter's bosses told her to wait in the courthouse while they decided what to do. Meanwhile, DePasquale proceeded with the hearing. Shortly before it ended, Ritter finally heard from her bosses and asked the judge to postpone the hearing and listen to arguments against keeping her out. He refused. Days later Robert Bernius, a thirty-year-old Gannett lawyer, traveled to the courthouse, armed with blank sheets of paper, a stapler, and a notary stamp. After Ritter told him what had happened, Bernius bought lunch for a courthouse secretary, paid her five bucks to use her typewriter, and banged out a motion to lift the ejection order and obtain the hearing transcript.[36] His core argument: the public and press had been deprived of their First, Sixth, and Fourteenth Amendment rights "to attend and disseminate news of the hearing."[37] Judge DePasquale rejected the motion and refused Gannett's request to explain why he thought it was necessary to close his courtroom. He offered no insight about how the two defendants would be prejudiced by an open hearing and why there weren't alternatives to barring the public and the press.[38] Instead DePasquale sealed the hearing transcript. An appellate court nullified DePasquale's order. But the New York Court of Appeals, the state's highest court, reversed that ruling, dismissing the public's interest in an open hearing as "mere curiosity."[39] Even though Judge DePasquale eventually released the sealed hearing transcript, Gannett appealed to the U.S. Supreme Court.

In *Sheppard v. Maxwell*, the Supreme Court told judges to control their courtrooms. In *Nebraska Press Association v. Stuart*, the court floated the idea that judges could control their courtrooms simply by closing them. In agreeing to hear *Gannett v. DePasquale*, the court would decide if a judge who closed his courtroom acted properly.

First Amendment lawyers began to organize themselves into a "media bar" in the 1970s as cases involving prior restraint (Pentagon Papers) and reporters' privilege (*Branzburg v. Hayes*) began to flow to the Supreme Court. But they didn't know what to make of the Gannett case because "this whole issue of closing courtrooms came out of nowhere."[40] It "snuck into the court."[41] And they certainly weren't thinking about Gannett, which hadn't been involved in high-profile First Amendment cases that "had captured the public's imagination."[42] Some thought Allen Neuharth, the "brash and blustery media mogul who built the Gannett empire"—and president of the American Newspaper Publishers Association at the time—was engaging "in a bit of showmanship."[43] So when *Gannett v. DePasquale* reached the Supreme Court, the dumbfounded First Amendment fraternity could only ask, "Where did this come from? Why didn't we have a moot court [a grueling run-through to make sure lawyers arguing before the Supreme Court didn't damage the cause of the First Amendment]? Why weren't we consulted about this?"[44] What's more, they thought the case was an "awful" First Amendment test. It dealt with a pretrial hearing, not a trial. A "procedural" matter, not the "core of the criminal justice system."[45] And it was going to be heard by a court stocked with four Nixon appointees. How likely were they to discover a First Amendment right of the press to set foot in a courtroom?[46]

To Gannett lawyer Robert Bernius, there was nothing sneaky at all. How could a case that had risen through the New York court system and reached the nation's highest court sneak anywhere?[47] Plus he had amicus briefs from the American Civil Liberties Union, the National Association of Broadcasters, and the New York chapter of Sigma Delta Chi, the nation's oldest organization representing journalists.[48] Floyd Abrams, a First Amendment lawyer who had worked on the Pentagon Papers, *Branzburg*, and *Nebraska Press Association* cases, submitted an amicus brief on behalf of the *New York Times*.[49] Bernius thought he had a winner. And it appeared that he did—until he didn't.

Following the oral arguments the Supreme Court justices met in conference to discuss and vote on the case. The First Amendment "right" went practically nowhere. Most justices either didn't see it or feared it would open the door to all kinds of access, from grand jury proceedings to executive sessions, perhaps even conferences involving court justices.[50] But the Sixth Amendment's guarantee of a "public trial" caused a split. It appeared that a five-justice majority favored reversing DePasquale's court closure. Justice Harry Blackmun began to draft what he and others assumed would be the court's opinion.[51] The Sixth Amendment issue boiled down to this: Was a defendant's right to a public trial—or, in this case, a public pretrial hearing—his and his alone? If he waived that right, could the courtroom be closed? Or did the public and press have a Sixth Amendment right to a public trial, too? If so, would a judge have to make "findings"—present a specific, on-the-record rationale before conducting a secret hearing?

Blackmun thought the public and press did have a Sixth Amendment right. He and other justices that made up the supposed majority noted that most criminal cases (upward of 90 percent) never went to trial. The defendants in this very case, Greathouse and Jones, pleaded guilty to a lesser charge. No trial.[52] Pretrial hearings, argued Blackmun, may be the only chance for the public to learn how the police obtained a confession, to witness the conduct of the judge and lawyers, and to assess the truthfulness of witnesses. In short, the only chance to decide whether justice was being served. But Justice Potter Stewart, who believed he was writing a dissenting opinion, backed Judge DePasquale, arguing that the Sixth Amendment's guarantee of a public trial was the defendant's right alone. There was no need for the public to worry about whether justice was being served because the prosecutor, who represented The People, would see to that. Even if the Sixth Amendment guarantee extended to the public and press, it was only for trials, not pretrial hearings. As for "any" First Amendment right—and Stewart didn't think there was one— Judge DePasquale held a hearing and gave the First Amendment argument "all appropriate deference." And rejected it. He handled it properly. End of story.[53]

The battle lines were drawn, but the majority, never that firm, began to crumble. On May 31, 1979, months after the conference and well after the justices circulated their draft opinions, Justice Lewis Powell, the majority's supposed "swing vote," informed Blackmun that he'd changed his mind. He felt more in tune with Stewart's views on the Sixth Amendment. He had also concluded that *Gannett* was really more of a First Amendment case and would write a separate opinion to explain. The majority had flipped.[54] With just a few weeks remaining in the court's term, Stewart scrambled to recast his dissenting opinion into the Supreme Court's majority opinion. It would not be pretty. On July 2, 1979, the court ruled 5–4 to uphold Judge DePasquale. It also dropped a twenty-one-word bombshell. Potter Stewart wasn't the only justice who appeared to use the words *trial* and *pretrial* interchangeably. But when his majority opinion declared, "we hold that members of the public have no constitutional right under the Sixth and Fourteenth Amendments to attend criminal trials," the nation's newspapers were horrified.

The next day's *Washington Post* reported the decision on the front page. "A closely divided Supreme Court ruled yesterday that members of the public have 'no constitutional rights' to attend criminal trials." Then came the firestorm.

"A Disastrous Assault" fumed a Fourth of July editorial in the *Los Angeles Times*: "The U.S. Supreme Court, turning its back on the Constitution and on two centuries of open judicial process, has taken the nation further down the ominous path to secret trials."

A day later, the *New York Times* lead editorial, headlined "Private Justice, Public Injustice," weighed in: "Now the Supreme Court has endorsed secrecy in language broad enough to justify its use not only in a pre-trial context but even at a formal trial."

The *Washington Post* editorialized: "The justices reached this startling conclusion by brushing aside . . . one of the basic sentiments upon which this country was founded: Distrust of secret trials, bred by the excesses of the Star Chamber and the Spanish Inquisition."[55]

New York Times columnist Anthony Lewis, a two-time Pulitzer Prize winner and a pioneer of legal reporting, called the ruling extreme—an example of "all-or-nothing jurisprudence." But he took a swipe at his own profession, urging the press "to foreswear absolutes. The . . . claim of recent years that its freedom has no limits has done the press no good. If the press began recognizing that these are difficult issues involving more than one interest, it could more effectively criticize the facile simplicity of a Gannett decision."[56] Justice William Brennan, perhaps the court's fiercest defender of the First Amendment, sounded a similar theme in the fall of 1979, saying the press's "excessive" reaction to the 1972 *Herbert v. Lando* state-of-mind ruling had impaired its credibility when it expressed "quite correct" opposition to *Gannett v. DePasquale*.[57]

Allen Neuharth—the Gannett "showman"—called the ruling "another chilling demonstration that the majority of the Burger court is determined to unmake the Constitution. This case is not simply a matter of free press vs. fair trial. Rather, it is the Supreme Court saying that the judiciary is a private judicial club, which can shut the door and conduct public business in private."[58] And out in Riverside, California, fifty miles and almost a world away from Los Angeles, Norman Cherniss, the pipe-puffing executive editor of the *Press-Enterprise* wrote, "It has been pointed out that 90 percent of all criminal cases are settled in the pretrial stage. This, then, is no minor exception to the open courtroom. Nor is it merely another one of this court's anti-press rulings, for the public would be specifically excluded, too. But worse is what it augurs as far as this court is concerned for main trials themselves." The July 5 editorial, headlined "Closed Court," concluded, "Once again, this is one of the court's Draconian decisions involving the press, representing the public, and the tragedy of the ruling is underscored by the court's emphasis not only on the desirability of closed proceedings, but the absolute right to them."

A few weeks after the July 2 ruling a Maryland judge closed a preliminary hearing for a man accused of arson.[59] That September the South Dakota Supreme Court locked arms with the Burger court, ruling that the public had no right to attend a criminal trial.[60] On July 3, 1980—a full year after the ruling—the *Washington Post* reported that judges had closed their courtrooms for all or part of criminal proceedings more than 260 times.

The Supreme Court justices, normally immune and aloof from the masses, felt the heat when they hit the speaking circuit after the 1979 term ended. Chief Justice Burger said judges had been misinterpreting the rule that was meant for pretrial proceedings only.[61] Justice John Paul Stevens suggested that judges might be rubber-stamping to shut their courtrooms.[62] And Justice Blackmun, whose majority opinion had morphed into a bristling dissent, said the *Gannett* majority opinion meant exactly what these lower-court judges thought it meant: thanks to the Supreme Court, full trials, not just hearings, could be closed to the public and the press.[63] Justice Lewis Powell, the defector from the original court majority, dropped a hint: *Gannett* didn't settle anything, at least not as far as the First Amendment was concerned.[64] Powell's flip-flop had a double-barreled impact: It allowed the court to deprive the public and press of a Sixth Amendment right of access. But Powell's concurring opinion had opened another public access avenue. "Because of the importance of the public's having accurate information concerning the operation of its criminal justice system, I would hold explicitly that petitioner's reporter had an interest protected by the First and Fourteenth Amendments in being present at the pretrial suppression hearing." Some would view this opinion as a turning point—arguably *the* turning point—in securing a constitutional right of courtroom access for the public and the press.[65]

Lee Levine, a First Amendment lawyer who would play a key role in preparing the national amicus briefs in support of the *Press-Enterprise*, said *Gannett* "emboldened judges to start closing stuff . . . emboldened media lawyers to get involved and emboldened the Supreme Court to [say] 'Hey, this was a Sixth Amendment case. We haven't heard a First Amendment case. Hint, hint.'"[66] In October 1979, just three months after its *Gannett* decision, the Supreme Court voted to hear a case in which a judge closed an entire trial.

Richmond Newspapers, Inc. v. Virginia (1980)

John Paul Stevenson had already been tried three times for stabbing a hotel clerk to death in 1975. The Virginia Supreme Court tossed out his second-degree murder conviction, ruling that Stevenson's bloodstained shirt had been improperly admitted into evidence. Trial two ended in mistrial. So did trial three. When Stevenson returned to the same court for the fourth time, he asked Judge Richard H. C. Taylor to close his courtroom to the public. The prosecutor didn't object. The two reporters in the room didn't immediately object, though Richmond Newspapers challenged the ruling in a hearing later that day. Judge Taylor, citing a state law that "gives me that power [to ban the public] specifically," cleared the courtroom of everyone except witnesses when they were called to testify. During the hearing to fight the closure, the paper's lawyer argued that Judge Taylor hadn't cited any evidence to justify his action and that he had failed to consider fair-trial alternatives that stopped short of banning the press and the public. Judge Taylor was not convinced. He observed that the courtroom's "layout" made him "think that having people in the Courtroom is distracting to the jury. . . . When we get our new Court Building . . . the rule of the Court may be different."[67]

The newspapers appealed Taylor's ruling, and the U.S. Supreme Court, perhaps eager to dig out of a self-excavated hole, took the case. On July 2, 1980, one year to the day after ruling in *Gannett*, the Supreme Court ruled 7–1 (Justice Rehnquist dissenting) that the public and the press have a First Amendment right to attend criminal trials. It was a remarkably swift, "lightning speed" turnaround.[68] Justice Harry Blackmun, whose *Gannett* opinion had flipped from majority to dissent,[69] seemed to revel in the I-told-you-so moment. "It is gratifying . . . to see the Court wash away at least some of the graffiti that marred the prevailing opinions in *Gannett*. No fewer than 12 times in the primary opinion in that case, the Court . . . observed that its Sixth Amendment closure ruling applied to the trial itself."

Richmond was all about the First Amendment, which had barely managed a cameo in *Gannett*. Now it was now center stage. Chief Justice Burger, whose plurality opinion attracted more support (just two justices) than any of the other six *Richmond* opinions, found himself in his accustomed position of trumpeting a press-friendly result. "We hold that the right to attend criminal trials is implicit in the guarantees of the First Amendment; without the freedom to attend such trials, which people have exercised for centuries, important aspects of freedom of speech and of the press could be eviscerated."

Burger blended his historical perspective with simple yet eloquent insight. "People in an open society do not demand infallibility from their institutions, but it is difficult for them to accept what they are prohibited from observing. When a criminal trial is conducted in the open, there is at least an opportunity both for understanding the system in general and its workings in a particular case."

A year earlier, only Justice Powell had detected First Amendment right of access to courtrooms. Now, almost overnight, a court majority had fallen into step; never mind that there wasn't a word about public access to courts in the Constitution or Bill of Rights. Chief Justice Burger dutifully cautioned against "reading into the Constitution rights not explicitly defined," then plunged ahead: "the Court has acknowledged that certain unarticulated rights are implicit in enumerated guarantees. For example, the rights of association and of privacy, the right to be presumed innocent, and the right to be judged by a standard of proof beyond a reasonable doubt in a criminal trial . . . appear nowhere in the Constitution or Bill of Rights. Yet these important but unarticulated rights have nonetheless been found to share constitutional protection in common with explicit guarantees."

Justice John Paul Stevens called it "a watershed case. Until today, the Court has accorded virtually absolute protection to the dissemination of information or ideas, but never before has it squarely held that the acquisition of newsworthy matter is entitled to any constitutional protection whatsoever."

In a chewy bit of prose, Justice Brennan wrote, "What countervailing interests might be sufficiently compelling to reverse this presumption of openness need not concern us now." What really mattered was that the Supreme Court had struck down a law that gave "unfettered discretion" to judges and lawyers to close their courtrooms.

The chief justice sketched out a framework for ejecting the public and press from criminal trials by chronicling what the Virginia judge had *not* done: "[T]he trial judge made no findings to support closure;

no inquiry was made as to whether alternative solutions would have met the need to ensure fairness; there was no recognition of any right under the Constitution for the public or press to attend the trial. . . . Absent an overriding interest articulated in findings, the trial of a criminal case must be open to the public."

The *Gannett* tide had turned. "It will take a while to figure out all the implications of the Supreme Court decision yesterday," said the *Washington Post* in an editorial headlined "Opening Those Closed Doors." "So for the moment we will just note with great satisfaction that the court has put a stop to the growing tendency of trial judges to do their work in secret."[70]

"Secrecy Is Our Enemy," declared the *Los Angeles Times* headline over an editorial that called *Richmond* "not only a victory for the press but also a triumph for an open system of criminal justice."[71] The *New York Times* editorial headline latched onto Justice Blackmun's tagline: "Wiping the Graffiti Off the Courtroom." The editorial faulted the "loose language" in *Gannett* for encouraging "judges everywhere to close courtrooms for all phases of the judicial process." But while the *Times* shared Blackmun's gratitude for the *Richmond Newspapers* graffiti removal operation, it was far from satisfied. "[M]ost court business these days could be called 'pretrial.' The Gannett ruling itself now needs overruling when the chance arises."[72] The daily newspaper in Riverside, California, agreed: "The decision that criminal trials must be open was not made absolute, and the press has never argued that right should be absolute. . . . Remembering that the overwhelming percentage of criminal cases are decided short of formal trials, the welcome decision in *Richmond* makes it no less imperative that the court, by the very same reasoning employed in the new landmark, bring last year's [*Gannett*] decision on pretrial hearings into line and broaden the guarantee to press and public."[73] Even as he wrote that editorial, *Press-Enterprise* executive editor Norman Cherniss probably didn't foresee that a closed preliminary hearing in his own backyard would be the vehicle that brought the Supreme Court into line.

Globe Newspaper Co. v. Superior Court (1982)

If the momentum propelling the public and press into American courtrooms was destined to stall, it would surely happen in a case involving underaged victims testifying in a rape case. The 1979 trial in Norfolk County, Massachusetts, involved three alleged victims: two sixteen-year-old girls and one a year older.

Citing a Massachusetts law, the judge closed the entire trial to the public and press. The prosecutor stated for the record that the judge had done this on his own and not at the state's request; the defendant objected to the closure. By the time the Globe Newspaper Company's appeal of the courtroom closure reached the state's Supreme Judicial Court, the trial was over, the defendant acquitted. While Massachusetts's highest court ruled that the law didn't require the entire trial to be closed, it said the state law *did* require that sex-offense trials be closed when minor victims testified. The Globe Newspaper Company, publisher of the *Boston Globe*, appealed to the U.S. Supreme Court.

Chief Justice Burger backed the trial judge, writing, "There is clearly a long history of exclusion of the public from trials involving sexual assaults, particularly those against minors." But this time Burger was writing a dissent. By a 6–2 vote, the court, echoing *Richmond*, held that the Massachusetts law violated the First Amendment.[74]

Justice William Brennan, who wrote the opinion, conceded that the state had a compelling interest in protecting "minor victims of sex crimes from further trauma and embarrassment." But "as compelling as that interest is, it does not justify a mandatory closure rule." A judge's decision to close the courtroom could be decided on a "case-by-case basis." And there was much to consider in each case: "the minor victim's age, psychological maturity and understanding, the nature of the crime, the desires of the victim, and the interests of parents and relatives."

In *Nebraska* and *Richmond* the court made it clear that the First Amendment did not give the press absolute immunity from prior restraint or an absolute right of access to criminal court proceedings. Now, in *Globe*, it was telling judges—and states—that they had no absolute right to ban the public and the press from the nation's courtrooms. Not even in a rape case when a minor victim testified. Judges could only close their courtrooms if they show it is "necessitated by a compelling governmental interest, and is narrowly tailored to serve that interest."

That language would echo throughout the nation as well as in Supreme Court opinions that would be handed down in the very near future.

9

Building the Case

If there were an Oxymoron Hall of Fame, *legal briefs* would be sacredly enshrined alongside *jumbo shrimp*. Even the strict rules of the U.S. Supreme Court push the common interpretation of *brief* beyond eye-glazing limits. The brief submitted by the petitioner—the *Press-Enterprise*—could not exceed fifty pages. Same for the respondent, Riverside County. Administrative reforms instituted by Chief Justice Burger required the newspaper's brief to be fronted by a light blue cover. Riverside County's had to be light red. Friend-of-the-court briefs were required to have a green cover and limited to thirty pages. All briefs had to be printed on "heavy paper."[1] The *Press-Enterprise* and Riverside County briefs had to be "compact, logically arranged . . . and free from burdensome, irrelevant, immaterial and scandalous matter" under threat of being "disregarded or stricken by the Court."[2]

Though briefs to the Supreme Court can be long and indigestible, there is a good (and mercifully brief) reason: They are the guts and heart of the case. They offer the best chance to make the case *and* to educate the justices, to tell them something they don't know, something that could sway their opinion. In a 2010 speech at the University of Virginia law school, Justice Antonin Scalia called historic details the "heart and soul" of briefs.[3] But he complained that the court was increasingly flooded with time-wasting amicus briefs penned by lobbyists trying to "assure the [trade] association members that their staff is on the job."[4] After the speech Scalia told Washington DC attorney Bruce Sanford that the broadside had not been aimed at two particularly memorable friend-of-the-court briefs containing rich historical nuggets that the justices' own law clerks had not mined. Sanford had been the lead writer of those 1980s briefs. Both had been written to bolster the court-access cases argued by the *Press-Enterprise*.[5]

Justices and, more often, their clerks read briefs before the lawyers show up for oral argument. If an argument doesn't appear in the brief, lawyers dare not trot it out when they address the court. If briefs do not conform to the rules—length, cover color, and so on–they can be tossed before justices and clerks ever get a look at them. "One of the things you do before you send your thing to the printer is you get the old ruler out," said Jonathan Kotler, a lawyer who represented California newspapers during the court-access battles in the 1970s and 1980s and who once argued a civil rights case before the U.S. Supreme Court. "The justices don't want to hear any cases. If the Supreme Court had its druthers, they'd hear nothing. In order to get to the Supreme Court from an administrative and technical standpoint, it has to be dead-on perfect. They will and they have bounced perfectly good cases because somebody violated the rules on page sizes, margins."[6]

The Supreme Court received eight briefs in what became known as *Press-Enterprise I*. The newspaper and Riverside County each submitted one. Bruce Sanford's Washington DC law firm, representing big name newspapers and radio and broadcasting associations, filed a "national" amicus brief in support of the *Press-Enterprise*. An Oakland, California, law firm representing state newspapers and news organizations filed a "California" brief that also backed the *Press-Enterprise*.[7] The California attorney general and the California public defender's office submitted neutral friend-of-the-court briefs. Joseph Peter Myers, the attorney for convicted rapist-murderer Albert G. Brown Jr., filed a brief in support of Riverside County. Finally, the *Press-Enterprise* filed a reply to Riverside County's brief.

Before the *Press-Enterprise* and the state and national brief writers could coordinate their attack, they had to come up with a strategy. They weighed two options. The first was to argue that *Gannett v. DePasquale* was wrong, or at least incomplete because it hadn't addressed the First Amendment. They would have to persuade the justices, who in *Richmond* had given the public and press First Amendment access to criminal trials, that *pretrial* proceedings—including jury selection—should be covered, too. But that was risky. Justice Powell's was the only *Gannett* opinion that declared a First Amendment right of access to pretrial proceedings. Justice Potter Stewart's majority opinion, which rejected giving the public and press a Sixth Amendment right to attend pretrial hearings, strongly suggested that even if the First Amendment guaranteed "access in some situations," *Gannett* was not one of them. So challenging *Gannett* could backfire: the court could rule that the public and press had no Sixth or First Amendment right to attend pretrial hearings.[8] That left Option 2: argue that voir dire was actually part of the trial and "fit comfortably" in the landmark *Richmond* decision. They would have to convince the justices that from a policy standpoint voir dire should be open, and that from a historical standpoint voir dire had always been open.[9]

The *Press-Enterprise* Brief

John Boyd, who worked directly for Jim Ward, took the lead writing the *Press-Enterprise* brief. The Pepperdine University Law School grad, now in his late twenties, viewed the case as a no-brainer: *Richmond* established a constitutional right to attend criminal trials. Lower federal appeals courts had ruled that jury selection was part of the trial. The *Press-Enterprise*'s case was a logical extension of the law.[10]

Norman Cherniss, the newspaper's executive editor and house intellect, was never far from the brief-writing process, reading every word and changing any word. Ward, like everyone else on the Riverside front, had to scale the steep constitutional law learning curve. But leaving most of the writing to Boyd, he turned his attention to something he'd done well since his high school days in Sioux Falls. The "World's Greatest Attorney" had to become the "World's Greatest Schmoozer." He and Cherniss worked the phones and wrote letters, enlisting newspaper editors and lawyers to submit briefs on behalf of the *Press-Enterprise*. "The more high-powered, the better," thought Ward.[11] Prominent newspapers and reputable First Amendment lawyers would complement the less prominent Riverside paper and its virtually unknown attorney.

By February–March 1983, newspaper's brief was taking shape:[12] Judge Mortland had misapplied *Hovey*, which said nothing about slamming the courtroom door on the public and the press. In doing so, he had violated the newspaper's constitutional right as set forth in *Richmond* and *Globe*. Jury selection was an *integral part* of the trial. To ban the public and the press for weeks and then seal a transcript didn't come close to meeting the Supreme Court's "narrowly tailored" standard.

The brief contended that jury selection in California had always been "considered a part of the public trial guaranteed to the defendant by the Sixth Amendment." This openness helped assure the public that the justice system was not riddled with perjury and wink-wink collusion between police, prosecutors, defense lawyers, judges, or anyone else. The brief turned to Sir William Blackstone's eighteenth-century commentaries on English common law, which greatly influenced American law. Blackstone never said jury selection had to be open to the public. But the brief argued it was inconceivable that the people would insist on a jury system and then be denied access to the process of selecting jurors. Further, a lower federal court *had* declared jury selection was part of the trial and "could find no historical evidence that *voir dire* was ever conducted in private."[13] The brief dismissed "alleged privacy of prospective jurors," saying it only came up after the newspaper had been kicked out of the courtroom—and granted after the jury had been picked in secret.

As Boyd hammered out the brief under the watchful red pencil of Norman Cherniss, Jim Ward asked a young lawyer, also in her late twenties, to perform what amounted to grunt work: make sure the cases cited in the brief hadn't been overturned. Sharon Waters, a native Californian, had only joined the firm a year earlier. An Air Force brat who lived everywhere from Kansas to Guam,[14] Waters took the scenic route to Thompson & Colegate, which had never hired a female lawyer. The office manager threw her résumé in a wastebasket. A secretary fished it out and told the manager to pass it along to a partner—or she would. Ward invited Waters to Riverside but didn't show up for their appointment. He flew to Sacramento and interviewed her there. The next time Sharon Waters came to Riverside, she had a job.[15] Now, in early 1983, she was dutifully checking citations for a Supreme Court brief. But she was also reading the brief, and the more she read, the more she felt she had to say something "not because this would get me into the case but because this brief wasn't of the quality that should be filed." Her parents had always encouraged her to speak up—diplomatically. Don't make it personal. "So I took a deep breath and walked in." She told Ward the brief didn't flow, didn't read well. "I'm not stupid," said Waters. "If you go to the boss and criticize them, you run the risk that they're not going to take it well." But Jim Ward was worried, too. "We've been feeling like there's something wrong," he told her.

John Boyd, the lead writer, knew exactly what was wrong. "I had become fixated with the *Hovey* decision, which affected my writing."[16] A self-described conservative, Boyd felt California Supreme Court Justice Rose Bird "was going to do anything to frustrate the implementation of the death penalty in California." He wanted the U.S. Supreme Court to overturn *Hovey*—something Ward didn't think was necessary. "This was my chance to take a shot at the Bird Court."[17] He hoped to deliver that shot via the *Press-Enterprise* brief. But it just wasn't working.

When Ward told Waters, "Do whatever you want," she walked back to her office and sat down.[18] "I remember very distinctly sitting on the floor with all these pieces of paper. . . . This paragraph needs to go over here." In the pre-computer-cut-and-paste era (at least at Thompson & Colegate), Waters taped one wayward paragraph to another and stapled other paragraphs together. When she finished, the *Press-Enterprise* brief flowed. But it needed a conclusion and not just a summary. The justices had to know what the *Press-Enterprise* believed was at stake.

One man knew exactly what was at stake: "There is an ominous progression . . . a monster grows, and there has been a disturbing unwillingness on the part of California appellate courts to protect the public's First Amendment right of access. But if it is not confronted, the spread will continue. For if the procedures described are wise in capital case(s), why not in non-capital cases? Few courts would proudly argue for secret *voir dire* and permanently sealed transcripts of *voir dire* in all cases. Yet that is the direction; and if logic and law support what has already evolved in the wake of Hovey, logic and law will support the frightening extension of the application described."

A lawyer didn't write those words. A newspaperman did. "Norman wrote the conclusion," said John Boyd. "We told Jim Ward not to touch it. This is our client."[19]

Riverside County's Brief—and the *Press-Enterprise* Reply

The Riverside County Superior Court relied on its lawyer, the Riverside County counsel, to argue that Judge Mortland had properly closed Albert Brown's voir dire and sealed the transcript. The county counsel's office usually drafted ordinances and contracts, advised county agencies on matters ranging from code enforcement to child welfare, and tried to keep public bodies, including the elected Board of Supervisors, on the straight and narrow. It was essentially a law firm, though not necessarily a high-powered one. "A lot of attorneys who gravitate toward government jobs don't have that fire," said Katherine Lind, who rose to assistant Riverside County counsel during her decades-long career. "They're what I call hiders. The thought that you would go to the Supreme Court and argue probably scared the shit out of them."[20] But Glenn Salter and Joyce Reikes stood out. Bright and ambitious, they were instrumental in writing the county's brief. Salter would argue the case before the Supreme Court.

The brief conceded that voir dire was part of the trial.[21] Judge Mortland closed jury selection and sealed the transcript only after applying what the brief called the Supreme Court's "three-pronged standard of *Richmond Newspapers*."

FINDINGS

Judge Mortland listened to lawyers' arguments, including remarks by Albert Brown's lawyer, Joseph Peter Myers, who opposed releasing the transcript: "And I can think of several of the people interviewed who are now on the jury who were concerned that what they were telling us about themselves was, in fact, confidential. . . . One woman I certainly recall said, 'I couldn't say these things because there's a lady in the [jury] who knows my mother, and I would never want my mother to know about this situation.'"

When the lawyers finished, Mortland said: "I agree with much of what the defense counsel and the People's counsel have said and . . . regardless of the public's right to know . . . I just think there is certain areas that the right to privacy should prevail and a right to a fair trial should prevail."[22] This comment, said the county counsel, showed that Mortland had "incorporated" the lawyers' remarks, and this amounted to on-the-record findings. In its reply brief, the *Press-Enterprise* ridiculed that conclusion, saying Mortland's supposed findings were nothing more than "random recollections by attorneys."[23]

ALTERNATIVES

Mortland offered an alternative to "total *voir dire* closure" because he let the public attend three days of general questioning before closing "the death-qualification" and "other special areas" of questioning for six weeks. The newspaper countered that aside from the three-day opening, Mortland didn't consider any alternatives, including juror questionnaires "to pinpoint any possible privacy problems"; screening questions to be asked in voir dire; giving jurors numbers to shield their identities; or excusing jurors who declined to provide "intimate information." Excusing jurors had been Ward's idea of finessing the jury privacy issue. A judge could excuse these prospective jurors "as if they were sick, disabled or compromised."[24] The newspaper didn't dispute that Mortland had passed the third *Richmond* test—recognizing the "public's right to know." But that subject would come up during a tense exchange between Jim Ward and two Supreme Court justices.

The brief rejected the newspaper's claim that Mortland's "application of Hovey" violated the public's First Amendment rights, arguing that prospective jurors had to be questioned individually and out of public view so they would not influence each other's responses. "[P]ersons not yet even summoned for jury service could have read newspaper accounts of earlier *voir dire* and have been influenced by them."

Riverside County asserted that the California constitution granted jurors a right of privacy. It conceded that the U.S. Supreme Court hadn't ruled on juror privacy, but it insisted that trial judges had historically protected prospective jurors, even to the point of allowing them to refuse to answer certain questions. "Prospective jurors should not be forced to leave their rights at the doorstep of the courthouse; they should not be forced to divulge private matters . . . simply because they are performing their civic duty."

The county argued that protecting jurors' privacy rights protected the defendant's right to a fair trial. "In a case such as this one, where questions about sexual matters, politics, race, religion and the secrecy of the ballot box were thoroughly examined by the parties for the protection of the defendant's Sixth Amendment right, complete and candid responses from prospective [jurors] were mandatory." If the jurors were forced to respond in public, "they may simply lie."

Finally, the brief defended Mortland's decision to seal the jury selection transcript. "It could be potentially more disturbing and work a greater hardship on the jury system if prospective jurors gave testimony about their most intimate and personal lives with the belief that their responses were being held in confidence, and then later discovered that feelings and experiences they would never have otherwise revealed had been exposed because the transcripts were made public."

Friends of the Court

The *Press-Enterprise* settled on a two-pronged campaign, which Norman Cherniss explained in a memo to *Press-Enterprise* employees: "It was early decided . . . that rather than have a great number of friend-of-the-court briefs pecking away at the court, and probably saying pretty much the same things over and over, there would be two amicus briefs, one national and one state."[25]

Bruce Sanford, the Washington DC lawyer with Baker & Hostetler, which represented the Society of Professional Journalists, would be the lead writer of the national brief. The state brief would be written by members of Crosby, Heafey, Roach & May, the Oakland law firm that served as Gannett's principle First Amendment and libel attorney in California. Having lost a New York case, *Gannett v. DePasquale*, the giant chain and its lawyers would get another shot at a court-access case originating on the other side of the country. Most of the newspapers and organizations signing on to the briefs would kick in $750 each "to help offset various costs involved" in their preparation.[26]

The California Brief

The state brief, which represented nearly twenty newspapers, told the justices that what happened in Riverside was happening everywhere in California, from Shasta County in the north to San Diego County in the south: since the 1980 *Hovey* ruling "trial judges have been closing the *voir dire* phase of the trial in capital cases with alarming frequency."[27] Though *Hovey* addressed the danger of prospective jurors prejudicing *other* prospective jurors, it did not "intend that any portion of *voir dire* be conducted in secret." Yet the brief listed twenty-five capital cases in which juries *had been* picked in secret.[28]

Public confidence in the criminal justice system emerged as a central argument advanced by the *Press-Enterprise* and its backers. Closed jury selection, suggested the state brief, can actually result in an unfair trial. While lawyers can cross-examine witnesses to test their credibility, "there is comparatively limited ability to explore the backgrounds of potential jurors before commencement of the *voir dire*. . . . [I]n the absence of public exposure, a juror who withholds or gives inaccurate information during *voir dire* is more likely to go undiscovered than the untruthful witness." The brief noted that the jury system and "*voir dire* in particular" were under fire in California. The state supreme court had granted eight hearings for criminal defendants claiming that "the manner in which juries are selected for capital cases has prejudiced their fair trial rights."

It was impossible to ignore the elephant in the brief-writing room: juror privacy. Judith Epstein, a Gannett attorney who signed the state brief, was the lawyer who had warned Jim Ward that the privacy issue could send the *Press-Enterprise* case down in flames.[29] John Carne, the brief's lead writer, recalled that the effort to back the *Press-Enterprise's* appeal unfolded against the backdrop of the November 1978 Jonestown massacre in Guyana, South America, where hundreds of Peoples Temple members committed suicide, and nonmembers, including California representative Leo J. Ryan, were ambushed and murdered. "There was concern that the jurors in that case might be in some physical danger if their identities became known. We considered several procedures that would allow jury selection to go on observed by the press and public without revealing names in case the question of juror safety and the power of a trial judge to protect jurors came up."[30] The California brief declared that jurors had no constitutional right to privacy when their views were relevant to the charges in the case before them. It quoted a 1947 U.S. Supreme Court ruling in *Craig v. Harney*: "A trial is a public event. What transpires in the courtroom is public property." While not denying that jurors were entitled to some privacy, the brief argued that federal and California courts had "recognized" that these "zones of privacy cannot intrude into areas of legitimate public concern." Judge Mortland's blanket entitlement of privacy went too far. He had secretly impaneled a jury, held a trial, received a verdict, sentenced a man to death, and *still* refused to release the voir dire transcript. By doing so Mortland "impermissibly crossed the boundary separating legitimately protectable privacy interests from the First Amendment right of access to information about criminal trials."

The brief's closing paragraph essentially put the American justice system itself on trial: "In every case, where a person is either convicted or acquitted . . . important questions inevitably arise about the manner in which the jury is selected. Did the prosecutor unduly influence the jurors during their examination? Did the defense attorney adequately question prospective jurors to elicit prejudicial bias? Did the trial judge rule on challenges for cause in an evenhanded manner? Were the jurors candid and forthright . . . ? Were racial and sexual prejudices effectively eliminated? Such fundamental questions should not be permitted to fester in secrecy, but must be exposed to the cleansing light of public inquiry. Public confidence in the criminal justice system, as well as added protection for the rights of the accused, do not permit less."

The National Brief

Tim Hays and Norman Cherniss had to have felt immensely comfortable with Bruce Sanford as the point man on the national brief. Baker & Hostetler represented the Society of Professional Journalists, Sigma Delta Chi. Organized in 1909 and twenty-eight thousand members strong, the nonprofit group represented "every branch of print and broadcast journalism."[31] This brief would speak for a who's who in American journalism: the American Society of Newspaper Editors (of which Tim Hays had been president), the Associated Press, *Los Angeles Times*, *Miami Herald*, *New York Times*, *Washington Post*, *San Francisco Chronicle*, National Association of Broadcasters, Radio-Television News Directors Association, Reporters Committee for the Freedom of the Press, and more.

Sanford, who was in his late thirties, was no stranger to journalism or First Amendment issues. The editor of his Hamilton College (New York) newspaper, he worked for the *Wall Street Journal* between his junior and senior years and planned to accept the *Journal*'s job offer once he got his degree at New York University Law School. But he plunged into law instead. In 1970 he joined Baker & Hostetler in Cleveland, home of the *Cleveland Press*, which achieved notoriety for its coverage of the Sam Sheppard case. The *Press* was a Baker & Hostetler client. Sanford took an interest in the First Amendment at a time when few lawyers tilled that field. His work for United Press International gave him a platform on which to expound—and try to expand the First Amendment rights of the press.[32] When he made his pitch at judicial conferences, he was not strident. Many judges weren't well versed in First Amendment law simply because they didn't have First Amendment cases. Sanford called for accommodation and balance: the First and Sixth amendments were not in conflict. They could work in concert.[33] The national brief, strongly worded as it was, was not extreme.

Lee Levine's name rests just below Sanford's on the light green-covered amicus brief. Not yet thirty when the *Press-Enterprise* case came along, he had worked on his college newspaper, the *Daily Penn-*

sylvanian, and majored in political science, with a focus on Supreme Court issues. When he graduated from the University of Pennsylvania, he had to decide whether he "wanted to be a journalist who wrote about courts or a lawyer who represented journalists." He chose Yale Law School. Soon after he graduated, Levine went to work for Sanford, who was moving to Baker & Hostetler's DC office to start a national First Amendment practice.[34]

The national brief rode the coattails of *Richmond* and *Globe*, seeking to use the justices' own words to steer the Supreme Court to what the brief's authors viewed as the only logical conclusion: if the First Amendment granted the public and press access to criminal trials, that constitutional right had to extend to jury selection as well. Neither bellicose nor rigid, the brief at times resembled a tutorial, giving judges a how-to-close-your-courtroom guide provided by *United States v. Brooklier*, a 1982 federal appeals court ruling.[35] Judges stood a good chance of surviving "constitutional scrutiny" if, before banning the public and press from voir dire, they held a hearing and publicly explained why (1) a compelling governmental interest requires closure, (2) less restrictive alternatives to closure will be ineffective, and (3) closure will prevent the perceived harm. Why did judges have to jump through these hoops? The U.S. Ninth District Court of Appeals's *Brooklier* ruling explained: "Since the purpose of the findings is to enable the appellate court to determine whether the closure order was properly entered, the findings must be sufficiently specific." Had Judge Mortland done this in the Riverside case? No, said the national brief. *Brooklier* laid out three requirements, and Mortland had whiffed on all them.

Lee Levine thought the brief had to satisfy two Supreme Court factions. There was the "Burger Faction," though it was "hard to say who else" was in it, that "believed the First Amendment was a function of history. A First Amendment right had to show this history of openness." And there was the "Brennan Faction," named for Justice William Brennan. Again, Levine didn't know exactly who else this included, but it "seemed not to care about history." It cared about whether openness was "a good thing from a policy standpoint."

Levine boiled it down to "history" and "logic." To get five votes, "we had to make both arguments."[36] As a matter of policy, or logic, the brief argued that open voir dire "provides a fundamental safeguard on the fair conduct of judicial proceedings." To illustrate why open jury selection was necessary to ensure the "fairness and integrity of a criminal trial," the brief offered an account of a *St. Louis Post-Dispatch* reporter who, in 1972, observed jury selection in thirty-one criminal trials where a defendant was black. Out of seventy-seven prospective black jurors, fifty-six were "challenged"—or kicked out—by prosecutors. "While blacks [in the jury pool] reflected their proportionate number in the county's population, prosecutors had systematically excluded black jurors from cases involving black defendants. More-over . . . prosecutors altered their systematic striking of blacks when they learned [the] reporter's purpose in the courtroom."

At least in those cases a reporter saw what was going on and wrote about it. In the John Hinckley trial, jurors were chosen in secret. After Ronald Reagan's would-be assassin was found not guilty by reason of insanity, newspaper articles pointed out that relatives of several jurors were once confined to mental hospitals. "[W]hether this fact had any actual effect on the integrity of the trial," said the brief, "the resulting perception of injustice may have been avoided had full public scrutiny of *voir dire* been guaranteed at the outset."

Perhaps sensing that a *perception* of injustice in the criminal justice system might strike a chord with justices who cared about whether "openness was a good thing from a policy standpoint," the brief seized on Chief Justice Burger's words in *Richmond*: "A result considered untoward may undermine public confidence, and where the trial has been concealed from public view an unexpected outcome can cause a reaction that the system at best has failed and at worst has been corrupted." A secret voir dire could have the same effect. The brief noted the increasing use of "expensive survey techniques" to "select juries likely to reach preordained verdicts." Unless a judge could publicly and convincingly state the reasons for closing jury selection in these and other cases, public suspicion of injustice in the justice system would only fester and flourish.

When the brief turned to history, it did so with Chief Justice War-ren Burger in mind. He was an "Anglophile" who "really was into this English tradition of openness and was very much favorably dis-posed toward it."[37] When it came to defining and fleshing out con-stitutional law, Burger gave considerable weight to tradition and the historical record. His opinion in the *Nebraska Press Association* prior restraint case cited John Adams, Chief Justice John Marshall, and Aaron Burr. The authors of the national brief hoped to persuade their prime target—the chief—that open jury selection was nothing less than the "original intent" of the authors of the Constitution.[38]

The brief traced the evolution of juries to "before the Norman Conquest," when trials were "open-air" meetings and jurors were not neutral at all. They were "as much witnesses as judges of the facts." They knew the defendant. "Embarrassingly large and unwieldy," the number of jurors could surpass eighty people. The entire proceeding "was a decidedly public event." Things changed in the fourteenth and fifteenth centuries when new rules allowed jurors to be challenged. Now jurors were supposed to be neutral, and these challenges "were routinely determined in open court, as the first phase of the trial on guilt or innocence." The brief documented this history with such sources as *The Book of English Law* (6th edition, 1967) and *A Concise History of Common Law* (1929). But it still didn't have ironclad proof. Then Brian Harvey went to the library.

A West Virginian and graduate of Case Western Reserve Univer-sity law school in Cleveland, Harvey joined Baker & Hostetler after clerking for a couple of federal judges. He was in his early thirties when his B&H bosses dispatched him to the Library of Congress on a fishing expedition of historic proportions. The Madison Building of the Library of Congress, which had opened in 1980, had "a wonder-ful law library, a huge collection."[39] But no database. No sea of com-puter terminals. Nothing Brian Harvey was looking for, not that he really knew *what* he was looking for, was just a click away. But he did know this: "Chief Justice Burger's writing on the topics of open court-rooms focused a lot on how things were done in Jolly Old England and how those things were transported over to the colonies." To find out how Jolly Old England handled jury selection—or whether there was even a record of such things—would require primary research. Harvey went to the library because "I didn't have the sense, I don't think any of us [at the law firm] had the sense that any other briefs would cover the historical proportions."[40]

Harvey worked backward, scouring early U.S. Supreme Court rulings for names of reports that provided decisions and transcripts of trials that had taken place in the 1600s and 1700s. Then he went to the "database"—the card catalog—and identified the books that contained the reports he was looking for. Then he asked the library staff to bring him what were "essentially random volumes" from the stacks. They arrived in what looked like grocery carts filled with "big, thick volumes over two feet long and eighteen inches wide, quite theatrical in their appearance." The massive books reminded Harvey of "the kinds of things you would see in engravings of Scrooge and Marley." They were law reports—reports of trials—from the Old Bailey, the old English court. "They weren't kept in any secure room or properly dehumidified space. You'd pull them up and open them up and read the reports, and dust would fly and bindings would become injured."[41]

As Harvey pored over the reports from the Old Bailey cases, decoding words where an *s* looked like an *f* (ſ), he began to realize that he was onto something that might interest Chief Justice Burger and the so-called "Burger Faction": "It just became apparent that the public was there in the courtroom." During jury selection. In *Harriſan's Trial* (Harrison's Trial), which occurred in 1660, the defendant kept challenging one prospective juror after another. When the tenth prospective juror got the boot, the court reporter wrote, "Here the People ſeemed to laugh." That, said Harvey, "suggested this was a very public place."[42] Jury selection had been open since at least the seventeenth century. Harvey had found the ſmoking gun.

That openness, noted the brief, carried over to the "colonies"—to the open-court voir dire in a trial that had fascinated Chief Justice Burger since his law school days: the Aaron Burr treason trial of 1807, Chief Justice John Marshall presiding. Roughly 175 years later Riverside County Superior Court judge John Mortland conducted a secret, six-week voir dire and refused to release the transcripts.

The Final Three

The State of California's brief, submitted by Attorney General John Van de Kamp, supported neither the *Press-Enterprise* nor Riverside County but was a balancing act that offered something for both. It said Mortland's closure and sealing "were overbroad.[43] Absent articulated findings on the record, no justification is stated for denying public access to all of the transcript of the closed *voir dire* proceedings."

"On the other hand," the brief stated, "our partial review of the transcript of the closed *voir dire* proceedings gives rise to the belief there is a possibility that a limited closure was proper." The state urged the Supreme Court to tell Mortland to release the transcript—except portions that, in "articulated findings," he could justify keeping under wraps.

The state public defender's brief criticized the *Press-Enterprise* and Riverside County for dragging *Hovey* into the debate because that ruling said nothing about barring the public and press from the courtroom.[44] The brief took no position on a juror's right to privacy but "contemplated" situations where voir dire could be closed to protect a defendant's rights to a fair trial. The newspaper found this brief mildly helpful because it said that *if* Judge Mortland relied on *Hovey* to close his courtroom and seal the transcripts, he had made a mistake.

Joseph Peter Myers, who defended Albert Brown, zeroed in on jury privacy.[45] He found it "interesting" that the national brief had singled out John Hinckley Jr.'s closed voir dire as an argument for open jury selection. "How could either party to that trial (defense or prosecutor) have expected jurors to reveal such 'skeletons in their closets' if the proceeding had not been closed? Truthful answers to *voir dire* questioning on that particular subject matter . . . was absolutely essential in connection with the trial." If jury selection had been open, prospective jurors "would not have been able to fulfill their duties and their oaths." They would have refused to answer or lied.

Myers allowed that the "historical search" for the origins and openness of the jury system" was interesting, but it was basically irrelevant to the "difficulties posed by modern communications media" that "intrude into the ancient system that criminal trials represent." Contrary to the *Press-Enterprise*'s contention, Myers said Judge Mortland had offered specific findings to support his orders for closure and sealing. But these findings came out in a hearing requested by the state attorney general roughly fifteen months after the jury convicted Albert Brown and voted for the death penalty.[46] Then Myers did what only he and a handful of other people could have done: he took the Supreme Court justices into Judge Mortland's closed courtroom.

Myers recounted the secret voir dire during which "[a] number of female jurors revealed that they were victims of sexual abuse, and that there had been a claim within one family of an interracial rape. . . . Other jurors dealt with intimate feelings about race and sex, as well as their religious and political preferences and ideas. Still others deal with the gruesome photographs which were to be introduced as evidence in the trial. Obviously, at a time when the popularity of the death penalty is ever-increasing, jurors were asked about that issue—and those who believed in non-imposition of such a penalty did not have to face public revelation of that now unpopular stance."

Myers said the newspaper's effort to "preserve" the jury selection process "is based upon a rejection of one of the most obvious traits of human beings—that they desire and need privacy. If jurors must choose between preserving their own rights and the protection of their families from potentially disastrous publicity, and the rights of a defendant or the prosecution to know their views, that choice may destroy the integrity of the jury system."

10

The Diaz Case Advances

With the briefs submitted, about all Jim Ward and Deputy County Counsel Glenn Salter had left to do was take a little trip to Washington DC, where, on Wednesday, October 12, 1983, they'd argue before the justices of the United States Supreme Court. But the secret voir dire wasn't the only case now commanding the *Press-Enterprise*'s and Ward's attention. Another court-access case was snaking its way through the justice system. On October 5, three days before jetting off to Washington, Ward appeared in a California appellate court to argue for the release of the preliminary hearing transcript for Robert Diaz, the accused serial killer charged with injecting fatal doses of lidocaine, a drug commonly used to treat heart problems, into a dozen patients. Prying loose the transcript was a small part of a much grander scheme. Ward and the newspaper hoped to convince the California court that the public and press had a constitutional right of access to preliminary hearings. This fight had begun fifteen months earlier, with the *Press-Enterprise* sitting on the sidelines.

When, at Diaz's request, Judge Howard Dabney closed the preliminary hearing on July 6, 1982, the newspaper didn't object. "It was not unheard of to close preliminary hearings in the most sensational cases," recalled James Bettinger, the paper's city editor at the time. In fact, the preliminary hearing of Albert Greenwood Brown Jr., convicted murderer of Arlington High School sophomore Susan Louise Jordan, had been closed to the public.[1] It was not unusual to close these hearings, said Bettinger, "because of the potential for evidence that might later not be admitted at trial."[2] There was also the potential of prejudicing the public, including a jury pool, if valid evidence was presented in open court.

If closed pretrial hearings were not unusual in Riverside County, they seemed borderline epidemic nationally—a direct result of the U.S. Supreme Court's 1979 *Gannett v. DePasquale* ruling that upheld the closure of a pretrial suppression hearing. "Post-*Gannett*," said First Amendment lawyer Lee Levine, "there was a noticeable increase in the phenomenon of pretrial hearings being closed. Before that, nobody ever cared. Following *Gannett*, it happened a lot."[3] And it was happening in California, too, from San Diego to San Luis Obispo to San Jose.[4] The *Press-Enterprise* had taken up the cause against secret jury selection when Riverside County judges kept closing voir dire in death penalty trials. But when it came to opposing closed preliminary hearings, the *Press-Enterprise* was not exactly the leader among California newspapers. And it appeared to be *following* the Riverside County district attorney.

After Dabney banned the public and media, including the three major television networks, from his courtroom, the Diaz preliminary hearing lasted forty-one days. When it ended in late August, the newspaper finally weighed in. "The *Press-Enterprise* would like to request that the transcripts of the preliminary hearing of Robert Diaz be released to the public," reporter Chris Bowman told the judge in open court. "[T]he matter is of legitimate public interest and the press has been excluded for the past eight weeks." Dabney refused. Instead, he sealed the four-thousand-page transcript "to insure that a defendant has a fair trial."[5] By early 1983 the Diaz trial had been assigned to Riverside Superior Court judge John Barnard, a former navy submarine officer, appointed to the bench by Governor Ronald Reagan. Riverside County also had a new district attorney. Grover Trask took office several months after Dabney closed the Diaz hearing. He had come up through the ranks and believed the "People's Business"—after all, the DA *was* "The People"—demanded "transparency and openness as a basic right."[6] Once he took over in November 1982, that belief became policy.[7] In February 1983 it was the DA, not the *Press-Enterprise*, that took the lead in trying to persuade Judge

Barnard to release the Diaz preliminary hearing transcript. Prosecutor Patrick Magers, who had gone along with Judge Dabney's preliminary hearing closure, told Barnard that nearly nine months had passed since that hearing ended, and "we feel that the interests of the public has dulled in this case . . . the public's right to know outweighs any possible denial" of Diaz's right to a fair trial. But Deputy Public Defender John Lee countered that his client had a right to be tried in Riverside County and that right would be jeopardized if the transcript were released. Suggesting that much evidence presented in the preliminary hearing "may be found inadmissible at trial," Lee said releasing the transcript would result in a "trial by paper."[8] Lee was particularly troubled by possible unsealing of "intemperate" remarks Judge Dabney had made on the last day of the preliminary hearing.

Dabney, a former assistant district attorney, had been a judge for only five years. One prosecutor had predicted, "He'll probably be the most competent man on the bench in a year or two."[9] But the same prosecutor said Dabney had a less-than-ideal temperament. A public defender added that the judge "always has a short fuse."[10] As the Diaz hearing drew to a close, Dabney acknowledged that his comments might not be appropriate. Then he let it fly: "When we talk about violence, it seems to me this is the most dangerous type of criminal. At least a person who has a knife and a gun, you know who you have to protect yourself against, but these people all came into this hospital expecting that their lives would be lengthened by this experience; and I think Mr. Diaz is an extremely dangerous man."[11]

Though the *Press-Enterprise* lawyers were in the middle of doing something they had never done before—preparing a brief to the U.S. Supreme Court in the closed voir dire case—they now threw their support behind DA Trask. Sharon Waters went down to the courthouse and told Judge Barnard that releasing the Diaz transcript was much different from a daily "blow-by-blow" coverage. The basic principle was "the public's right to know . . . the harm of releasing the transcript is certainly not as great as [it] would have been if the preliminary hearing had been open at all times."[12] In papers filed with the court John Boyd said the logical extension of the public defender's argument for keeping the transcript sealed "would mean that there would be no news coverage of any judicial-criminal proceedings prior to trial."[13] Barnard refused to unseal the transcript. After invoking the U.S. Supreme Court's 1979 *Gannett* ruling, he concluded, "There is a reasonable likelihood that making all or any part of the transcript public might prejudice the defendant's right to a fair and impartial trial."[14] Those two words—*reasonable likelihood* of prejudice—would become the state standard for closing a preliminary hearing. They would also become a target of the *Press-Enterprise*.

District Attorney Trask appealed Barnard's ruling, asserting that the judge had "abused his discretion." But in March 1983 the state court of appeal in San Bernardino rejected the DA's appeal without comment.[15] The *Press-Enterprise* then filed its own appeal, contending that keeping the transcript sealed "endangers the public's right to a free press and access to public hearings." In April 1983, again without comment, the court of appeal shot down the *Press-Enterprise*. Trask decided to drop the case, but *Press-Enterprise* editor Tim Hays continued the fight. When the *Press-Enterprise* asked the California Supreme Court to hear the closed voir dire case, all it heard was "HEARING DENIED." (Six days later, Dabney closed the Diaz hearing.) But now, however slightly, the legal landscape had shifted. By the time the newspaper brought the Diaz case to the state's highest court, the U.S. Supreme Court had agreed to hear the voir dire appeal. In May 1983 the California Supreme Court didn't say "HEARING DENIED." It didn't take the Diaz case, either. But it did order the state court of appeal, which had already refused to hear the sealed-transcript arguments *twice*, to hold a hearing. It was set for Wednesday, October 5, 1983—exactly one week before Ward would argue the voir dire case before the U.S. Supreme Court.

While it's tough to find a "Perry Mason" moment in a sealed transcript case, the run-up to the October 5 hearing featured genuine courtroom drama. Just six days before the hearing—on September 30—Robert Diaz waived his right to a trial by jury and decided to take his chances with Judge Barnard, who had never heard a death penalty case.[16] Once Diaz opted for no jury, Barnard changed his mind about the preliminary hearing transcript: he saw no reason to keep it sealed. But he agreed to delay a ruling on whether to release it until after the state court of appeal held its hearing on the morning of October 5 in nearby San Bernardino. Barnard said he would then listen to further arguments about the transcript that afternoon.[17] In a seventy-five-minute hearing before three state court of appeal justices, Diaz lawyer John Lee argued that releasing the transcript would set a precedent that would threaten a defendant's Sixth Amendment right to an impartial jury. *Press-Enterprise* attorney Jim Ward framed the debate as a delicate constitutional balance. "The public has a right to observe its government and judiciary in action," he told the justices. "The public which is personified by the press had its First Amendment rights taken away." Taken away without a specific finding that the defendant's rights were endangered.[18] It was essentially the same argument the newspaper was using in the voir dire case. It would be months before the court of appeal announced its decision.

That afternoon in Riverside, Judge Barnard might have expected to hear a debate between the defense and the prosecution. But the DA had flip-flopped. Months earlier prosecutor Magers argued that public interest in the case had "dulled" and the people had a "right to know" what was in the transcript. Now the DA's office was having second thoughts. What if Diaz changed his mind and asked for a jury trial? Or what if Judge Barnard died? Outside of court, Magers noted that the trial was just three weeks away. If the transcript was unsealed and Diaz asked for a jury trial, the trial might have to be moved to another county. Better to stick with the status quo. Barnard said he would announce his decision on the sealed transcript on October 14.[19] By that time Jim Ward would have argued the voir dire case before the U.S. Supreme Court.

11

Mr. Ward Goes to Washington

"The marble façade of the U.S. Supreme Court building proclaims a high ideal: 'Equal Justice Under Law.' But inside, an elite cadre of lawyers has emerged as first among equals, giving their clients a disproportionate chance to influence the law of the land. . . . They are the elite of the elite: Although they account for far less than one percent of lawyers who filed appeals to the Supreme Court, these attorneys were involved in forty-three percent of the cases the high court chose to decide from 2004 to 2012."[1]

On Saturday, October 8, 1983, Jim Ward, who was not even close to the "elite of the elite" back then, lifted off on a 7 a.m. flight from Ontario International Airport. Destination: Washington DC. An amateur historian and prolific writer, Ward compiled letters, snapshots, memos, newsletters, newspaper clippings, and other materials that document both *Press-Enterprise* cases. Each case is memorialized in its own large black three-ring binder that includes Ward's typewritten logs of his two trips to the U.S. Supreme Court.

John Boyd, Sharon Waters, and Norman Cherniss also boarded the plane to Washington. Ward had invited Tim Hays to sit at the counsel table during oral arguments. But for reasons either unexplained or forgotten the editor, who signed off on the Supreme Court battle and paid Ward's law firm $25,000 to fight it, decided not to go. Before the plane took off, Cherniss handed Ward an envelope marked "sealed orders."[2]

Ward and Boyd sat in the plane's nonsmoking section; Waters and Cherniss did not. It was a working flight. Ward instructed Boyd and

Waters to come up with a list of one hundred questions that would be fired at him by Supreme Court justices or by a panel of First Amendment lawyers who had been lined up for a practice session.[3] After a lazy, sight-seeing Sunday Ward got down to business. He and Boyd spent Monday morning at Baker & Hostetler with Bruce Sanford and other law firm lawyers. The Riverside duo became increasingly comfortable; they "had things under control." But during lunch, "people drifted in from all over the country." All were First Amendment lawyers, and they had converged on Baker & Hostetler turf for a "moot court"—the lawyers' version of a dress rehearsal.[4] Part of their job was to toughen up Jim Ward for the main event. By the end of the day Ward would feel a lot less comfortable than he had felt all morning.

These experts, including Robert Bernius, who represented Gannett when the Supreme Court heard *Gannett v. DePasquale* in 1979, assumed the role of Supreme Court justices. They convened in a conference room and listened to Ward present his case. At times, they were gracious, holding their fire for minutes at a time. But other times just seconds would pass before one of the "justices" interrupted to pepper Ward with questions. When he responded, they interrupted him again. "Your answers have to be snappier, quicker, sharper," they told him.[5] These "justices" had a stake in the First Amendment and, observed Sharon Waters, "didn't want little Riverside lawyers to screw up their issues." They "knew the Supreme Court justices better than any of us would ever hope to—which justices asked a lot of questions, what kind of answers might get us in trouble. The last thing you want to do is not answer a question the way a justice wants or, worse, make them ask the next question even louder."[6]

If there was one thing these lawyers hoped to drill into Jim Ward, drill it into him so deeply that no matter how nervous or flustered he might become, he would stick to the script, it was this: this case was about voir dire. Period. If any justice asked him if there was a First Amendment right to preliminary hearings or a hearing to suppress a confession, Ward would have to find a way to say, "That is not what this case is about, your honor. It's about voir dire."[7] Because if he strayed too far and asked for too much, the justices might find an excuse to not give him anything at all. And if the *Press-Enterprise* lost, the First Amendment and the lawyers sitting at that conference table would lose, too. By the time the intense, sometimes withering, session ended, Ward was wrung out, exhausted.[8] But it also paid off. The "justices" had anticipated virtually every question Ward would hear three days later.[9] But even though Ward knew the curveballs were coming, he would still have to be able to hit them.

Ward wasn't the only one getting prepped for the case. Less than three miles away the real Supreme Court justices were boning up on *Press-Enterprise Co. v. Superior Court.* Briefs for both sides had been submitted six months earlier. The justices' clerks digested them and composed memos summarizing the arguments and recommending how the justices should vote.

Elizabeth Taylor, a graduate of University of Virginia Law School and Yale Divinity School and now, in 1983, a clerk for Justice Harry Blackmun, carefully laid out the arguments on both sides in a forty-three-page memorandum. Numerous lines and phrases of her memo, one of thousands of documents Blackmun donated to the Library of Congress, were brightly highlighted in yellow, presumably by the justice himself. In addition to her summary and analysis, Taylor also offered her own unvarnished observations:

> "In case the existence of a first amendment right becomes an issue, I register my agreement that the press and the public do have a first amendment right of access to the *voir dire.*"[10]
> "As to most of the information sought during *voir dire*, it is difficult to believe that when a prospective juror receives notice that he is called to serve, he has an expectation . . . that what he says in court will be kept private. . . . [A] trial is a public event."[11]
> "I am satisfied that jurors should be protected as much as possible from wide ranging and unnecessary examinations of their personal lives. I am not satisfied, however, that the Court should articulate a juror right to privacy in this case."

"The trial court's failure to make findings supporting his closure order is the most vulnerable spot. . . . That failure . . . indicates that the court did not make the individualized determination of necessity that *Richmond Newspapers* and *Globe Newspaper* require."

In the concluding paragraph of her September 28, 1983, missive, Taylor wrote, "I would hold that the initial closure order was unconstitutional because it deprived the press and the public of their first amendment rights without articulating a compelling interest justifying closure."

She also recommended that the court order Judge William Mortland to release the voir dire transcript, withholding only "the information that is particularly sensitive and the jurors themselves request confidentiality."

David Charny submitted his twelve-page memo on October 6, less than a week before oral arguments. The Harvard Law grad and clerk to Justice Lewis Powell opened with a succinct statement of the issue: "May the state trial court in a criminal case close *voir dire* to the public and seal the transcript of the *voir dire* proceedings?" Powell read the memo carefully, circling and underlining words and writing in the margins in blue ink.[12] Charny wrote that "it seems unquestionable that *voir dire* is an integral part of the trial itself." Powell scribbled in the margins: "*Voir dire* is part of the trial."[13] The memo noted that the *Richmond* and *Globe* rulings found the "right of access particularly important to the functioning of the judicial process." And Powell, who in *Gannett v. DePasquale* was the only justice to argue for First Amendment access to pretrial hearings, inserted blue-ink check marks beside his clerk's specific examples: "fosters an appearance of fairness" and "permits the public to participate in the judicial process by observing and discussing its operation."[14] After citing the historical and practical arguments for open jury selection, Charny wrote that the trial court (Judge Mortland) "made no findings" when it closed voir dire. Wrote Powell: "No findings made."[15]

Charny dissected the privacy issue, separating a juror's personal information from a juror's attitudes. Riverside County's own brief "concedes courts have traditionally granted jurors a privilege to refuse to answer questions which might incriminate or embarrass them." But "jurors have no reason to conceal their attitudes on subjects such as the death penalty, the trustworthiness of policemen, or violent crime . . ." Even if some statements that jurors "purportedly" made during the Albert Greenwood Brown voir dire should be kept from the public, it was impossible for the Supreme Court to say so because "no findings in the record indicate that such statements were in fact made."

Charny concluded that the "orders closing *voir dire* to the public should be reversed because it is supported neither by findings made in this case nor by state interests as articulated in California law." Like Blackmun's clerk, Taylor, Charny recommended that the case be sent back to Judge Mortland so he could release *edited* transcripts that would protect the interests of the jurors. Sending it back would also "permit" Mortland to "fashion a remedy which better accommodates the competing interests here than would full disclosure of an unedited transcript."

12

The Audience of Nine

On Wednesday, October 12, at 9:05 a.m., Jim Ward and John Boyd reported to the Lawyers' Lounge on the first floor of the U.S. Supreme Court building. As per Supreme Court rules, they appeared in "conservative business dress in traditional dark colors." Ward's salt-and-pepper hair, dark-framed glasses, and somber black tie blended nicely with his gray three-piece suit, accented by a white handkerchief whose peaks jutted from the breast pocket. Boyd was a tad flashier: gray three-piece, no hanky, and a red-and-gold striped tie. The two quickly met up with Bruce Sanford and ran into their adversaries: Riverside County Counsel Gerald Geerlings and his deputies, Joyce Reikes and Glenn Salter. Salter would argue the case for the county.[1]

The lawyers were early. *Press-Enterprise v. Riverside County Superior Court* would not be argued until the afternoon. The Ward team stayed in the building, found the library, and tweaked the biggest argument of Jim Ward's life. He felt comfortable until it was time to go to lunch. That's when the nerves set in. He ran into Norman Cherniss, who slipped him an encouraging note on White House stationery, almost certainly supplied by Martin Salditch, the paper's Washington bureau chief. The note said, "Go get 'em Tiger," but it didn't seem to help. "Lunch was lousy," Ward wrote in his log. When they finally entered the small, ornate courtroom, Ward beelined to the spectator section and greeted "our contingent," which included his wife, two of his kids, and Uncle T, the "surrogate father" who stepped up after the eleven-year-old Ward's dad died in a plane crash. Cherniss and Sharon Waters sat together, with the executive editor gabbing away even though the spectators had been told there would be no talking—

even *before* the justices took the bench. A bailiff told Cherniss to be quiet, which worked for a while. When Cherniss started in again, the bailiff returned. "There will be no third time," he warned. "If I come back here again, it will be to escort both of you from the courtroom."[2]

Before the afternoon session began, Ward prevailed upon the marshal of the court to give him two quill pens, one left-handed, one right-handed. "I explained that was the only reason I had come to court!" He probably needn't have asked. "The quill pens at counsel table are gifts to you," say the Supreme Court rules, "a souvenir of your having argued before the highest Court in the land. Take them with you. They are handcrafted and usable as writing quills."[3]

In the 1980s there was only one tip to lawyers about how they should behave during oral argument: "*The court looks with disfavor on any oral argument that is read from a prepared text*" (emphasis in original).[4] Today the Supreme Court offers "Guidance for Counsel" that includes rules and suggestions that might have been penned by a high school vice principal: "Say nothing until the Chief Justice recognizes you by name"; "When the Justice speaks to you, do not look down at your notes, and do not look at your watch or at the clock located high on the wall behind the Justices"; "Preparing for your oral argument at the Supreme Court is like packing your clothes for an ocean cruise. You should lay out all the clothes you think you will need, and then return half of them to the closet"; "Please note that a legal sized pad does not fit on the lectern properly. Turning pages in a notebook appears more professional than flipping pages of a legal pad."[5]

Jim Ward probably would have ignored some of these suggestions. "It is better to use 'Your Honor' rather than mistakenly address the Justice by another Justice's name." Ward planned to address each justice by name. "Attempts at humor usually fall flat." Jim Ward, the champion high school debater, nationally ranked extemporaneous speaker, and "World's Greatest Attorney," was determined to "crack a joke."

"We will hear arguments next in Press-Enterprise Company against Superior Court of California," announced Chief Justice Warren Burger in his deep, rumbling bass. For the next thirty seconds, the court-room audience murmured, an unidentified justice said something unintelligible to Burger, who answered with an affirmative growl, and Jim Ward gathered himself behind the lectern.

When John Boyd, seated up front at the counsel table, surveyed the row of justices above him, he saw "people in black robes and rockers, tilting back. I thought I was in an old-folks' home."[6] From his vantage point at the lectern Ward saw a row of justices seated behind a bench that, by order of Chief Justice Burger, had been reshaped into a curve so the justices could see each other. Burger sat right in front of him.

To Burger's right sat Justice William J. Brennan Jr., seventy-seven, who had the most seniority among the eight associate justices. Born in Newark, New Jersey, Brennan was the son of a coal shoveler at a brewery. He held a Harvard law degree and practiced until he became a state judge. In 1956 President Eisenhower plucked Brennan from the New Jersey Supreme Court to fill the "Catholic seat" on the Supreme Court. Only one senator voted against his confirmation: Joseph R. McCarthy.[7] Known as the leader of the "liberal wing" of the Burger court, Brennan was a strong defender of First Amendment rights.[8]

Justice Byron "Whizzer" White, sixty-six, the second-most senior justice, sat immediately to Burger's left. The All-American football player from the University of Colorado went to Oxford on a Rhodes Scholarship but came home early after the outbreak of World War II. He ranked first his class at Yale Law School but took a leave after one year to play pro football with the Detroit Lions. He joined the navy after Pearl Harbor, eventually returned to Yale, graduated in 1946, and clerked for Supreme Court justice Fred M. Vinson. As a navy intelligence officer, he investigated the sinking of PT-109, skip-pered by John F. Kennedy. When Kennedy ran for president, White, by then practicing law in Colorado, worked to get JFK elected. White became a deputy attorney general, and Kennedy appointed him to the Supreme Court in 1962.[9] Something unheard of in recent decades: the Senate approved White's nomination with a voice vote.[10]

"He is a rocker," recalled Jim Ward in a 1986 speech at UC Riverside. "He rocks back and forth in his chair. The [Supreme Court] pages cannot get by behind him on the back stroke, so they wait for him to rock forward and then they dart behind his chair. A most feared cross-examiner . . . I took a tremendous risk with him."[11] It was White who would unwittingly give Jim Ward an opening to crack a joke. "I was able to do so at his expense."[12]

The Supreme Court's seniority-based seating chart continued to alternate from Burger's right to his left. Justice Thurgood Marshall, the seventy-five-year-old great-grandson of a slave, sat next to Brennan.[13] The son of a dining car waiter and a school teacher, the court's first black justice was the top-ranked graduate in his Howard University Law School class.[14] In 1965 President Lyndon Johnson named Marshall as his solicitor general—the person who represents the federal government before the U.S. Supreme Court. Marshall initially balked at the appointment, but Johnson sealed the deal by telling him, "I want folks to walk down the hall of the Justice Department and look in the door and see a nigger sitting there."[15] Two years later LBJ appointed Marshall to the Supreme Court. Unlike Brennan and White, who breezed to confirmation, Marshall encountered hostile southern senators who picked away at him with questions about minute details of constitutional history.[16] He was confirmed 69–11.

Prior to joining the Supreme Court, Marshall was perhaps best known as the lawyer who oversaw the legal battles that led to the court's landmark school desegregation case, *Brown v. Board of Education* (1954). But as the longtime director of the NAACP's Legal Defense and Education Fund, Marshall became intimately familiar with another institution teeming with racism: American courtrooms in the South, where blacks were systematically excluded from juries. In Columbia, Tennessee, in 1946 Marshall "watched patiently" as the district attorney general "stacked the deck in his own favor by excusing every potential black jury member in the Maury County pool. . . . He was used to, and even welcomed, such tactics from his opponents because they often helped to establish solid grounds for appeals."[17] In 1949 lawyers under his supervision argued *Shepherd v. Florida* before the U.S. Supreme Court. Their opponent, Florida assistant attorney general Reeves Bowen, explained to the justices that jury selection in the Lake County case took place against the "historical background of the South," where elected officials "just don't think about Negroes as jurors" any more than they would "think of having Negroes on a list for a social function." The court overturned the conviction of the NAACP's clients.[18]

Tawdry as they were, these jury selections were open to the public. Civil rights lawyers like Thurgood Marshall personally witnessed the routine exclusion of black jurors. Now Marshall was about to listen to oral arguments in a case where an all-white jury had been picked in secret and convicted a black man of raping and murdering a white girl. The judge who sentenced that man to death had permanently sealed the voir dire transcripts.

Justice Harry Blackmun, seated beside Byron White, was appointed to the Supreme Court in 1970 by President Nixon after two failed attempts to fill the vacancy created by the resignation of Abe Fortas. Blackmun, seventy-four, was a Minnesotan and general counsel for the Mayo Clinic. Born into a family of modest means, he went to Harvard undergrad on a scholarship and graduated with top academic honors. Then it was on to Harvard Law. Blackmun and Burger, also a Minnesotan, were lifelong friends. On the court they were initially known as the "Minnesota Twins." But they grew apart, with Blackmun gradually sliding from conservative to centrist to liberal.[19] Blackmun, like other justices, was at times underwhelmed by the quality of Burger's opinions and believed the chief justice took this personally.[20] Early in his tenure, 1973, Blackmun authored the opinion that made him famous—and infamous: *Roe v. Wade.*

Richard Nixon had much smoother sailing when he replaced Justice Hugo Black with Lewis Franklin Powell Jr. Nominated in October 1971, Powell was confirmed 89-1 and took his seat, next to Thurgood Marshall, early the following January.[21] Born in Suffolk, Virginia, Powell, seventy-six, graduated from Washington and Lee University School of Law. During World War II he became a decorated intelligence officer for the Army Air Force. He chaired the Richmond school board from 1951 to 1961, during the aftermath of the Supreme Court's *Brown v. Board of Education* desegregation order. Under his leadership the board's integration efforts produced only modest results, but Richmond schools remained open, no mean feat amid a wave of school closures in the South.[22]

William H. Rehnquist, fifty-nine, was the fourth and last Nixon appointee. Though named to the court along with Powell (Rehnquist succeeded Justice John Harlan), Rehnquist's road to confirmation was much bumpier because of his conservative Republican pedigree. He worked in Barry Goldwater's 1964 presidential campaign and served as a deputy attorney general under Nixon.[23] Nixon knew what he wanted in a Supreme Court justice: a conservative view on criminal justice and a commitment to judicial restraint. He thought Rehnquist fit the bill.[24] More than one quarter of the United States senators voted against his confirmation in December 1971. A native of Wisconsin, Rehnquist attended Stanford as an undergrad, earned a master's in political science at Harvard, and returned to Stanford for law school, graduating first in his class. When Burger retired in 1986, President Ronald Reagan elevated Rehnquist to chief justice. In a swipe at Burger, the liberal justice Thurgood Marshall said of the conservative chief justice Rehnquist, "He has no problems, wishy-washy, back and forth. He knows exactly what he wants to do and that is very important as a Chief Justice."[25]

President Gerald Ford made just one appointment to the Supreme Court (President Jimmy Carter, who succeeded him, made none). Ford replaced the liberal firebrand William O. Douglas with the bow-tied John Paul Stevens. A Phi Beta Kappa from the University of Chicago and a graduate of Northwestern University School of Law, Stevens joined the navy on the eve of Pearl Harbor and spent his war years as a code breaker. After graduating from law school, he clerked for Supreme Court Justice Wiley Blount Rutledge and then returned to Chicago, where he specialized in antitrust law and led a corruption investigation of the Illinois Supreme Court.[26] Like Blackmun, Stevens became more liberal as the court skewed more conservative. He was one of the court's most frequent modern-day dissenters.[27] Stevens, sixty-three, sat to Burger's right, at the end of the bench.

Sandra Day O'Connor graduated from Stanford Law School and turned down a Los Angeles law firm that offered her a job as a secretary. Now fifty-three, she sat in the last seat to the chief justice's left—and right next to an old friend and law school classmate, William Rehnquist. President Reagan named O'Connor the first woman on the Supreme Court (or, as she sometimes called herself, "F.W.O.T.S.C.") in 1981. Born in El Paso, Texas, in 1930, Sandra Day met John O'Connor at Stanford. They settled in Phoenix in 1957, where they raised three sons, and Sandra Day O'Connor carved out a career as an elected official, first in the state senate, where she became majority leader, and later as a trial court judge. Arizona's Democratic governor appointed her to the state appeals court, and Reagan picked her up to replace Justice Potter Stewart.[28] Regarded as conservative, O'Connor also had the independent, plain-speaking streak of a westerner.[29] Ward and the moot court "justices" had a carefully conceived strategy for the oral argument. Justice O'Connor singlehandedly blew it up.

Warren Burger, seventy-six, was appointed chief justice by Richard Nixon in 1969, just five months after Nixon became president.[30] With his white mane, square jaw, and deep, resonant voice, Burger could have been a walk-on from central casting. And his backstory was no less compelling: One of seven kids, he grew up on a farm outside of St. Paul, Minnesota. In high school he was student council president and lettered in four sports. As a young adult he sold insurance by day while attending night classes for six years, including law school.[31]

Some justices regarded Burger as disorganized, unprepared, inarticulate, and unreliable during the conference—where all justices met to discuss and vote on cases. The chief's case summaries could either be incomplete or framed by his own opinion of how an issue should be resolved. Not always an accurate notetaker when recording the views of fellow justices, Burger would sometimes assign a majority opinion to a justice who happened to be in the minority.[32] He was thought to be "pompous," "prickly," and "starchy," "more chief housekeeper than chief justice," whose "imprint on the Court's jurisprudence was not always readily identifiable."[33]

But the caricature of a snobbish bumbler belied a certain shrewd-ness. Over the years the chief justice developed a reputation for seiz-ing opportunities to write opinions that placed him in good standing with the press—an institution Richard Nixon, who appointed him, detested. "If you look through his First Amendment cases," former Justice John Paul Stevens told the *New York Times* in 2011, "I think you'll find that when the First Amendment claim was upheld, he might well write it. But where it was denied, Byron White would get it."[34] Burger even managed to portray himself as a First Amendment champion when he was in the minority. He argued that the Pentagon Papers case should be sent back to lower courts for more hearings. But six justices voted to immediately allow the *New York Times* to publish. When the 6–3 ruling came down, it was Chief Justice Burger who read the short opinion from the bench and later told reporters and an American Bar Association audience the case was "actually unanimous."[35]

Burger excelled at presiding over oral arguments.[36] And the opin-ions he wrote in *Nebraska* and *Richmond* captured attention of First Amendment lawyers for their elegance and for Burger's abiding respect for and reliance on history. And now, on the afternoon of October 12, 1983, the other justices sat in silence as the chief justice of the United States looked down at the lectern and said, "Mr. Ward, you may pro-ceed whenever you are ready."

13

"I Will Be Back"

Jim Ward gazed up at the majestic landscape: red velvet drapery, jet-black robes, and nine justices of the United States Supreme Court. It was just after 2 p.m., October 12, 1983. He had been preparing for this moment for months—ever since the court agreed to hear the case. Or maybe since the day Norman Cherniss called to tell him a reporter had been kicked out of a courtroom. Or possibly since that Sunday afternoon in Sioux Falls that changed a young boy's life but left a deep reservoir of self-confidence and ambition undisturbed. Now, the forty-eight-year-old business lawyer heard himself say, "Mr. Chief Justice and may it please the court."[1]

But just seconds later, he stumbled. "This is a court co-closure case . . ." Ward couldn't believe it. Of all the words to trip over. *Closure*. That's what his case was all about. And here he was, an obscure lawyer representing an equally obscure newspaper and flubbing a word, arguably the *key* word that Supreme Court justices had been struggling with for years. But as the jazz artist Miles Davis wisely counseled, "It's not the note you play that's the wrong note—it's the note you play afterwards that makes it right or wrong." Ward chuckled to himself and played on. The right notes began to flow. The gaffe had steadied him. Calmed him down. He relaxed into an up-tempo, conversational tone that lasted for nearly twenty seconds—until the chief justice, sensing that the "World's Greatest Attorney" needed a little coaching, interrupted.

CHIEF JUSTICE WARREN BURGER: I want to be sure not to misunderstand you. You said in a capital case. Your presentation . . . is not limited to capital cases, or is it?

WARD: The case below was limited to a capital case—
BURGER: But—

Ward got the hint.

WARD: Obviously, we would be happy with the pronouncement
that affected the *voir dire* in all sorts of criminal cases, Mr.
Chief Justice.

As the argument began, Justice Harry Blackmun jotted a note, perhaps to remind himself who was addressing the court: "Mr. Ward . . .
greying & glasses," an apparent reference to the lawyer's hair color
and spectacles.[2] Such notations, rarely flattering, were typical for
Blackmun, who also graded attorneys on their presentation. On a
scale of 1 to 10, Ward received a 5.[3]

WARD: We are asking this Court to pronounce that the California
Supreme Court case of *Hovey* versus Superior Court should be
construed and applied consistent with the right of access (that
the Supreme Court granted in *Richmond* and *Globe*).
JUSTICE WILLIAM REHNQUIST: Well, we can't actually do that
for you, can we, Mr. Ward? We can't announce how the decision of the Supreme Court of California should be construed.

Ward expected to be challenged, but this was the *first* challenge,
and it came from a sharp, conservative intellectual whose tone was
less than congenial. Ward didn't budge.

WARD: It would be our position that this Court could most
assuredly pronounce that the case should not be interpreted
to impact upon our First Amendment rights.

Rehnquist backed off, and for the next three-plus minutes Ward
told the justices about the Susan Jordan rape-and-murder case: the
trial, the conviction, the six weeks of closed voir dire, the sealed transcripts. He told them that other California judges were closing jury
selection, too. Judge Mortland hadn't just shut his courtroom for
"death-qualifying" questions but for, and here Ward quoted Mort-

land, "any other special areas that counsel may feel some problem with regard to." Ward recounted the newspaper's futile efforts to get the voir dire transcripts unsealed—and walked into a trap.

> WARD: At the conclusion of the argument, [Judge Mortland] verbalized that "the right of privacy of the jurors," to use the court's words, "should prevail, and that the public's right to know"—
> REHNQUIST: Neither of those rights are in the Constitution, are they, either of them, the juror's right to privacy or the public's right to know?

The question may have come up in the moot court rehearsal,[4] but hearing it posed by a Supreme Court justice rattled Ward so much that his knee-jerk response threatened to undercut the *Press-Enterprise*'s entire case.

> WARD: I agree with that, Justice Rehnquist.

Seconds later, another justice jumped in where Rehnquist left off—and threw Ward a lifeline.

> JUSTICE JOHN PAUL STEVENS: Did you agree there is no right to know in the Constitution?
> WARD: I am sorry, Justice Stevens. That was . . . I perhaps was a bit quick with my answer.
> STEVENS: I think you might as well sit down if you agree with that.

Ward, who was intent on cracking a joke, found himself the butt of one as laughter rumbled through the courtroom. But when Burger spoke the laughter stopped.

> BURGER: Will you read the passage [in the Constitution] that tells us that [the public has a right to know]? Or cite it to us?
> WARD: I cannot, Justice . . . Mr. Chief Justice, at this point in time, cite the passage from the Constitution.

But it would take more than that to control the damage. Ward reminded the justices that it was actually Judge Mortland who had used those "perhaps inappropriate" terms—"right to know" and "the right of privacy of jurors"—as part of his "rationale for having closed the courtroom." The tortured response finally ended the discussion, and Ward moved on. Virtually uninterrupted for five minutes, he told the justices that *Hovey* had nothing to do with isolating the public and press from potential jurors, that Mortland's "findings" to close his courtroom were as inadequate as they were brief, and that unsealed transcripts were a poor substitute for closed jury selection. "The transcript is, at best, a second-best alternative."

In the log he composed shortly after his trip to Washington, Ward wrote that Justice Brennan threw him "creampuff questions." Following the tense exchanges with Rehnquist, Stevens, and Burger, Ward welcomed the full tray of pastries.

JUSTICE WILLIAM BRENNAN: May I ask you, Mr. Ward, are you going to argue that there are no circumstances under which there may be closure of the *voir dire*?

WARD: I would not espouse an absolute rule.

Brennan then escorted Ward through the thicket of voir dire closure.

BRENNAN: Who would have the burden of proof [to show a courtroom should be closed]?

WARD: The burden would be on those seeking closure.

BRENNAN: And by what standard of proof?

WARD: I would think that the–

BRENNAN: Clear and convincing [evidence that *not* closing the courtroom would harm a juror or defendant]?

WARD: I would believe that clear and convincing would be the appropriate standard, because we are dealing with the First Amendment right of access.

BRENNAN: I gather you would argue, Mr. Ward, that the presumption should be that the *voir dire* should be open.

WARD: Yes, most assuredly Justice Brennan . . .

When the creampuffs ran out, Justice O'Connor stepped in.

JUSTICE SANDRA DAY O'CONNOR: Mr. Ward, do you think that prospective jurors do have any rights concerning questions that may be of a very personal or private nature to have the process closed—that have to be considered by the trial court?

There it was: juror privacy. The issue that haunted some lawyers in the *Press-Enterprise* camp and was the linchpin of Riverside County's case.

WARD: Assuming for the moment, Justice O'Connor, that there is some right of the juror to refrain from responding to a question for whatever reason . . . I can conceive of no circumstance why it would be necessary to close the courtroom in order to solve that problem for the juror, because there are reasonable alternatives available to the court to avoid any damage to any perceived right of the juror in those circumstances.

O'CONNOR: Such as what alternatives?

WARD: The most obvious being, of course, that the court could excuse the juror before invading any perceived right of privacy, because the defendant has the right to a fair and impartial juror and a fair and impartial jury, but not to a specific juror . . . I submit that a juror with a perceived privacy problem is no different than a person who has an illness or for some particular reason, is going to have an operation the following week and cannot sit on the trial, or has some physical infirmity or disability.

For the next three minutes, Burger and Brennan questioned Ward about juror privacy and press access to voir dire as well as juror questionnaires. Then, Justice O'Connor broke in again, leading to the most memorable and tense exchange of the *Press-Enterprise I* oral argument.

O'CONNOR: Mr. Ward, would your supposed rights [of access] extend beyond *voir dire* and into, for example, the plea-bargaining process between the prosecutor and defense counsel?

This was a red flag, alarm bell, and air raid siren all rolled into one blunt question. Ward had been expecting it. With the moot court session still fresh in mind, he didn't hesitate to answer.

WARD: We do not make that suggestion at this time, Justice O'Connor.

O'CONNOR: You're saving that for tomorrow?

The audience began to laugh. Just before their plane left for Washington, Norman Cherniss had handed Ward an envelope jokingly marked "sealed orders." It contained newspaper clips of Ward's October 5 appearance before the state court of appeal in the Robert Diaz preliminary hearing case. O'Connor's question may have called that week-old argument to mind.

WARD: Yes, your Honor. I will be back.

More laughter. Then he repeated his original answer.

WARD: No, I . . . we do not make such a suggestion at this time.

Ward had done exactly what he had been trained to do: stuck to the script and resisted the bait to stretch the scope of his argument. He had even basked in the warmth of audience laughter right along with Justice O'Connor. Having sidestepped a land mine, he engaged in a nearly three-minute exchange with Justice Rehnquist about what was and what was not part of the trial. Jury selection? Continuance hearings? And when Rehnquist asked a rather innocuous but speculative question, Ward gave the same answer, nearly verbatim, that he had given moments earlier: "We are not prepared to indicate at this time . . ." And Justice O'Connor pounced.

JUSTICE O'CONNOR: When you say, we are not prepared to do it at this time, it is sort of an unsatisfactory answer. What do you really think about it? It is not whether you are arguing it today. It is how do you analyze it?

John Boyd, sitting at the counsel table, had closely followed the back-and-forth between his boss and the justices. Some asked softball questions, as if to say, "Here's the question that I know you want to answer." But O'Connor was throwing heat. "She wanted to strike a balance on court access. There was no such thing as an absolute right and she wanted to know where this access doctrine was going."[5]

What's more, O'Connor had told Ward his answer was "unsatisfactory" in what Ward described as "her school marm voice." And when she asked him, point blank, "What do you really think about it?" Ward thought, "I don't have any alternative. Guys like (Robert) Bernius and (Bruce) Sanford were saying, 'For God's sake don't let them get you off talking about these other issues. They'll think it's too extreme.' I thought it was perfectly clever to say we're not making this argument at this time, but that wasn't good enough."[6] With O'Connor's question dangling in the chamber, Ward asked himself why he was really standing at the lectern, why had he come all this way, from the Riverside County Courthouse to the United States Supreme Court?[7]

WARD: All right, Justice O'Connor, I am sorry. You are quite right. It is a very fair question and comment. My position would be that openness should prevail.

With Ward's time winding down, Justice Byron White mused, "I suppose the whole case could go off just on whether this [jury selection] is part of the trial or not." Ward said it "definitely" was part of the trial, but added that even if someone didn't think so. . . . White interrupted him. If jury selection *wasn't* part of the trial, *Richmond's* constitutional guarantee of public and press access might not apply to the *Press-Enterprise* case.

WARD: Yes, that's true, so let's keep [it] as part of the trial.

Jim Ward had cracked his joke, and the audience laughed merrily. Soon, the red light on the lectern signaled that his time had expired, and the chief justice cut him off. Ward departed, and Burger summoned the newspaper's opponent.

BURGER: Mr. Salter.

Glenn Robert Salter, a 1975 graduate of Loyola Law School in Los Angeles, was a thirty-two-year-old deputy county counsel for Riverside County. The native Southern Californian and the only child of a SoCal Edison lawyer played baseball as a kid: good glove, weak bat. "I figured I wasn't going very far," he told the *Daily Journal*, a California legal newspaper. He majored in English at the University of Redlands and set his sights on a PhD in American literature. But his mom persuaded him to take a shot at law school. The first year changed his life. "In some sense," he told the *Journal*, "it was a little bit like going into literature because you're dealing with stories." But in law, he noted, they're true stories.[8] Salter, described in Justice Blackmun's notes as "balding, sandy"[9]—apparent references to his hair and lack thereof—would prove to be an articulate and measured, if not entirely persuasive, advocate. Blackmun's grade for Salter: 4.[10]

> GLENN SALTER: Mr. Chief Justice, and may it please the Court, this case presents a situation which calls for the delicate balancing of three fundamental interests, the Sixth Amendment right of a defendant to a fair trial, the First Amendment right of the press to gather and report the news, and the First Amendment and penumbral rights of the prospective jurors to a right to privacy. The issue as we perceive it is not whether there is a right of access by the public to *voir dire* proceedings. Rather, we see the fundamental issue to be the extent of the juror's right to privacy.

Moments earlier, Justice Rehnquist had asked Jim Ward whether the "right to know" was in the Constitution. Now, Rehnquist pressed Salter.

> REHNQUIST: What provision of the United States Constitution do you think guarantees a juror's right to privacy?

Salter said there wasn't one—not in the Constitution, not in the Bill of Rights. But he said the right has "roots even deeper than the Bill of Rights," and that the Supreme Court had said as much. He cited a case and might have explained it. But Justice Thurgood Marshall jumped in.

JUSTICE MARSHALL: Could a juror refuse to answer a judge's question on the *voir dire* on the grounds that it would violate his right of privacy?

Salter said yes and cited a California case where a prospective female juror refused to say what her husband did for a living because prospective male jurors had not been asked what their wives did for a living.

MARSHALL: You mean, you have the right of privacy not to tell your husband's work?

Salter conceded, "It was not a privacy issue" and Marshall pressed on.

MARSHALL: I am asking for the right of privacy point. Some juror says, under my right of privacy, you don't have a right to question me.

SALTER: I am unaware of any case which has supported that, but I believe that a juror would have that right.

Marshall kept at it. "I don't understand how you get the juror's . . . First Amendment right. . . . Suppose . . . we have a case where a juror was drunk. Could that juror say, you can't question me because it would violate my right of privacy?" When Salter eventually gave a qualified yes, Marshall again asked where it said so in the Constitution. (Listening to the exchange, Jim Ward found Marshall was "abrasive, rude and argumentative." He actually felt sorry for Salter and later said so to the *Press-Enterprise*'s gruff Washington bureau chief, Martin Salditch. Salditch put it in his story. Norman Cherniss took it out.)[11]

Salter changed the subject from a drunken juror to a "question which probably came up in the very case we are dealing with, how did you vote on . . . the death penalty issue? I think a defendant has a legitimate right in asking that question. I also think that a juror could legitimately say, I'm sorry, but the ballot box is secret, and you cannot compel me to answer."

REHNQUIST: So how do they decide that? Or is that why the *voir dires* take six months in California?

The audience dissolved into laughter.

Justice Lewis Powell, taking notes, wrote: "Salter—Jurors have a '*const.* right' to privacy & therefore [a right] to object on this ground to answering a question. (cited no cases)."[12]

JUSTICE STEVENS: May I ask if the *voir dire* in this particular case is in the record before us? Is it available to us?

SALTER: The *voir dire* was not made available.

STEVENS: Have you examined it?

SALTER: No, I have not . . .

STEVENS: . . . Because I was just wondering if there is any way to find out what percentage of this massive inquiry really involved confidential matters, or privacy matters . . . I had the impression that maybe three or four percent of the questions involved something fairly sensitive, but the rest of it was fairly routine. But are you telling me everything in this massive examination is sensitive?

SALTER: Not having read it, I could not tell you . . .

JUSTICE MARSHALL: Do you know of any case before this Court that we were denied the right to see what we were passing upon? Including the Pentagon Papers?

Salter said the county had not "intended in any way to deprive this Court of seeing any information that it thought was relevant . . . and we would certainly be more than willing to make it available." Marshall said he didn't want to see the three-thousand-page transcript, and Justice O'Connor asked Salter if there were any "feasible alternatives" to permanently sealing it? Could "sensitive responses" have been deleted? Could prospective jurors have been given numbers to shield their identities? The justices seemed concerned that what Stevens called "this massive examination" was completely under wraps. Salter said that even the *Press-Enterprise* hadn't suggested any alternatives until it filed a reply to the county's Supreme Court brief. Questionnaires weren't the answer, he said, because the newspaper would want to see them. Giving jurors numbers wouldn't work, either. It all came back to the core of the Riverside County case: juror privacy.

SALTER: I think the problem in a small community would be that if the public is allowed to come into the courtroom, even if a juror had, instead of a tag that said Juror on it, it said Number 18, someone in the audience may very well know who that person is, and so that person may very well say Juror Number 18, who happens to be someone next door to me, answered the question this way.

Anonymous responses, he added, really weren't that anonymous.

SALTER: If the question is, have you or anyone in your family ever been sexually abused, it is very difficult to either . . . screen that question or to rephrase that question in a way that does not require the prospective juror to provide the same basic information . . .

Salter rejected Ward's idea of simply excusing jurors who don't want to answer intimate questions. But he took it a little too far.

SALTER: It is not at all unusual for one juror to see another juror offer an excuse, and have the trial judge allow that juror to be let go. A prospective juror who does not wish to serve will simply mimic that excuse, and so you have the problem of . . . getting valid responses and that they will not offer you simply excuses to avoid their jury duty and their public duty.

JUSTICE STEVENS: Mr. Salter, I find that argument rather strange. You are implying that most members of the panel will give false excuses when under oath during a *voir dire*? Just because somebody ahead of them said they needed a babysitter, everybody else is going to make the same statement? Should we not presume that the citizens will tell the truth . . . ?

SALTER: I think we need to presume that they will tell the truth. Unfortunately, there is somewhat of a prevalent trend nowadays for people to either want to serve or not want to serve. It is very difficult if you come to a case and the trial judge says, this case should probably take six weeks to try. It may take five months for *voir dire* questioning.

STEVENS: ... [T]hat is an argument you are making in favor of closing the *voir dire* to the public?

SALTER: I am not suggesting per se that the jurors would lie simply to get off a jury.

Now on the homestretch, Salter told the justices that the key issue was whether Judge Mortland followed the Supreme Court's *Richmond* standards before he barred the public and the press from jury selection. Salter insisted that the judge had satisfied all three standards: He recognized the public and press right to attend a trial; he considered alternatives to closure; and he stated his reasons for closure on the record. But when he asserted that Mortland had "adopted" an alternative to closure by allowing lawyers to question jurors about subjects "traditionally governed by the right of privacy," Rehnquist didn't buy it.

JUSTICE REHNQUIST: But they didn't allow the press to sit in on the questioning, did they?

SALTER: That's correct.

REHNQUIST: Well, how is that an alternative?

SALTER: It represents an alternative because we ... believe that the right to privacy should not be invaded unless there is a compelling state interest. We are allowing that ... for the very limited purpose of giving the defendant a fair trial. But there is no reason that that should be extended or expanded so that the press or the public can delve into those private areas of a person's individual life.

When Salter concluded, Chief Justice Burger told Jim Ward that he had two more minutes and asked if there was anything else he wanted to say.

WARD: Yes, Mr. Chief Justice. This is a closure case. We do not believe it is an appropriate case for deciding right of juror privacy. Not only is it a case devoid of any record regarding the matter of juror privacy, but it is devoid of any juror claiming any right. All that we have are vague references by counsel and the court to the possibility of some sensitivities of jurors. We have no evidence at this point and on this record that any juror objected to any question, or that there was indeed any invasion of any right . . .

Burger posed a hypothetical: Suppose a potential juror had a confidential matter he didn't want to be asked about, explained it to the judge, and asked to be excused.

BURGER: . . . [W]ould you waive any inquiry, any claim to a right to know what the reasons were?
WARD: Yes, most assuredly, Mr. Chief Justice. We would have to.

14

"The Presumption of Openness"

On Friday October 14, two days after the oral arguments, the justices of the United States Supreme Court convened to decide the Albert Brown closed voir dire case.

The same day, Riverside County Superior Court judge John Barnard unsealed the transcript of the preliminary hearing for accused serial killer Robert Diaz. "The transcript was boring!" wrote Jim Ward beneath the *Press-Enterprise* clip in his scrapbook. The only "excitement" was Judge Howard Dabney's "intemperate" comment as the hearing ended: "[A]nd I think Mr. Diaz is an extremely dangerous man." The *Press-Enterprise* appeal, which sought public access to preliminary hearings, was still creeping along in the California courts.[1]

At 9:55 that Friday morning a buzzer sounded—or was supposed to—in the chambers of each Supreme Court justice. It was their five-minute warning to meet in the conference room next to the chief justice's chambers.[2] The walls of the large, rectangular, high-ceilinged room were lined with carved American oak; the windows were framed by fluted wood pilasters; the red carpet dated back to 1935.[3] When they entered the room, the justices engaged in the traditional handshakes before taking their seats. Chief Justice Burger sat at one end of the long table. Justice William Brennan, who had the most seniority among the associate justices, sat at the other end. The next three senior justices sat on one side of the table, while the final four crammed together on the other side. The justices were the only ones in the room. No clerks or other staff members were allowed. The custom was meant to enhance respect for the court by demonstrating, as Justice Louis Brandeis once put it, "We do our own work."[4] Justice, and later Chief Justice, William Rehnquist elaborated: "If a justice is to participate meaningfully in the conference, the justice must himself know the issues to be discussed and the arguments he wishes to make."[5] If anyone knocked on the door, Sandra Day O'Connor, the junior justice, would answer. She would also perform other menial clerical tasks. The justices considered exempting her from these duties because they didn't think it would look good to have the first woman justice catering to her colleagues "like a nursemaid." They ultimately decided to treat her just like any other newcomer.[6]

Chief Justice Burger opened the discussion of *Press-Enterprise Co. v. Superior Court*, most likely summing up the case, outlining the issues and explaining what the lower courts decided.[7] The other justices followed in order of seniority. When they finished, the voting began, again starting with the chief justice.[8] Each justice had a tally sheet or scorecard—a piece of paper that was completely blank except for the justices' names. This allowed them to take notes as their colleagues revealed their views—and their votes.[9]

"Rev," wrote Justice Powell in the space labeled The Chief Justice. This meant that, in Powell's view, Burger had voted to reverse Judge Mortland's order to close his courtroom during voir dire. Taking notes as the chief spoke, Powell wrote: "Judge should not close without an explanation . . . jurors may ask to be excused . . . there [are] less restrictive ways to deal with problems than this judge did . . . we should try to provide standards."

But Justice Blackmun seemed uncertain about what Burger had decided. In The Chief Justice box, he wrote "+ or -?" (the plus sign meant affirm, minus meant reverse). Burger, who was first to speak, did not know how the vote would go and may not have wanted to tip his hand too early and lose the chance to write a majority opinion. Blackmun's handwritten notes on Burger's remarks included: "Juror has a right to assert a reason privately . . . for good cause shown trial judge may close . . . important to give some guidance (about standards for closure)."[10]

The Powell and Blackmun scorecards show that Justices Brennan, White, Powell, and Rehnquist declared that voir dire was part of the trial. If it was part of the trial, the *Richmond* rules came into play, and, said Rehnquist, "this requires trial court to make findings" before jury selection could be closed to the public.[11]

The *Press-Enterprise* had not argued for an absolute constitutional right to open jury selection. But it *had* argued against automatic, arbitrary, and largely unexplained closures of voir dire. According to Blackmun and Powell, the justices agreed. Jury selection couldn't be closed "without making any findings," said Brennan. But they *could* be closed for "proper reasons," said White. Powell said judges "must identify reasons why entire *voir dire* is closed."

Justice Brennan wrote and most likely read aloud what appears to be a conference statement, asserting that the *Press-Enterprise* case was "squarely controlled by *Globe* and *Richmond Newspapers . . . voir dire* is clearly part of the criminal trial. . . . As far as I can discern, the judge [Mortland] utterly failed to consider alternatives to complete closure." A judge could "invite jurors to raise any private matters in chambers" instead of "total closure and sealing of the complete transcripts." Prospective death penalty jurors could be questioned "outside of the hearing of each other" in open court.[12]

If the justices had problems with Judge Mortland's less-than-rigorous reasoning to eject the public and press from jury selection, they were equally unhappy with his decision to seal the entire Albert Brown voir dire transcript. Once again it came down to balance. The *Press-Enterprise* had not argued for unfettered access to the transcript. But it had strenuously protested the permanent sealing of the six-week proceeding. That protest seemed to resonate. Justice Powell's notes on his own conference remarks read, "Reasons must be given [to seal the transcript]. A general statement as to privacy of parties and implied assurance to jurors of confidentiality are not enough." Justice Blackmun's notes have Powell saying a trial judge must explain why the transcript is "not suitable for publication generally." Justice O'Connor agreed that "we have to remand on the transcript,"[13] meaning Judge Mortland would have to wade through thousands of pages and release everything that did not invade juror privacy.

Powell's score sheet showed nine votes to reverse. Blackmun, unsure about where Burger stood, tallied eight reversals with a "+ or -" for the chief. Clearly, the court decided that Mortland had improperly closed his courtroom during jury selection in the death penalty trial of Albert Brown. The court also voted that Mortland should release the voir dire transcript without compromising the privacy of jurors. The *Press-Enterprise* appeared to be headed toward a lopsided victory, but not before the majority opinion weathered agonizing and tart criticism, much of it centering on that now-familiar bugaboo: juror privacy.

The very day Jim Ward and Glenn Salter squared off at the Supreme Court, Kingsley Browne, who clerked for Justice Byron White, wrote a "POST-ARGUMENT MEMO." Taking note of the "sensitive subjects" apparently raised in the Albert Brown voir dire, he declared, "I have great difficulty accepting the view that the public has a First Amendment right to know such intimate personal details of a juror's life."[14] Browne's memo acknowledged the logic of the *Press-Enterprise* argument that open voir dire would discourage a juror from lying. But the problem, he wrote, "is not lying. It is that he may be less forthcoming about the details of his feelings if he knows they are being made public." This could threaten the defendant's right to a fair trial. While it appeared that Judge Mortland failed to consider "less restrictive alternatives" to ejecting the press and the public, Browne questioned whether any of the measures suggested by Jim Ward would actually protect a juror's privacy. Questionnaires could be made public. Screening questions that lawyers might ask jurors seemed naive in a state where lawyers were allowed to ask prospective jurors virtually anything. Giving jurors numbers might work in a big city, but in a small town? As for releasing transcripts after a trial, Browne fretted that the next jury in the next case would be on notice that even if the voir dire were secret, the secret would eventually get out.

How, then, to balance the public's and jurors' interests? Deleting "sensitive" material in the three-thousand-page transcript would "pose significant administrative burdens on the trial court." Allow the press and public in the courtroom during the "dull and boring" parts and kick them out when things got too personal and sensitive? Browne mused that reporters and the public would have "to be on roller skates." White's clerk finally struck a note of resignation. "I suppose that this case should be reversed and remanded. Because of the significant rights involved, however, I think that trial courts should be granted great discretion in their decisions to exclude the press and public from *voir dire.*"

Chief Justice Burger assigned the opinion to himself. On December 17, 1983, he sent the first draft to the justices. It did not meet with rave reviews. Justice Harry Blackmun, once Burger's close friend, seemed to ridicule a lengthy, footnoted passage about the history of juries. Beside the narration, which began, "As the jury system evolved in the years after the Norman Conquest . . ." Blackmun scribbled: "The great historian!" When the history lesson spilled onto the next page, Blackmun wrote, "more of the same."

If Blackmun came off as snide, his clerk, Elizabeth Taylor, was withering. In a blunt "Mr. Justice" memo to her boss, she began, "This is not a great opinion."[15] Her biggest concern was that Burger "assumes that jurors have a right of privacy that . . . must be balanced against the first amendment interests in favor of openness." Recognizing such a "right could unnecessarily complicate the lives of trial judges trying to conduct *voir dire.*" And how would this juror's right be balanced against a defendant's constitutional right to a fair trial? "Could a juror simply refuse to answer questions posed in *voir dire*?" Burger "makes no effort to examine the implications of recognizing a juror privacy right." Taylor acknowledged that jurors have an "interest" in not revealing highly personal information. That interest didn't carry the clout of a constitutional right, but "in most cases that interest coincides with the interest of the defendant and the state in encouraging juror honesty." Hence, constitutional muscle was not needed to protect juror privacy.

Taylor was specifically troubled by a passage of Burger's draft that went beyond referring to rights of the accused and embraced the "the right of prospective jurors to privacy." Blackmun had caught that, too, underlining the word *privacy* on his copy of the Burger draft. Burger evidently got the message about juror privacy. In his January 6, 1984, rewrite he said, "Of course, the right of an accused to fundamental fairness in the jury selection process is a compelling interest." But the "right of prospective jurors to privacy" had disappeared.

"The cj's new draft is lots better," Taylor wrote to Blackmun the same day.[16] Burger now spoke of a juror's *interest* instead of *right* all the way through—except when he wrote, "Even then a valid privacy right may rise to a level that part of the transcript should be sealed." Taylor suggested that if Blackmun decided to endorse—or "join"— Burger's opinion, he could ask the chief to change that lone *right* to *interest*. Or, she wrote, "I also think it may still be worth writing separately [a concurring opinion]. I am drafting something short for your perusal." If Blackmun made that suggestion, Burger ignored it. Blackmun wrote a concurring opinion.

Juror privacy wasn't the only subject in Burger's opinion that ignited controversy. Justice Thurgood Marshall took great offense to a "gratuitous" passage: "We cannot fail to observe," wrote Burger, "that a *voir dire* of such length [six weeks], in and of itself undermines public confidence in the courts and the legal profession. . . . Properly conducted it is inconceivable that the process could extend over such a period." In a "Dear Chief" letter, Justice Brennan went to bat for Marshall. Noting that he had joined the chief's opinion, Brennan wrote that he would "feel more comfortable if you could accommodate Thurgood's concern as expressed in his opinion concurring in the judgment. Can you do so? Sincerely, Bill."[17]

Two days later, January 6, Burger replied: "Dear Bill, I am always open to good ideas that will improve an opinion or enhance accuracy, and I can readily agree with some of what Thurgood has written. However, it is hardly a novelty for opinions of this Court to comment on state practices that affect the administration of justice. As to dropping the observation on the absurdity of taking six weeks to pick a jury for a case which should take only a matter of days to try, I am not prepared to omit that observation. Regards, WEB."[18]

On January 18, 1984, the U.S. Supreme Court ruled 9–0 that Judge Mortland had been wrong to close his courtroom to jury selection in the capital case of Albert Greenwood Brown Jr.[19] Burger wrote for the majority, but three justices who agreed with the decision weighed in with concurring opinions to amplify their views. One of those justices, Marshall, refused to join—or have any part of—the majority opinion because he thought Burger's critique about the length of the voir dire was out of line.

Justice John Paul Stevens's concurring opinion emphasized that open voir dire wasn't just desirable for the sake of "judicial administration." This First Amendment ruling, like the ones that came before it, provided "protection to all members of the public from abridgement of their rights of access to information about the operation of their government, including the Judicial Branch." Stevens also defended Burger, though not by name, for identifying "the public interest in avoiding the kind of lengthy *voir dire* proceeding that was at issue in this case."

Justice Blackmun, drawing heavily on clerk Elizabeth Taylor's recommendations, emphasized that the court was not ruling on the "asserted right" of juror privacy. Recognizing such a "right" would "unnecessarily complicate the lives of trial judges attempting to conduct a *voir dire* proceeding. Could a juror . . . refuse to answer without a promise of confidentiality until some superior tribunal declared his expectation unreasonable? Could a juror even refuse to answer a highly personal, but relevant, question on the ground that his privacy right outweighed the defendant's need to know? I pose these questions only to emphasize that we should not assume the existence of a juror's privacy right without considering carefully the implications of that assumption." Blackmun also noted that "no juror is now before this Court seeking to vindicate that right," and that since Judge Mortland and California law recognized an "interest" in protecting juror privacy "to encourage juror honesty," there is "no need to determine whether a juror has a separate assertable constitutional right."

While the other justices wanted Mortland to release the entire voir dire transcript except for passages that invaded a juror's privacy, Justice Marshall's concurring opinion took a different approach. "The constitutional rights of the public and press to access all aspects of criminal trials . . . are most severely jeopardized when the courts conceal from the public sensitive information that bears upon the ability of the jurors impartially to weigh the evidence presented to them." The "preferable method," he wrote, was to "redact transcripts in such a way as to preserve the anonymity of jurors while disclosing the substance of their responses."

Marshall then voiced his "strong disagreement with Burger's "gratuitous" comments. "The question whether *voir dire* proceedings in this case extended for too long a period is not before this Court. . . . [W]e know few of the facts that would be required to venture a confident ruling on this question. Some of the circumstances of which we are aware, however, cast considerable doubt on the majority's judgment."

Marshall was not just writing as a Supreme Court justice but as a veteran civil rights lawyer who, unlike his colleagues, had spent his early career in courtrooms in the segregated South, where black defendants, having been framed, were convicted of murder by rigged, all-white juries. "Albert Greenwood Brown Jr.," Marshall wrote, "was accused of an interracial sexual attack and murder. Given the history and continuing legacy of racism in our country, that fact alone should suggest that a greater than usual amount of inquiry may have been needed in order to obtain a fair and impartial jury in this case. I find it not at all 'inconceivable' that the *voir dire* process could have legitimately extended over six weeks."[20] A capital case involving an interracial sexual attack "was bound to arouse a heightened emotional response from the affected community. . . . [The] use of unusually elaborate procedures to protect the rights of the accused" might result in "heightened respect for the judiciary's unshakable commitment to the ideal of due process even for persons accused of the most serious crimes."

Finally, Marshall said that unless the length of the voir dire somehow "violates federal law," the court had no business "stray[ing] beyond its proper role when it lectures state courts on how best to structure such proceedings."

Chief Justice Burger, writing for the majority, declared, "No right ranks higher than the right of the accused to a fair trial." But in the very next sentence he wrote, "[T]he primacy of the accused's right is difficult to separate from the right of everyone in the community to attend the *voir dire* which promotes fairness." It boiled down to a balancing act, and the court concluded that Judge Mortland's actions had fallen short of even attempting to strike that balance.

"The great historian," as Blackmun dismissively called Burger, wrote of the "presumptive openness of the jury selection process in England" that "carried over into the proceedings in colonial America. . . . Public jury selection thus was the common practice in America when the Constitution was adopted." In the passage documenting this "presumptive openness," Burger cited the Old Bailey case that Brian Harvey, the young Baker & Hostetler lawyer, had excavated during his dig at the Library of Congress. The 1660 voir dire during which "the defendant's persistence in challenging jurors provoked laughter in the courtroom" was clear evidence of the public's presence.

Judge Mortland closed voir dire for six weeks after explaining, "I agree with much of what defense counsel and People's counsel have said and I also, regardless of the public's right to know, I also feel that's rather difficult that by a person performing their civic duty as a prospective juror putting their private information as open to the public which I just think there is certain areas that the right of privacy should prevail and a right to a fair trial should prevail and the right of the people to know, I think should have some limitations." After reading that passage in Burger's first draft, Justice Powell commented in bright red ink, "Hardly an elegant example of the English language!" But it was also vague language—much too vague to balance the rights and "interests" of the public, press, defendant, and jurors.

Quoting *Richmond Newspapers* (1980), Burger wrote: "People in an open society do not demand infallibility from their institutions, but it is difficult for them to accept what they are prohibited from observing." He then quoted *Globe Newspaper Co.* (1982): "Where . . . the State attempts to deny the right of access in order to inhibit the disclosure of sensitive information, it must be shown that the denial is necessitated by a compelling governmental interest, and is narrowly tailored to serve that interest."

The chief refreshed and amplified those rulings in *Press-Enterprise Co. v. Superior Court*: "The presumption of openness may be overcome only by an overriding interest based on findings that closure is essential to preserve higher values and is narrowly tailored to serve that interest. That interest is to be articulated along with findings specific enough that a reviewing court can determine whether the closure order was properly entered." The majority opinion concluded that Mortland's "prolonged closure was unsupported by findings" that Albert Brown's right to a fair trial and jurors' privacy interests were in jeopardy. Even if Mortland had come up with compelling reasons to close his courtroom, he "failed to consider whether alternatives were available" to protect those rights and interests.

Burger did acknowledge jurors' have "privacy interests." Prospective jurors should have the chance to tell the judge—in chambers, on the record and with attorneys present—about public questions that might embarrass them. A "valid privacy right," he wrote, could justify sealing "part of the transcript." But Mortland had sealed all of it. Permanently.

In his first draft Burger had written: "Sensitive material reasonably entitled to privacy could have been stricken without such a sweeping order. Some effort should have been directed to identifying such material." That was too weak for Powell and Marshall. "Not strong enough," Powell scribbled in blue ink. "Judge should be directed to disclose the transcript except for confidential portions." Wrote Marshall: "I fear that the Court may give the wrong impression . . . by intimating that merely 'some' effort to segregate sensitive material will suffice to quiet First Amendment concerns." Burger got tougher in his published opinion. "Those parts of the transcript reasonably entitled to privacy could have been sealed without such a sweeping order; a trial judge should explain why the material is entitled to privacy."

Building on *Richmond* and *Globe*, the Supreme Court delivered a double-barreled rebuke of Judge Mortland's secret jury selection and sealed transcript. The court ordered him to review and release the three-thousand-page transcript in a manner "not inconsistent with this opinion." The ruling did not strike down *Hovey*, the California Supreme Court ruling that prospective death penalty jurors must be questioned "in sequestration." Mortland didn't explicitly mention the case when he closed his courtroom. Nothing in the uc Santa Cruz study cited in *Hovey* suggested jurors' attitudes about the death penalty were influenced by the presence of the public and press during voir dire. The justices found a First Amendment right to attend jury selection without repudiating the California Supreme Court decision. But if it hadn't been for *Hovey* and California judges' interpretation of it, *Press-Enterprise Co. v. Superior Court* never would have reached the U.S. Supreme Court.

15

A Halt to the "Ominous Progression"?

As the congratulatory calls and letters poured in and somberly delighted newspaper editorials blanketed the country, Norman Cherniss was, as he might have put it, not the most exuberant celebrant of the Supreme Court's 9–0 ruling. "I don't want you to think we get much fun out of all this," the *Press-Enterprise* executive editor told a *Los Angeles Times* reporter the day the court announced its decision. "None of it's cheap." Added Cherniss, "I guess it's a victory, I hope so. . . . We do try to pick what is important. We're not ones to be screaming all the time."[1]

Though it was almost unheard of to see a local story on page one of the *Press-Enterprise*, the newspaper's victory in a case that originated with the vicious rape and murder of a Riverside high school girl was the lead front-page story on January 19, 1984: "Supreme Court Says Open Jury Selection Is to Be the Rule." It was not a banner headline that shrieked across the top of the page. It was an understated, three-deck headline, above the fold but below the *Press-Enterprise* logo, apportioned over just two columns.

The *Press-Enterprise*'s editorial, published the same day, read much like the Supreme Court's balancing act. "Candor and privacy are never to be dismissed as unimportant; but neither are they to be convenient excuses for taking the judicial process behind closed doors when such closure cannot in fact be justified."[2] The editorial made it clear why the newspaper had gone to the "effort and expense" to challenge Judge Mortland's ruling. "While *Press-Enterprise v. Superior Court* is, of course, a First Amendment case—in which not only this newspaper but many others and many news organizations across the country have had a part—it is not, and was never meant to be, simply a press case. The 'right of access' is not limited to the press, and the decision makes that clear. The value of openness lies in the fact that people not actually attending trials can have confidence that standards of fairness are being observed." The editorial concluded: "There has been an ominous progression in California courts, among others, toward greater secrecy, and it can be hoped that the Supreme Court brought this to a halt."

In its editorial headlined "Justice in Plain Sight," the *Los Angeles Times* called the ruling "a victory for the *Riverside Press-Enterprise*, a persistent champion of open court proceedings."[3] The *New York Times* editorial, "Justice in the Open," had a scolding tone: "[T]oo many judges, intoxicated with the desire to run a courtroom as a personal fiefdom, still focus on the fine print that mentions rare circumstances when closing the courtroom might be justified in terms of fairness or the privacy of jurors and witnesses. So once again this week the Supreme Court had to lay down the law to the judges. The winners were justice and the public no less than the press. . . . Openness would seem especially vital for a trial so likely to stir strong community interest. Do the jurors who are chosen seem representative of the community? Do those who are dismissed lean for or against the death penalty? Is one side or the other striking too many prospective jurors of one race, sex or class? These and other questions can be answered only by observing the process."[4]

"It is difficult to fathom," wrote the *San Francisco Chronicle*, "just what motivated Riverside Superior Court Judge J. William Mortland" to close voir dire and seal the transcript. "The court judge explained somewhat lamely that questioning of jurors sometimes involved 'sensitive areas that do not appear to be appropriate public discussion.' This kind of vague waving away of the public carries little persuasiveness."[5]

The *New York Times* and *Washington Post* played the court's ruling on page one. Deep in her story *New York Times* reporter Linda Greenhouse noted that "the decision treated the jury-selection process as part of the trial itself. It therefore did not overrule the 1979 [*Gannett*] decision in which the court refused to find a constitutional right of access to attend pretrial hearings."[6] But now some wondered whether *Gannett*, a Sixth Amendment case, could survive what appeared to be the Supreme Court's First Amendment avalanche. The neighboring *Redlands (CA) Daily Facts*, a paper even smaller than the *Press-Enterprise*, picked up the scent. "Five years ago, the high court rejected arguments that the press and the public had the right to attend a pre-trial hearing in a New York murder case. We hope, in its quest for openness, the high court will take another look at closed pretrial hearings when a similar case is brought before it for judgment."[7]

Glenn Salter, the losing attorney, could not be reached by the *Press-Enterprise*. But his Riverside County colleague, Deputy County Counsel Joyce Ellen Manulis Reikes, put the best face on defeat. "It seems to me," she told the newspaper, "that the court made it very clear that jurors have a right to privacy that can, in certain circumstances, override the First Amendment right of public access relative to *voir dire*. It seems we may have lost the battle, but we won the war."[8]

Not surprisingly, Sharon Waters, the young lawyer who retooled the *Press-Enterprise* brief, had a much different view. "Judge Mortland really messed up," she reflected decades later. "He never read the transcript. He never looked at whether there was any part that could be released to the public without jeopardizing jurors' privacy interests. The [Supreme] Court ordered, 'Judge, you read that transcript and you decide which part has to be kept confidential. Do the balancing.'"[9] Mortland "felt scolded by the ruling," recalled *Press-Enterprise* court reporter Ron Gonzales. "He felt belittled. He took it personally."[10] He wasn't going to simply hand over the transcript, either. Joseph Peter Myers, Albert Brown's attorney, told Gonzales that he would ask Mortland to call the more than one hundred people questioned during jury selection back to court, "where they would be allowed to say whether they want their answers sealed—and ask the judge to order the *Press-Enterprise* to pay attorney fees for jurors who want lawyers."[11]

John Boyd and Sharon Waters had worried that Ward would stumble during oral argument. They were nervous that something would go wrong.[12] Despite his professed self-confidence, Ward had the jitters, too. He ordered Boyd to say, "Good job, Jim," no matter how well—or poorly—he handled himself. But Boyd didn't have to fake it. "In a heartfelt way," wrote Ward, "he said much more flattering things."[13]

Despite the worries and misgivings about a business lawyer making his constitutional law debut before the U.S. Supreme Court, Bruce Sanford, the lead writer of the national amicus brief, said the *Press-Enterprise* and Ward were the right messengers at the right time. "With Burger and Rehnquist, the court was changing from the liberal court of the sixties and seventies. This Court wasn't wild about the *New York Times* and *Washington Post*. They liked that it wasn't the same old players bringing the case. Here you had a medium-sized paper saying it's very important in our community to cover criminal trials. It was so much more appealing than the big newspapers swaggering in. People can minimize the optics or the atmospherics in the way cases are presented. But I don't."[14]

1. Howard H "Tim" Hays. *Press-Enterprise* owner Howard H "Tim" Hays believed "openness is the most important characteristic of free government." Photo by *Press-Enterprise*; courtesy of Southern California News Group.

2. Norman A. Cherniss. Executive editor Norman A. Cherniss was the journalistic and intellectual force behind legal battles that led the *Press-Enterprise* to the U.S. Supreme Court. Photo by Fred Bauman, *Press-Enterprise*; courtesy of the author.

3. (*above*) Mel Opotowsky. The newspaper's point man on *Press-Enterprise II*, senior editor Mel Opotowsky was a hard-nosed newsman and well versed in First Amendment law. Courtesy of Mel Opotowsky.

4. (*right*) James D. Ward. The only thing "Mr. Everything" lacked was experience in constitutional law. But it didn't matter. Courtesy of James D. Ward.

5. U.S. Supreme Court justices that heard the *Press-Enterprise* cases.
Bottom row, left to right: Thurgood Marshall, William J. Brennan,
Chief Justice Warren E. Burger, Byron R. White, Harry A. Blackmun.

Top row: John Paul Stevens, Lewis F. Powell, William H. Rehnquist, Sandra Day O'Connor. Photo by Robert S. Oakes, *National Geographic*; courtesy of the Supreme Court of the United States.

Rev 9-0

No. 82-556 , PRESS-ENTERPRISE v. SUPERIOR COURT   Conf. 10/14/83

The Chief Justice *Rev.*

Transcript is not in record. (?)
Jurors may ask to be ~~and~~ excused
Judge should not close w/o an explanation
There "less restrictive" ways to deal
with problems than this judge did
We ~~do~~ should try to provide
standards.

Justice Brennan *Rev.*

Voir dire is ~~~~ part of trial.
The TC ~~~~ went much too far w/o
making any findings.

Justice White *Rev.*

Should apply *Richmond Newspapers*
TC ignored our decision

6. First page of Justice Lewis F. Powell's notes during the conference and vote for *Press-Enterprise I*. Chief Justice Burger said there were "less restrictive" ways to handle jury selection "than this judge did"; Justice Brennan said voir dire was "part of the trial" and Judge Mortland "went much too far without making any findings; and Justice White said Mortland "ignored our decision" in *Richmond Newspapers v. Virginia*. At the top of the page, Powell writes "Rev 9–0," a unanimous victory for the newspaper. Courtesy of the Washington and Lee University School of Law.

16

Smacked Down Again

Less than a week after the Supreme Court ruling, Norman Cherniss received a brief note on official stationery with *(Personal)* in the letterhead: "Dear Norman: Although I express no opinion hereby regarding the legal issues involved, I wanted to send you my congratulations on your unanimous victory before the United States Supreme Court. Not bad for a first try! Best wishes. Sincerely, Rose."[1] California chief justice Rose Elizabeth Bird had written the *Hovey* opinion that served as the launching pad for the newspaper's trip to the U.S. Supreme Court. Cherniss had editorially blasted *Hovey* as a "rambling decision." The Bird court, with the exception of the chief justice herself, had refused to hear the newspaper's appeal. Now, "Rose" sent a gracious message to her friend.

This relationship, and Cherniss's even closer friendship with state supreme court justice Stanley Mosk, troubled Jim Ward, who repeatedly urged Cherniss to "refrain" from communicating with them while the newspaper pursued its court access appeals.[2] As it crusaded for open courtrooms, the *Press-Enterprise* never failed to insist that public confidence in the judicial system was at stake. Any appearance of coziness and favoritism between Cherniss and the justices who might be asked to hear yet another closed-courtroom case would do little to boost public confidence in either the California Supreme Court or the *Press-Enterprise*, not to mention the justice system and media in general.

The ongoing correspondence became particularly troublesome after January 12, 1984–just six days before the *Press-Enterprise's* 9–0 voir dire triumph—when the state court of appeal in San Bernardino ruled that Riverside County Superior Court judge John Barnard had acted correctly in refusing to unseal the preliminary hearing transcript of accused serial killer Robert Diaz.[3] "[S]ince there is no right of public access to preliminary hearings arising under either the federal or state Constitutions," said the court, "there is no constitutional right to transcripts of such hearings." This was the first appellate court interpretation of the state law, amended in 1982, that said preliminary hearings "shall be open and public" unless judges find that keeping them closed is "necessary" to protect the rights of the defendant.[4] What did *necessary* mean? The legislature left that to the courts. Now, a higher court had spoken. The justices said a judge would have to find, as Barnard had found, "a reasonable likelihood of substantial prejudice" to the defendant's rights. The *Press-Enterprise* argued for the much higher standard set forth in a 1982 *federal* appeals court ruling: "a substantial probability that irreparable damage" to a defendant's fair trial right would result from an open-court proceeding.[5] Norman Cherniss told *Press-Enterprise* readers that no decision about an appeal to the California Supreme Court would be made until the ruling had been studied more closely.[6]

With the study complete, Cherniss wrote to his friend, the chief justice, to arrange a San Francisco get-together. "Dear Rose," he began on February 28, 1984, "[M]y next San Francisco meeting . . . is scheduled for Saturday, April 28, which would make Friday, April 27, the day I would hope to get together with you again. . . . I should tell you, however, for whatever it may be worth in this regard, that we filed a new petition for certiorari with your court last Tuesday."[7]

On March 15 the California Supreme Court agreed to hear the *Press-Enterprise*'s appeal asking the court to "clarify the public's right to attend preliminary hearings in criminal cases.[8] A week later, Cherniss, in his sly-and-dry style, wrote to his close friend Justice Stanley Mosk. "I have to tell you that my lawyer feels that you should stop making these personal contacts while we have a case pending before your court. . . . I have to tell you that he has gone so far as to suggest that if you do not refrain from all efforts to contact me in the immediate future, that I ought to complain to the Chief Justice when I get together with her in a few weeks. Naturally, neither he nor I would want this to become necessary. I hope you'll take this in the spirit meant."[9]

Several weeks later Cherniss's disengagement from the state supreme court justices appeared to be complete. In an April 26 letter to Ward, Cherniss wrote: "Dear Jim, I phoned the chief justice's office this morning, not only to confirm our appointment, but to mention again the circumstances that might make an appointment ill-advised." When the chief justice called back, she "was very friendly, and agreed in a very nice way, that it probably wouldn't be a good idea to get together while review was pending. She expressed her appreciation that I called the pending review to her attention and, I thought, but could not be sure, that as she hung up she turned to someone and said something like that's more than that damned Ward would have done."[10]

As the banter continued and the newspaper's case rose to the state supreme court, there were other important developments in the Diaz case: On March 29 Riverside County Superior Court judge John Barnard found Robert Diaz guilty of twelve counts of first-degree murder. Less than two weeks later, after five days of poring over testimony and taking solitary walks along the beach at Corona del Mar, Barnard sentenced Diaz to die in the gas chamber.[11]

On October 3, 1984, Norman Arnold Cherniss, who had a history of heart trouble and a tendency to brush aside suggestions that he take better care of himself, died of a heart attack. He was just fifty-eight years old. His death shocked and saddened journalists and jurists throughout the country.

John Siegenthaler, editorial director of *USA Today* and editor and publisher of the *Nashville Tennessean*, remembered Cherniss—whom he had known since their Harvard/Nieman Fellowship days in 1959—as a man who "had an ability to say what he believed with compelling logic and devastating satire that made what he said all the more difficult to ignore. He stood for what was the best in American journalism even though he came from a smaller newspaper in terms of circulation."[12] Howard Simons, managing editor of the *Washington Post* and also in that Nieman Class of 1959, told the

Press-Enterprise, "He was the philosopher among us. There are bright editors and smart editors, but he was the most thoughtful among all of them."[13] California Supreme Court justice Stanley Mosk, a pall bearer at his friend's funeral, remembered Cherniss as a man "sincerely dedicated to the First Amendment and the freedom of the press. . . . He has done a great deal in opening up government and the judiciary to inspection of the press. In my opinion, he is the finest journalist I have known."[14] Wallace Turner, the San Francisco bureau chief for the *New York Times*, said Cherniss "was able to shape the paper and make a showcase of what a relatively small newspaper in a small city could be."[15]

Perhaps more than anyone else in journalism or law, Tim Hays understood the magnitude of the death of the man who grumbled, "My daddy never owned a newspaper." Cherniss was a "monumental loss" to the *Press-Enterprise*, said Hays. "His talents were so unique and so totally committed to journalism that he established a national reputation for a paper of modest size. He had many opportunities to move on to larger audiences. It was our good fortune that he preferred the intimacy of a smaller paper and of this particular paper."[16]

The *Press-Enterprise*'s October 5 editorial page masthead still listed Norman A. Cherniss in bold type. Quietly beneath his name: Executive Editor, 1971–1984. The lengthy editorial concluded with Cherniss's four-year-old remarks to graduates of UC Berkeley's School of Journalism: "This is your day, of course, *your* commencement, but cheered as I ordinarily am by the bright-eyed, the young and coming, I think I'll break with tradition here and pay special respect to the practitioners. I'm talking about the genuinely seasoned journalists who . . . keep their zest, their enthusiasm for what they're doing, their profession, their craft, their calling . . . I can explain it, I think, by borrowing . . . from some anonymous person's description of life in the French court under one of the Louis: It may not be the best life, but it spoils you for anything else. For those who belong in it, I think that's true of journalism."

These tributes and remembrances appeared in the *Press-Enterprise* the same day as a scheduled court hearing concerning the Albert

Brown voir dire transcript. Nearly ten months had passed since the U.S. Supreme Court ordered Judge William Mortland to release most of the transcript to the public. That he still had not done so enraged Norman Cherniss.[17] Mortland finally released an edited version of the three-thousand-page transcript on April 19, 1985—fifteen months and one day after the Supreme Court's unanimous ruling in *Press-Enterprise I*.[18]

The California Supreme Court had scheduled an early October session to hear the *Press-Enterprise*'s appeal for public access to preliminary hearings. But when Cherniss died, that hearing was postponed. Now, on October 15, the state supreme court convened to hear *Press-Enterprise v. Superior Court*, otherwise known as *Press-Enterprise II*. Jim Ward represented the newspaper. Ephraim Margolin, a San Francisco lawyer representing California Attorneys for Criminal Justice and the National Association of Criminal Defense Attorneys, appeared on behalf of Robert Diaz.[19] Margolin, who took the case at no charge, argued that there was only one absolute right: the defendant's *constitutional* right to a fair trial. The public and press had a "qualified" right of access to a preliminary hearing, but judges could shut the public out if they found a "reasonable likelihood" that a defendant's right would be imperiled. A stronger standard, such as the "substantial probability of irreparable harm" pushed by Ward, would make it almost impossible to close a hearing, Margolin argued.[20]

When Chief Justice Bird said the press could get the transcript after the preliminary hearing, Ward replied, "We live in a now society. . . . Timeliness is important." Diaz, he said, made "loud and vocal objections to his treatment by [Judge Howard Dabney, who conducted the preliminary hearing]. There were allegations of indiscreet remarks by the judge." But in the months between the hearing and the release of the transcript, Dabney "was elevated" from municipal court to superior court. An open preliminary hearing, said Ward, would have resolved those allegations.[21] Bird said the public and press could still learn the facts of the case during the trial, but Ward replied that only 10 percent of criminal cases filed ever go to trial. Margolin told the court that preliminary hearings provide only a partial, one-sided view of the case because the defense rarely *puts on* a defense. He said a preliminary hearing is like a melody played by a single instrument: the cello. "You get basically a skewed melody."[22]

In his prepared remarks to the court, Ward wrote: "My firm, my associates and I, have been involved in a war in connection with this matter of right of access to the trial court for some years now. . . . We have faced it in the frontline trenches. We are confronted with defense counsel who, feeling a need to protect themselves from malpractice, make every motion and seek every remedy available to them. . . . We are confronted with trial judges who . . . are constantly concerned about reversal. Given that scenario, and given a standard as easy to justify closure as 'reasonable likelihood of substantial prejudice,' trial judges will always close." But Ward warned that such closures were risky. "We are dealing with a populace that mistrusts us. We are dealing with a populace which finds that we lawyers and judges are not properly handling the criminal justice system. They accuse us . . . of turning criminals loose on the streets. In such a situation of distrust and fear, we have to resort to openness and education of the public that the criminal justice system is a[s] good as we can possibly make it. We must . . . avoid the overtures of those who would cause the courtrooms to be closed unnecessarily."[23]

Ward and the *Press-Enterprise* had the support, including two amicus briefs, of a number of newspapers and news organizations, including Knight-Ridder Newspapers, the *San Jose Mercury News*, the California Newspaper Publishers Association, Copley Press, and the Times Mirror Co. Three days after the hearing, Ward wrote a thank-you letter that included a rather all-encompassing prediction. "I predict that they will not pronounce a constitutional right of access to the preliminary hearing. They will interpret [state law] and find a standard somewhat more stringent than [reasonable likelihood of substantial prejudice] but not as stringent as substantial probability of irreparable harm. I would not be surprised, however, if we suffered a total setback at their hands."[24] He turned out to be partially right. On the last day of 1984, the California Supreme Court handed the *Press-Enterprise* a total setback. By a 6–1 vote—a majority that included Chief Justice Bird and Justice Stanley Mosk—the court declared that the public and press had no constitutional right to attend a preliminary hearing and that such hearings must be closed if there is a "reasonable likelihood" that an open courtroom would endanger a defendant's right to a fair trial.

17

"Expanding the Right of Access"

John J. Lee, the public defender who had represented convicted murderer Robert Diaz, called the California Supreme Court's ruling "fantastic." Tim Hays called it "disappointing" but hadn't decided whether to appeal to the U.S. Supreme Court.[1] True, that court unanimously ruled for the newspaper in the voir dire case. But even Riverside County had conceded that jury selection was part of the trial. By its very name, a *preliminary hearing* was a different animal, and *Gannett v. DePasquale* had already said the public and press had no *Sixth Amendment* right to attend one. But if the *Press-Enterprise* hadn't decided whether to appeal the Diaz ruling, at least there was a rationale to do so. San Diego lawyer Ed McIntyre, who represented Copley Press and frequently fought alongside the *Press-Enterprise* in court-access cases, explained the 9-0 ruling in *Press-Enterprise I* wasn't just a voir dire case. "The thrust of the decision," he said, "is toward openness."[2] *Constitutionally required* openness. *Press-Enterprise* lawyer John Boyd put it in much plainer terms. The Supreme Court had imposed tough standards for closing voir dire, but California courts had set relatively weak standards for closing preliminary hearings. Boyd's analysis: "Hey dummies! Don't you get it?"[3]

Three months after the Bird court's rebuke, the *Press-Enterprise* filed an appeal with the U.S. Supreme Court. Jim Ward's petition, submitted on March 29, 1985, sought to put the Supreme Court on the spot by appealing to its self-imposed obligation to resolve conflicts that emerge in lower courts.[4] In the federal courts, declared the newspaper's petition, "there is generally unanimity that the public's constitutional right of access extends to pretrial criminal proceedings." But since this was not an absolute right, the standards to keep the public and press out of preliminary hearings were literally all over the map. The Third Circuit Court of Appeals (Philadelphia) said trial judges could not close a pretrial hearing unless they made "specific findings" that alternative measures "will be insufficient to preserve the defendant's rights." But the Ninth Circuit (based in San Francisco) said pretrial hearings could only be closed if there was a "substantial probability that irreparable damage to the defendant's fair-trial right will result." Way down yonder in New Orleans, the Fifth Circuit was far more laid back, saying defendants only had to show that their constitutional right to a fair trial is "likely to be prejudiced." The Second Circuit (New York) said a pretrial hearing could be closed with "a showing of a significant risk of prejudice."

This mish-mash of standards didn't even include state courts. Eleven states had decided "that a right of access to pretrial criminal proceedings arises under the First Amendment or under state law or both." Yet, noted the *Press-Enterprise* petition, "there is a divergence of opinion" about when that right could be yanked. Then there were the six states, including California, that did not recognize a constitutional right of access to pretrial hearings. "It is imperative," lectured the *Press-Enterprise*, "that the Court now resolve this issue." Until it does, "uniform recognition and protection of this important right will not occur."

Ward accused the California Supreme Court of "utterly" ignoring the U.S. Supreme Court, which had so recently concluded that open criminal proceedings help encourage "all participants to perform their duties conscientiously, discouraging misconduct and abuse of power by judges, prosecutors and other participants." Public access also serves "a community therapeutic function by allowing the public to see that justice is done." The U.S. Supreme Court used these "benefits" to lay the foundation for a First Amendment right of access to criminal trials (*Richmond*, *Globe*, and *Press-Enterprise I*). Now, Ward argued, that right should be extended because "the preliminary hearing in California has almost all the attributes of a trial." And it is often the "only judicial proceeding . . . that takes place during a criminal prosecution because so many cases are disposed of without trial."

Finally, the petition zeroed in on what it perceived to be the California Supreme Court's reliance on a flimsy standard to close pretrial hearings: the "reasonable likelihood of substantial prejudice." The California Supreme Court's "loose standard" makes courtroom closures the rule, not the exception, and violates the First Amendment rights of the public.

Once again the *Press-Enterprise* had backup. Copley Press lawyers McIntyre and Hal Fuson delivered a friend-of-the-court brief on behalf of California newspapers and organizations representing editors, publishers, radio, and television. Largely echoing the *Press-Enterprise* petition, the brief told the Supreme Court that California's preliminary hearings were "routinely closed, often with no evidence of prejudice to the defendant's fair trial right" and based upon "an unsubstantiated recitation" of "reasonable likelihood of prejudice."[5]

"After every preliminary hearing," the brief concluded, "a person is either bound over for trial or charges are dismissed and the accused returns to society." (Or a defendant avoids a trial by pleading guilty to a lesser charge.) "Such judicial decisions cannot be allowed to occur in secret. Unless the Court acts to establish a strict standard based on the First Amendment, the public in California will continue to be prohibited access to this critical stage of the criminal process."

The Riverside County Counsel, representing the Superior Court, dismissed the *Press-Enterprise*'s contention that the Supreme Court had to clean up a constitutional mess.[6] There was no need to go that far because California's amended Penal Code "already recognizes the public's right of access to preliminary hearings." Granted, the state didn't recognize a *constitutional* right of access, but state law clearly stated "the examination shall be open and public" and closed only when the judge finds it "necessary" to protect the defendant. "The fact that the California [Supreme] Court rejected the constitutional argument does not [mean the U.S. Supreme Court should take the case] since a ruling on the issue will not affect the public's right to access in California one way or the other."

The county also argued that this case was, in effect, too weird—it said "uncommon"—to serve as vehicle for a Supreme Court ruling.

One judge closed the preliminary hearing and sealed the transcript, and the trial court judge kept the transcript sealed to guarantee the defendant's right to a fair trial before an impartial jury. "However, in what can be considered a most uncommon, if not rare occurrence in a trial involving death penalty potential, Defendant Diaz ultimately waived his right to a jury trial." This, said the county, reduced the case to "highly speculative" musings about the possible effects of an open preliminary hearing on a jury that would never be picked.

The county then sought to torpedo the *Press-Enterprise* argument that California's "loose" standards paved the way for routine closures of preliminary hearings. Whereas the newspaper argued that "reasonable likelihood of substantial prejudice" was much too weak, the county described it as "simply a first step. The press and public then have the right to overcome the defendant's showing, and can raise all of the issues at that time." "Simply stated," concluded the county, "the instant case does not present the Court with a clear constitutional question which must be answered, and thus the Petition for a Writ of Certiorari should be denied."

On September 30, 1985, six months and a day after the *Press-Enterprise* submitted its petition, the Supreme Court justices cast their initial votes on whether to hear the case. More than two and a half years had passed since the justices voted to hear *Press-Enterprise I*, and different law clerks were weighing in on *Press-Enterprise II*.

"VB"—very likely Vicki Been, Justice Blackmun's law clerk—seemed lukewarm about the *Press-Enterprise* case. "The issue whether the right of access applies to preliminary hearings is a tough one that the court probably will eventually have to resolve. I think that it might be best to allow the lower courts to grapple with the problem a while longer however." She recommended that Blackmun vote to deny the newspaper's petition—unless three other justices voted otherwise. In that case he could deliver the deciding vote to hear the case.[7] "Deny," urged "Lee"—most likely A. Lee Bentley III—in a handwritten note to his boss, Justice Powell. "The Court may want to resolve this issue one day, but . . . this is not yet a serious conflict that needs to be resolved.

This case would seem more worthy of a grant if the California statute barred the press from all preliminary hearings."[8]

These handwritten recommendations appeared on a twelve-page typewritten "Preliminary Memorandum" by Scott Nelson, who clerked for Justice Byron White. Nelson said the *Press-Enterprise*'s claim that courts are divided on the question of a First Amendment right of access to preliminary hearings was "somewhat exaggerated" because "most of the cases"—including "all of the federal cases"—the paper cited involved jury selection or suppression hearings, not preliminary hearings, "where the traditional concern for secrecy reflects a well-founded fear that the public may mistake the evidence introduced to establish probable cause as proof of guilt."[9] He acknowledged that the *Press-Enterprise* did cite two state court decisions, one in New Jersey, the other in Utah, that "expressed the view that the First Amendment right does apply to preliminary hearings." Even so, both courts based their rulings on their state constitutions, and both used the same standard for closure—"reasonable likelihood of prejudice"—that the California Supreme Court had embraced. "Given that all three courts arrived at the same standard on grounds other than the First Amendment, their [conflicting views on a First Amendment right of access] does not strike me as one that must be resolved."

Still, wrote Nelson, "the issue presented is one that the Court might want to resolve." Though the Diaz preliminary hearing wasn't exactly the same as, say, the murder trial in Richmond "the [*Press-Enterprise*] is correct in noting that many of the concerns underlying the right of access to trials are equally applicable where preliminary hearings are concerned. In addition, [the newspaper] points out that the courts have been somewhat confused about the proper [standards] for closure of a proceeding to which there is a right of access. . . . Thus, if the Court is inclined to continue its project of expanding the right of access, and if it believes that the 'reasonable likelihood of prejudice' standard for closure is inadequate . . . a grant here would be a possibility." But the memorandum seesawed one last time. The Supreme Court had recognized a difference between preliminary hearings and "other proceedings" that now received First Amendment protection;

California already provided a "significant level of protection" for public access on nonconstitutional grounds; and there wasn't a "square conflict." Concluded Nelson: "I recommend denial."[10]

When the first ballots were cast on September 30, five justices, including the chief justice, checked *D* for deny. But three justices—Brennan, Marshall, and law clerk Nelson's boss, Byron White, checked *G* for grant. Justice Blackmun wrote "Join 3," indicating he'd provide the fourth vote. It appeared that that the court had voted to give the newspaper a hearing, but according to Justice Powell's notes on a copy of the September 30 ballot, Byron White asked that the case be "relisted" so he could think it over. When the justices voted again on October 11, Justice Powell noted that White had not changed his mind. "Grant. No change in vote."[11] With White holding firm, Blackmun joined the trio.

A *Press-Enterprise* headline trumpeted the result: "Supreme Court Agrees to Hear Appeal on Closing of Hearings." The Riverside paper was headed back to Washington.[12] "It certainly is historic and highly unusual for the court to hear cases in the same area involving the same newspaper," said Bruce Sanford, the First Amendment lawyer who had been lead writer of the national amicus brief in *Press-Enterprise I*.[13] Tim Hays, the *Press-Enterprise's* publicity-shy editor and publisher, would have deferred to Norman Cherniss to explain why the paper was so "gratified" by the court's decision to take the case. But Cherniss had been dead for more than a year, so it was left to Hays to tell his own readers: "The people of Riverside County must have access to their courts if they are to understand how they operate and have confidence in their fairness. Preliminary hearings are vital to this. . . . Relatively few people have the time to attend court proceedings. Most people depend on their newspaper to represent them and report to them. This is why we have made such an effort to keep the courts open."[14]

18

Needle in a Haystack

Once the Supreme Court agreed to hear *Press-Enterprise II*, the brief writers from California to Washington DC stirred to life. Like veteran heavyweights who knew each other's moves, *Press-Enterprise* and Riverside County lawyers punched and counterpunched, hoping to land their best shots well before they actually faced off in oral arguments.

Once again the *Press-Enterprise* had a crowd in its corner: Bruce Sanford and Lee Levine, the Baker & Hostetler lawyers who wrote the national amicus brief in *Press-Enterprise I*, again took the lead on behalf of the nation's largest newspapers, newspaper chains, TV broadcasters, and various national news organizations. One of the firm's young lawyers, Janet Rehnquist, worked so hard on the case that she earned the lawyerly equivalent of a byline in the brief submitted to the Supreme Court. Some members of the firm wondered whether the mere participation of Rehnquist might lead her father, Justice William Rehnquist, to disqualify himself from hearing the case. But she and the firm did not represent the *Press-Enterprise* or Riverside County, so there was no reason to assume the justice would step aside.[1] Yes, the amicus brief was crafted to sway the justices, but by deepening their understanding of the issue, not through a crass lobbying campaign. (And, yes, most brief writers would probably say the same thing.)[2] Perhaps to the dismay of the newspaper and its attorney, Justice Rehnquist heard the case.

California newspapers and news organizations weighed in with an amicus brief of their own. The Riverside County DA's office submitted a brief in support of the *Press-Enterprise* even though it had not objected to the closure of Diaz's preliminary hearing or the sealing of the transcript.[3] Ephraim Margolin, the San Francisco criminal defense lawyer who had argued on Robert Diaz's behalf at the California Supreme Court, filed a brief to the U.S. Supreme Court, again on Diaz's behalf. It urged the Supreme Court to reject any First Amendment right to attend preliminary hearings. Naturally Riverside County countered the *Press-Enterprise* with a brief of its own, but as in *Press-Enterprise I*, it had no friend-of-the-court backing from other California county counsel offices or associations or superior courts.

Press-Enterprise Brief

Back in early 1983, Sharon Waters had the gumption to tell Jim Ward that the brief for *Press-Enterprise I* was not working. Now she was the lead brief writer of *Press-Enterprise II*. She wasn't flying solo, of course. Jim Ward was still very much in charge. And there was a new point man in the newspaper's First Amendment crusade.

Mel Opotowsky, at various times managing editor/features and administration and day editor, was above all else an aggressive, tough-minded newsman. The New Orleans native arrived at the *Press-Enterprise* in 1973 after fifteen years at United Press International and *Newsday*. His impact, manifested by an acid, Groucho Marx–like wit and a robust skepticism of politicians and government bureaucrats, was immediate. "Mel brought this urban combativeness and willingness to kind of be really gruff," said James Bettinger, the paper's ex–city editor. "There was unrest about Mel and what he was asking people to do, which was to be more aggressive and less deferential."[4] His blistering "Day Notes" were the stuff of newsroom legend. "We had a stenographer on this story," he once wrote. "Now, let's get a reporter on it." Longtime court reporter Chris Bowman went "the extra mile" to avoid the unpleasant and inevitable encounters when Opotowsky spotted a hole in a story. "There was something about those pale blue eyes peering at you over his black reading glasses that would slip down his nose. He didn't have to say anything."[5] Opotowsky, observed Robert LaBarre, another longtime *Press-Enterprise* reporter, "dramatically improved the paper's ability to cover spot news."[6]

Norman Cherniss had made sure that Opotowsky kept his distance from the First Amendment cases. This was Cherniss's turf, jealously guarded. But Opotowsky was as bright as he could be hard-edged. He seemed as well versed in First Amendment law as the lawyers themselves. He was also, said Sharon Waters, "rabid, rigid, passionate and less pragmatic" than Cherniss. This would not be helpful in the Diaz case because the *Press-Enterprise* was asking the Supreme Court to break new ground: rule that the public had a *constitutional* right to attend preliminary hearings. "We would talk to [Opotowsky] about why we weren't going to make certain arguments [such as urging public access to grand jury proceedings]," recalled Waters. "He agreed, but he was not happy about it."[7] But, like Norman Cherniss, he was happy to edit every word of the *Press-Enterprise* brief.

While it didn't convey an air of inevitability about stretching the right of access, the brief quickly invoked the unwritten law of momentum.[8] It cited Justice Potter Stewart's majority opinion in *Gannett v. DePasquale*, which said the court hadn't ruled out the possibility of First Amendment right of access to pretrial hearings. Then it rolled out the trio of ensuing Supreme Court rulings—*Richmond*, *Globe*, and *Press-Enterprise I*—to show the "Court consistently found a First Amendment right of access in court proceedings." True, these cases involved actual trials. But "the constitutional right of public access cannot be arbitrarily foreclosed to the preliminary hearing simply by characterizing the proceeding as pretrial" since the preliminary hearing "in California . . . has all the procedural attributes of the trial itself."

There's a neutral magistrate, or judge, whose powers are "indistinguishable" from trial judges. This magistrate could determine the credibility of witnesses, what weight to give their testimony, and even dismiss a case or reduce a crime from a felony to a misdemeanor. There were lawyers in the courtroom—prosecutor and defense. Defendants had a right to present a defense, call and cross-examine witnesses, introduce evidence that might prove their innocence. "While the ultimate determination of guilt or innocence is obviously not made in the preliminary hearing, in all other respects it closely resembles the trial itself."

Beyond that, the preliminary hearing was often the only judicial proceeding that looked anything like a trial since upward of 90 percent of cases never got beyond a preliminary hearing. Citing the most recent Annual Report of the California Judicial Council, the brief said that in fiscal year 1983–84, California superior courts "disposed of 66,534 defendants accused of felonies. But just 6,710 cases went to trial." In the nearly five thousand cases that went through Riverside County courts, there was just one trial for every six preliminary hearings.

Once again the *Press-Enterprise* emphasized the importance of open courtrooms to the "functioning of a democratic society" and attacked the California Supreme Court's embrace of "reasonable likelihood of substantial prejudice" as the standard to shut the public out of preliminary hearings. Compared to the U.S. Supreme Court's language in *Richmond, Globe,* and *Press-Enterprise I,* that standard would be "unconstitutional" if the court found a First Amendment right of access to preliminary hearings.[9]

By accepting the "reasonable likelihood" standard, the California Supreme Court had endorsed "secret proceedings" where secrecy was not justified. When Judge John Barnard first considered the request to unseal the Diaz preliminary hearing transcript, almost six months had passed since that hearing ended. Hoping to keep the transcript sealed, Diaz's lawyers submitted eighty "mostly old and often irrelevant news clippings," more than half of them nearly twenty-one months old. The transcript itself, said Barnard, was "as factual as it could be. . . . It's not extremely inflammatory or exciting." Yet Barnard still concluded there was a "reasonable likelihood" that making the transcript public would harm Diaz's chances for a fair trial. When Barnard finally did release it in October 1983, the transcript had been sealed for more than thirteen months.

The *Press-Enterprise* proposed a much tougher standard to close a preliminary hearing: the "three-prong test" first advanced by Justice Harry Blackmun in his *Gannett v. DePasquale* dissent. A pretrial hearing could be closed only if a judge found a *substantial probability* of the following results:

Irreparable damage to the defendant's fair-trial right will result
from conducting the proceeding in public.

Alternatives to closure will not protect adequately his right to a
fair trial; and

Closure will be effective in protecting against the perceived harm.

"A close analysis," the brief concluded, "establishes that the criminal justice system in America, and specifically in California, is not a trial system but predominantly a pretrial system." The Supreme Court must therefore go beyond *Richmond, Globe,* and *Press-Enterprise I* and extend First Amendment access to "pretrial proceedings, particularly preliminary hearings."

Riverside County Brief

Riverside County's brief attacked the *Press-Enterprise* arguments from top to bottom.[10] Once again Deputy County Counsels Glenn Salter and Joyce Reikes were its primary authors. This time Reikes would argue before the Supreme Court.

The county brief dismissed the need for a constitutional right of access to preliminary hearings because California law already kept these hearings open except in the face of a "reasonable likelihood of substantial prejudice." This protected the defendant's Sixth Amendment right to a fair trial and the public's First Amendment right of access to courtroom. That was enough. Constitutional protection wasn't necessary.

The county disputed the *Press-Enterprise*'s claim that preliminary hearings were virtually indistinguishable from trials. A trial decided innocence or guilt while a preliminary hearing's most fundamental function was to "prevent innocent persons from being deprived of liberty" because of "baseless allegations." The preliminary hearing "serves to protect the rights of the accused . . . it does not and has never been intended to serve as a basis for guaranteeing the public a right of access."

Whereas the *Press-Enterprise* brief reminded the justices that their most recent court access decisions had come down strongly on the side of the public, the county noted that the U.S. Supreme Court, in *Gannett v. DePasquale,* had already recognized that, at the pretrial stage, "the defendant's Sixth Amendment right is superior to the public interest in openness of proceedings." Translation: No constitutional right of public access.

The *Press-Enterprise* argument that the majority of criminal cases did not go to trial—and that, in Riverside County, "only one trial took place for every six preliminary hearings"—underwhelmed county lawyers who faulted the newspaper's brief for failing to "to cite any historical statistics" to show that the preliminary hearing-to-trial ratio was "significantly different now than in the past." The county scoffed at the notion that statistics should be "used to support the establishment of a federal constitutional right of access." And it didn't buy the *Press-Enterprise*'s characterization of preliminary hearings as so "pivotal" in the administration of justice that public access was increasingly vital. It cited a 1975 California Supreme Court case that noted, "the Alabama preliminary hearing is far less 'critical' than its California counterpart because its sole purpose is to determine if there is sufficient evidence . . . to justify bringing the case before a grand jury."[11]

Turning to the specific case, the county defended Judge Howard Dabney, who closed Robert Diaz's preliminary hearing and sealed the transcript, and Judge John Barnard, who kept the transcripts sealed, arguing that both men "acted in a manner consistent with [Diaz's] Sixth Amendment constitutional right and the public interest."

Before he closed his courtroom, Dabney discussed the national publicity the case had received as well as the one-sided nature of preliminary hearings when, for tactical reasons, the defense doesn't present a case. This "evidence of his concerns" showed that Dabney had properly arrived at the conclusion that an open hearing would result in "reasonable likelihood of substantial prejudice."

Judge Barnard, who presided over the trial, noted that Diaz essentially threatened to push for a change of venue if the transcript was released.[12] This, said the county, showed that Barnard had considered alternatives to keeping the transcript sealed and decided that moving the location of a projected eighteen-month trial would impose a "severe hardship" and not protect Diaz's fair trial right.

Finally, the county asked where this First Amendment access issue was headed next: To grand juries? Straight into the DA's office itself, where decisions to prosecute are made? It was a logical question, and the Supreme Court justices would practically taunt Jim Ward with it a few months later.

The National Brief

The national brief aggressively tried to discredit the assumption that pretrial publicity threatens a fair trial.[13] "*Pretrial publicity,*" it began, quoting the Supreme Court's own words in *Nebraska Press Association v. Stuart* (1976), "*even pervasive, adverse publicity, does not inevitably lead to an unfair trial.*" It sought to show that the supposedly dire effects of media coverage on jurors were way overblown. It cited several studies, including a 1982 review of sixty-three thousand appeals of criminal convictions in all fifty states over a five-year period. "[I]n only twenty-one cases did the state highest appellate courts overturn a conviction based all or in part on prejudicial publicity." The U.S. Supreme Court itself, noted the brief, had overturned just one such conviction. Even high-profile defendants such as John DeLorean, John Hinckley, Dan White, Angela Davis, and John Connally were acquitted by juries "despite substantial adverse pretrial publicity."

The brief then praised an open Los Angeles preliminary hearing for launching important national conversations. The nineteen-month "McMartin" hearing, which ended in January 1986–months *after* the *Press-Enterprise II* briefs had been submitted—centered on allegations of sexual abuse of preschool children. The very fact that it was open to the public and press led to "nationwide examinations" of child abuse and day care facilities; it "sparked a public debate" about the preliminary hearing process itself; and it "resulted in the creation of [federal] day care guidelines." The ripple effects of a public preliminary hearing," concluded the brief, "illustrate the necessary dependence of an informed discussion of public affairs on open judicial proceedings."

What happened to the McMartin defendants *after* the preliminary hearing may have bolstered the case for public access even more. After "the longest preliminary hearing in California history," a judge decided the seven defendants were most likely guilty and should stand trial. But a week later—just a month before oral argument in *Press-Enterprise II*—the recently elected Los Angeles County DA dismissed all charges against five defendants, calling the evidence "incredibly weak."[14] "Fortunately," wrote Loyola Law School professor Gerald Uelmen, "the McMartin preliminary hearing was open to the press and public." Uelmen's newspaper column concluded, "[O]ne must wonder whether . . . a prosecutor would have greater reluctance to take such a step were the preliminary hearing conducted in secret, for fear of being accused of participating in some sort of cover-up. . . . The McMartin case may provide the strongest argument to convince the U.S. Supreme Court that the press and public should have a constitutional right of access to preliminary hearings."[15] Jim Ward would make that point to the Supreme Court justices a month later.

There was another argument, perhaps an even stronger argument than McMartin, that Bruce Sanford and Lee Levine hoped to pitch to their favorite target: Chief Justice Burger. "Judicial proceedings in criminal cases," declared their brief, "have traditionally been conducted in open court." Now, all they had to do was prove it. The brief tracked the arc of "preliminary hearings" from sixteenth-century England, where they were actually secret investigations, to post–American Revolution "preliminary hearings," which evolved into judicial proceedings with a *neutral* judge and became decidedly "public affairs." This was a broad-brush history. The lawyers needed more.

Adrienne Wieand was in her midtwenties, fresh out of the University of Virginia School of Law and now a first-year associate with a big Washington law firm. Baker & Hostetler was paying her a lot of money, and like a lot of new lawyers, she was feeling a little insecure— "worried about whether they made a mistake by hiring you."[16] One day the firm's heavyweights told her, "'Go start digging.' What was I supposed to do? Research. See one thing, go to the next thing and go to the next thing. They had a historical angle from the start. They wanted to add something that somebody else was not going to come up with. That was the plan." It was a typical assignment for someone with her modest seniority. "You go off on these wild goose chases" because the senior attorneys "don't want to spend money on somebody" who bills at a higher rate.

Off Wieand went to the Library of Congress, where "Lexis [a new legal database] was just getting going, but you really didn't trust it. Back then the belief was that there was no substitute for just rolling up your sleeves and getting in the books." Every day for a week, she rolled up her sleeves and "sat on the floor, pulling out books," convinced she wouldn't find anything. She paged through volumes of federal cases—digests of the *oldest* of the old federal cases—looking for a heading that said *preliminary hearings*. She wasn't looking for a decision that said, "Preliminary hearings shall be open" because she knew it didn't exist. But she came across a trial that caught her interest: the 1807 treason trial of Aaron Burr, Chief Justice John Marshall presiding. What caught her eye was "just an observation . . . just background information" about the preliminary hearing. Chief Justice Marshall had convened it to determine whether probable cause existed to charge Burr with treason. The court reporter gave this account: "At ten o'clock MARSHALL, Chief Justice, took his seat on the bench, in the court room, which was densely filled with citizens. . . . On the suggestion of counsel that it would be impossible to accommodate the spectators in the court room, the chief justice adjourned to the hall of the house of delegates."

In *Press-Enterprise I*, Brian Harvey, another young Baker & Hostetler associate, made his pilgrimage to the Library of Congress and uncovered evidence that back in "Jolly Old England" jury selection had been open to the public. Chief Justice Burger cited that evidence in the 9–0 ruling for of the *Press-Enterprise*. Now, in a discovery that she called "purely kind of a fluke," Adrienne Wieand felt the jolt of her own "Ah-ha!" moment. "In the earliest days of the Republic, these [preliminary hearings] were presumed to be open. I wrote it up in a memo and remember everyone being very excited about this. I remember getting a pat on the back. I surprised myself. I wasn't really sure what I was doing. We found the needle in the haystack."

Baker & Hostetler lawyer Lee Levine remembers exactly where he was when he learned about the needle: standing in a hallway, talking to

Wieand on a pay telephone, just before he and Bruce Sanford went into a meeting. "We were skeptical that she would find anything" because preliminary hearings dating back to the 1600s "had been thoroughly researched in the *Gannett* case. We thought the best we were going to be able to do was draw a distinction between [closed] preliminary hearings in England, which were prosecutorial, and those presided over by an independent decision-maker. We were going to point to the error [in the argument] that a preliminary hearing in California bore any resemblance to [a] preliminary hearing in 1600 or 1700." But Wieand had discovered an *open* preliminary hearing with Chief Justice Marshall on the bench. And not just any open preliminary hearing, either. "Chief Justice Burger had a standard after-dinner speech at judicial conferences," recalled Levine. "It was all about the Aaron Burr treason trial. I had heard him give that speech. Amongst lawyers who paid attention to the Supreme Court, his strong interest in [the Burr] trial was well known, which was why we were so excited when she called."[17]

Burger knew the Burr trial inside out. "While a night student at St. Paul College of Law, Burger and a few friends regularly convened what they called the 'smokers' club to reargue famous trials." Burger argued three, including Burr's. "Two decades later, in the spring of 1953, while serving as an assistant attorney general in the Eisenhower administration, Burger, a talented artist, painted in oil a still life of 'some familiar objects' in his office." One object was a book of case reports that included *United States v. Aaron Burr*. "When he sat at his desk in the Supreme Court . . . that painting hung on the wall above him."[18]

The California Brief

The "California" brief, representing dozens of newspapers and news organizations, told the justices that the "ability to report on preliminary hearings has been seriously compromised by the Diaz decision," handed down by a California Supreme Court "blinded by an unfounded fear of publicity."[19] It then introduced the "*Diaz* progeny"— courtroom doors that had slammed shut since California's highest court endorsed secret preliminary hearings and sealed transcripts.

In one case a judge closed not only a preliminary hearing but also the debate over whether the hearing should be closed. In another, a judge ruled that a defendant only had to establish the Diaz standard ("reasonable likelihood") to close "any proceeding"—trial or pretrial. "Diaz is a signal . . . that even trials can be closed without evidence, findings or satisfaction of a meaningful burden."

In another case an accused murderer used the Diaz standard to try to close his *arraignment*. Then he successfully moved to close the argument about whether to close the arraignment. Though the judge eventually kept the arraignment open, the public "was not even allowed to see the court's ruling" that kept it open.

A widow was charged with hiring five marines to kill her marine husband. In early December 1984, just weeks before the California Supreme Court issued its Diaz ruling, the press successfully challenged the defense effort to close the preliminary hearing. After the ruling the defense again moved to close it, providing "no evidence of prejudice" except for "a few news clips." Because the defense tried to close testimony from nearly all of the sixty-five witnesses, "press attorneys appeared again and again, opposing closure at a cost of thousands of dollars in legal fees." The judge ended up taking secret testimony from about fifty witnesses.

Finally there was the curious case of *People v. Prairie Chicken*. Blaine Prairie Chicken, of the Sycuan Indian Reservation in San Diego County, had been accused of biting a police officer's arm during a scuffle in a Laundromat. Prairie Chicken, who claimed he had AIDS, moved to close the hearing on account of pretrial publicity. The DA supported the motion to "protect the police officer's sensibilities." The judge decided that Prairie Chicken had produced zero evidence of prejudice but closed the hearing anyway and sealed the transcript. The judge, said the brief, was "more concerned about the police officer's potential embarrassment than public access."

The brief also argued that that the entire basis for closure was a "historical aberration." It noted that the Field Code, which required a judge to close a preliminary hearing at the defendant's request, had become part of the California law in 1851 but hadn't even been "invoked or enforced" until 1959. Further, it argued the code's provision that a defendant could unilaterally close a hearing was the brainchild of David Dudley Field, a lawyer and, very briefly, a U.S. congressman who had an ax to grind against the press.[20]

Though the legislature put a stop to automatic closures in 1982, the brief argued that the "Diaz standard practically guarantees closed preliminary hearings. . . . The public's ability to attend preliminary hearings is left to the unfettered discretion" of a judge, whose decision to boot the public and press won't be reversed by a higher court "so long as the magic words [reasonable likelihood of substantial prejudice] are said."

Brief by Robert Diaz's Lawyer

Ephraim Margolin devoted much of his brief to arguing that preliminary hearings do not rate a First Amendment right of access because they are very different from actual trials and, for that matter, from pretrial hearings where judges decide whether to toss out confessions or evidence.[21]

Preliminary hearings are inherently lopsided affairs where the prosecution's "burden" to show probable guilt is often "readily met" while defendants rarely tip their hand, preferring to not reveal their strategy before the case goes to trial. The result: public access would expose a jury pool "only and overwhelmingly to the prosecution's evidence."

In a trial or a pretrial "suppression" hearing "each side has an incentive to prevail." Publicity helps assure fairness. Not so with a preliminary hearing where "the defendant's lack of incentive to prevail . . . seriously detracts from any contributions to fairness to be gained by public access." Even Justice Lewis Powell, the lone justice in *Gannett v. DePasquale* to find a First Amendment right of public access to a pretrial hearing, "was careful to point out that 'not all pretrial matters are so important for public scrutiny as is a suppression hearing.'"

Margolin disputed practically every contention in the *Press-Enterprise* brief. He dismissed the newspaper's 1983–84 statistics about the ratio of California preliminary hearings to trials, arguing that, compared to 1978 figures, criminal trials in California were actually on the rise. He wrote derisively and a little darkly about the argument that an open preliminary provides a "community therapeutic value." Community "catharsis is achieved less by access to the proceedings themselves than by harsh penalties." Citing the extensive coverage and public access to the trial of Dan White, who murdered San Francisco's mayor and a gay county supervisor in 1979, Margolin asserted there was no community catharsis since White "was convicted only of manslaughter." Catharsis was achieved six years later, he wrote, when White committed suicide.

The brief rebutted the premise that the open McMartin preschool preliminary hearing served a public benefit by launching state legislation and national conversations about child abuse. It was the charges, not the preliminary hearing, that raised public awareness. The open hearing actually had "adverse" effects: "All out-of-custody defendants have moved from their homes, many to different states. . . . Daily reportage collapses seven hours of hearings into a few paragraphs of print or seconds of TV time . . . media attention is paid to the prosecution's case almost exclusively."

Finally, Margolin asserted that preliminary hearings had been closed to the public even before the U.S. Constitution was adopted. Once the Constitution was in place, preliminary hearings still didn't enjoy the same degree of openness as trials. He conceded that there had been a "trend" toward open preliminary hearings, but, citing a UCLA *Law Review* article, said the earliest case "was reported in 1898."[22] If Margolin was aware that the national brief, thanks to Adrienne Wieand, cited an open preliminary hearing that occurred ninety-one years before that, he did not mention it.

The Final Three

AMERICAN CIVIL LIBERTIES UNION

Over the decades, the ACLU had gone to bat for defendants, such as Dr. Sam Sheppard, whose right to a fair trial had been undermined by prejudicial press coverage. It had backed the press in such cases as

Nebraska Press Association v. Stuart, where judges essentially dropped the nuke by imposing gag orders.

Closure of any judicial proceeding, including preliminary hearings, the ACLU told the justices, "is an extraordinary step which should only be used sparingly."[23] The ACLU was not asserting an absolute right of public access but said it should not be denied without "specific findings that closure is essential . . . and narrowly tailored." The California Supreme Court had simply allowed closure "as a matter of right" and "eroded" the constitutional rights provided by the U.S. Supreme Court. "Accordingly," concluded the ACLU, the state supreme court's ruling "should be reversed."

ATTORNEY GENERAL OF CALIFORNIA

Attorney General John Van de Kamp's brief supporting the *Press-Enterprise* also made it clear that there was nothing absolute about a right of public access to courtrooms.[24] But judges who shut their courtrooms to the public must defend their decisions in public and in detail. The California Supreme Court, he wrote, had "erroneously concluded that the First Amendment right of access does not extend to preliminary hearings." As a result the AG urged the U.S. Supreme Court to "hold that the First Amendment does guarantee a right of public access to preliminary hearings, and to reverse the [California Supreme Court] decision."

RIVERSIDE COUNTY DISTRICT ATTORNEY

Though his policy of openness periodically wavered—and outright flip-flopped when it came to unsealing the Diaz preliminary hearing transcript—District Attorney Grover Trask's brief strongly backed the *Press-Enterprise*.[25] "In this case, the magistrate's [Dabney's] order closing the preliminary examination in its entirety, and the trial court's order sealing the preliminary examination transcript were overbroad. The magistrate and trial judge made no articulated findings which would justify constitutionally denying public access to the hearing or all of the transcript." He said the rulings were "based upon unfettered and arbitrary discretion . . . because of the lack of any constitutional guidelines or rules." Trask urged the Supreme Court to "establish specific guidelines and rules based upon the First Amendment to protect the public's right of access" to preliminary hearings. Any decision to shut the public out "must specify articulated findings that can be reviewed by the appellate courts on a case-by-case basis. This is not the case today in California."

19

"The Soil of Openness"

The blanket of snow covering Washington DC didn't faze Jim and Carole Ward, the Southern California couple who popped into town five days before the February 26, 1986, oral argument. Passages of Ward's written account of his return trip to the Supreme Court read like the rollicking adventures of a tourist-gourmet. There was French toast at Gadsby's Tavern in Old Town Alexandria. Dinner at a "sedate and excellent French restaurant." Lunch at the University Club. The "fun, trendy, cluttered" Filomena Italian restaurant in Georgetown. The clock exhibit at the Renwick Gallery. A trip to Bureau of Printing and Engraving. On moot court day, Ward even managed to drop by the office of a fellow South Dakota native. The man he hoped to see wasn't around, but weeks later, Senator George McGovern, the 1972 Democratic presidential nominee, dashed off a quick note. "Of course I remember our associations in South Dakota when you were a star debater at Washington High School. Let's get together."[1]

Less than three years earlier, Ward told Justice Sandra Day O'Connor, "I will be back." Now, he *was* back, even if his sendoff had been somewhat less than resounding. Ward's partners at Thompson & Colegate had been "ecstatic" and "joyous" about the Supreme Court's 9–0 ruling in the voir dire case.[2] But viewed through the harsh prism of profitability, *Press-Enterprise I* was not quite as thrilling. "We lost our ass," said Don Grant, a retired partner at the Riverside firm. "Once you became partner, you were basically autonomous. People didn't keep track of whether you showed up at eight-thirty or seven-thirty or whether you stayed till ten at night or left . . . in the afternoon to go play golf." There was no formal vote when Ward decided to take the first *Press-Enterprise* case; the firm billed the paper $25,000 for the Supreme Court battle—a cut-rate, flat fee to compensate for such thin experience in constitutional law.[3] But after *Press-Enterprise I*, the partners started paying more attention to billable hours. Started looking at "who was bringing in what."[4]

When the Supreme Court agreed to hear *Press-Enterprise II*, Ward had a chance to do what few lawyers have ever done: argue a second case before the U.S. Supreme Court. But at Thompson & Colegate the Age of Autonomy had ended. The firm had a new committee, and Ward needed its approval.[5] The committee voted to allow Ward to take the case. But this time it would cost the newspaper more: $50,000.[6]

As Ward, Sharon Waters, and John Boyd researched and wrote and rounded up state and national support for this potentially ground-breaking case, something didn't seem right. The *Press-Enterprise* money just wasn't flowing in. Recalled Ward: "The billing clerk at Thompson & Colegate whispered in the ear in one of my partners and said, 'He's giving away the store!' And they came down on me."[7] Actually, recalled Don Grant, they trapped him. Following one of their occasional tennis outings, the partners repaired to a favorite pizza joint for a few beers. On the day of reckoning, the partners slid into a booth. "Jim was trapped against the wall," recalled Grant. "He was cornered. The whole issue of the *Press-Enterprise* case was brought up."[8] They wouldn't let him leave until he explained his billing.[9]

"My understanding," said Grant, "is that there was some other firm snooping around that wanted to take the case. I don't know who they were, but somebody was showing interest in taking this over—maybe even doing it for free. It was very upsetting to Jim. He wanted to keep the case. So he ended up quoting $25,000 for the sec-ond go-around. It was against all of our instructions." Trapped in the booth, Ward fought back: You guys play golf and ski, he supposedly told his partners. The *Press-Enterprise* case is *my* hobby.[10] "He used the exact word," said Grant. "This is my hobby. He was enjoying it, learning as he goes along."

Ward said he didn't recall the pizza booth confrontation. Nor did he remember agreeing to the $50,000 fee. "As if to say I really betrayed my partners by promising one thing and doing something else—I think it's totally inaccurate. We simply did not dictate to one another about fees in that manner. I think Don's recollection is flawed."[11] Ward was forced to "do a big memo of justification" for his billing. He totaled up all the hours and all the billing. "Obviously, it was lower than I could have charged, but I just thought it was fair and it was right."[12] It was a memo, said Ward, that his partners never acknowledged. "They never said aye, nay, or boo. They never said, 'Yeah, you convinced me.' I don't think they were giving up their point that, 'Ward, you gave away the store. You billed at too low a rate.'"[13]

The *Press-Enterprise* Supreme Court case had become so toxic that John Boyd, who was trying to make partner, was pulled aside by a senior partner and advised not to go to Washington. Ward wrote in his log: "I thought he [Boyd] should be included. He was disappointed but his future was more important than this trip. I offered his airline and hotel reservation to all the partners, but no one wanted to go."[14] Sharon Waters made the trip, as did the *Press-Enterprise*'s Mel Opotowsky.

As the Wards prepared to board their flight to Washington DC, they bumped into Deputy County Counsel Joyce Reikes at California's Ontario International Airport. She, too, was on her way to the capital, where she would oppose Ward in the *Press-Enterprise* case. Ward was "amazed" that Reikes and her son were flying into Dulles Airport, which was fifty miles farther away from the Supreme Court building than National Airport.[15] Reikes's more indirect route to the Supreme Court could have been a metaphor for her legal career.

The daughter of a firefighter, Reikes grew up in Brooklyn and received a scholarship to the Jewish Hospital School of Nursing, located in the same borough. She settled into Riverside as the wife of a doctor. But a "difficult divorce" in 1970 turned her life upside down.[16] The single mother of three small boys balked at returning to nursing. She wanted "independence"; she wanted to work for herself.[17] Her divorce lawyer suggested law school. "It came as a bolt from the blue," she said. "In two weeks, I was in love with it."[18] Reikes was forty when, in 1976, she graduated from Riverside's Citrus Belt Law School, which had opened in the basement of a bank building five years earlier. She passed the bar exam and went to work for a small Riverside firm. Four years later she hired on with the county counsel as the office's only woman lawyer. By day she handled matters ranging from antitrust to right-to-die to cryonics, once arguing that the county coroner should be allowed to thaw a woman's head.[19] By night she taught at Citrus Belt. Among her subjects: constitutional law.[20]

Close friends and colleagues regarded Reikes as bright, even brilliant, ambitious, and ultracompetitive. "She loved being in court," said Dorothy Honn, longtime lawyer in the county counsel's office. "She was always well prepared. She could argue with the best of them." Not quite fifty years old, Joyce Reikes would get to argue *in front* of the best of them.[21] And she would savor it as the highlight of her professional life.[22]

On Monday, February 24, Baker & Hostetler once again hosted a four-hour moot court session. Ward, the "star debater" and largely unscripted extemporaneous speaker, had become accustomed to the discipline of these rigorous rehearsals (there had been an earlier session in Los Angeles). This time, about twenty lawyers who would masquerade as "justices" converged on Bruce Sanford's office. Some had big First Amendment cases on their résumés. Others, like Janet Rehnquist and Adrienne Wieand—"a cute young attorney who dug up the critical information on Aaron Burr"—had worked on the *Press-Enterprise* case for Baker & Hostetler. "We did three run-throughs of the argument with different judges and each time I was critiqued," wrote Ward. "I was not too tired as I had too much adrenaline flowing." Afterward, Ward treated the "California delegation" of moot court lawyers to dinner La Chaumière in Georgetown—"great seafood combo with lobster sauce."[23]

As Ward and Reikes prepared for the court battle, the Supreme Court justices got up to speed on *Press-Enterprise II.*

"In a case that received widespread publicity," began clerk David Sklansky in a twenty-six-page memo to Justice Harry Blackmun,

"Robert Diaz was charged with the murder of twelve hospital patients." After summarizing the closure of the forty-one-day preliminary hearing and the sealed transcript's odyssey through the California courts, Blackmun's clerk wrote, "My analysis will be relatively terse" because all the briefs were "very good" and because "you have already staked out a pretty clear position on the question of press access to judicial proceedings, which I see no reason for you to alter."[24]

Blackmun had staked out that position in his 1979 dissent in *Gannett v. DePasquale*, arguing that the press and public had a Sixth Amendment right to attend pretrial hearings. Now, seven years later, Blackmun found himself comfortably in the majority that had pronounced a First Amendment right of access to criminal trials. Wrote Sklansky in his February 20, 1986, memo: "I think the public right of access to criminal trials, whether found in the First Amendment or the Sixth Amendment, should extend to preliminary hearings of the sort held in California."

Sklansky credited the *Press-Enterprise* brief and those of its "friends" for "having the better of" the historical debate. "Although preliminary examinations were held in secret under English common law, the "inquisitional" proceeding differed from the "modern" hearing held before a neutral judge. "It is to that process that our tradition fairly consistently has allowed public access." He then set about the delicate task of reconciling the 1979 Justice Blackmun with the 1986 Justice Blackmun. In *Gannett* Blackmun made a clear distinction between suppression hearings (i.e., whether to admit evidence or confessions) and preliminary hearings: "[B]ecause of the critical importance of suppression hearings . . . the pretrial suppression hearing at issue in this case must be considered part of the trial." But preliminary hearings "are not critical to the criminal justice system in the same way . . . and they are not close equivalents of the trial itself."

Sklansky argued that Blackmun's support of open preliminary hearings in *Press-Enterprise II* "would not be inconsistent with your opinion in *Gannett*" because "you were talking about the old kind of preliminary hearings, not what the procedure has matured into in states such as California." Perhaps to reassure the boss that his views then and now were stitched together by a thread of consistency, Sklansky resorted to grammar. "Significantly, you spoke about preliminary hearings [in *Gannett*] only in the past tense" mainly in the context of common law. "It seems plain enough that you did not mean to rule out the possibility that preliminary hearings, if conducted in such a way that they *are* 'critical to the criminal justice system' and 'close equivalents of the trial itself . . . ,' would qualify for a public right of access."

Sklansky had little sympathy for Riverside County's arguments. Maintaining that a preliminary hearing, during which the defense might call no witnesses, "will create public confusion and lead to prejudice . . . seems profoundly misguided . . . the cure for incomplete information is more information, not secrecy. There is no reason that potential jurors cannot be educated, either through the media or in the courtroom, regarding the difference between a preliminary hearing and a trial."

Finally, the memo, liberally highlighted in yellow, presumably by Blackmun himself, said the court should not just say the California Supreme Court was wrong to find no First Amendment right to public access; it should set the standard for "what the defendant must show in order to justify closure." And that standard should be consistent with the court's recent opinions, including *Press-Enterprise I*.[25]

Justice Lewis Powell had been the first and only justice to declare a First Amendment right of access to pretrial hearings in *Gannett v. DePasquale*. His defection from the initial but shaky majority in that Sixth Amendment case has been credited with opening the door to the string of First Amendment victories in *Richmond*, *Globe*, and *Press-Enterprise I*.[26] Yet Powell voted not to hear *Press-Enterprise I*, though he eventually voted to give the public and press a First Amendment right to attend jury selection. He also voted against hearing *Press-Enterprise II*. And now he wrote to his clerk, "I am far from at rest in this case."[27] Though his previous votes showed "I am generally inclined toward the openness of trial procedures," Powell worried about "pervasive" pretrial publicity "that makes a subsequent trial difficult if not impossible." Defendants "certainly" must be "protected" from that. But Powell also observed that some briefs in the case emphasized that "the presence of the media often assure fair procedures and serve a public purpose." Powell needed to know more about California preliminary hearings. Were they like grand juries? Like trials? The agonizing justice concluded: "Bob, I will not want a long bench memo. I would like a summary of your views, and your recommendation." Bob appears to be Robert Allen Long Jr., a 1985 graduate of Yale Law School who went to work for Powell in 1986.[28]

"Bob" urged the justice to reverse the California Supreme Court. "Virtually all of the policies that favor a constitutional right of access to criminal trials support a right of access here. Further, I find such a holding consistent with your views as expressed in *Gannett v. DePasquale*."[29] In blue ink Powell underlined "consistent with your views" and wrote "my" above "your." The clerk's memo noted that even as it ruled against the *Press-Enterprise*, the California Supreme Court "acknowledged the benefit in the openness of such a proceeding, and the similarities between a preliminary hearing and a trial." ("Yes . . . like a trial," wrote Powell in the margin beside a passage he had bracketed in blue ink.) As for the similarities between California preliminary hearings and grand juries, the clerk could detect none. The preliminary hearing was not "an arm of the prosecution," and its focus was to "test evidence against a defendant, not to produce evidence against a defendant."

The Riverside County Superior Court's reasons for *closing* a preliminary hearing "could . . . be applied to trials in general," contended the memo. And the Supreme Court had already rejected most of those arguments. The county's alarm that granting a right of access to preliminary hearings would lead to access to prosecutor's files and grand jury proceedings struck the writer "as just silly."

Like Blackmun's clerk, Powell's wrestled with history. Criminal trials had been open while the earliest (British) preliminary hearings had been closed. But "Bob" eloquently reconciled the difference. "In the end, I think that the larger point should not focus on the history behind particular proceedings, but rather on the fact that the roots of this country's judicial processes are set in the soil of openness."

Powell's clerk, like Blackmun's, urged the justices not to leave the California Supreme Court, and others, in the dark about what standards had to be met before a preliminary hearing could be closed. He suggested that the court could use the same standards his boss, Powell, laid out in the 1984 *Waller v. Georgia* case that upheld a *defendant's* Sixth Amendment right to an *open* pretrial hearing.[30] The standards Powell set down in *Waller* had been drawn from an earlier 1984 case: *Press-Enterprise I.*

20

"Hands over His Face"

By Wednesday, February 26, the snow had given way to an unseasonably warm 70 degrees in Washington DC. Jim Ward and Sharon Waters checked in at the Supreme Court clerk's office well before the scheduled 11 a.m. oral argument. "She looked terrific," Ward wrote of his young colleague. "It was the first time I had ever seen her in a skirt and I stupidly failed to compliment her. I later rationalized that I didn't want to make her uncomfortable."[1] Ward and Waters ran into Riverside County DA Grover Trask and his wife and two kids. Joyce Reikes, who would argue on behalf of the county, arrived with her nineteen-year-old son, Mark. "We had all made this a family affair," wrote Ward, whose "entourage" included his sister, a couple of cousins, and his aunt Wilma and uncle Toad, who had been Ward's surrogate father since the long-ago plane crash killed his dad. Soon, they began to fill the Supreme Court chamber along with Tim and Helen Hays. The *Press-Enterprise* editor and publisher had not made the trip in 1984. Other spectators that day included Janet Rehnquist, the justice's daughter, who had worked on the national brief in support of the newspaper; John O'Connor, husband of Justice Sandra Day O'Connor; and Mel Opotowsky, the *Press-Enterprise*'s point man who had devoted so much time to the case. Earlier, perhaps thinking it was a winning strategy, Opotowsky handed Ward a note very similar to the one the newspaper's lawyer received from Norman Cherniss in 1984. Written on White House stationery, it read, "Go get 'em again, tiger!"[2]

"Mr. Ward," said Chief Justice Warren Burger, "I think you may proceed whenever you are ready."[3]

The last time Burger told Ward he could proceed, Ward stumbled over a word that was central to the newspaper's case. This time, he nailed it. "Mr. Chief Justice and may it please the court. This is a court *closure* case involving specifically the question of access to the preliminary hearing in a criminal case."

The hour-long argument pitting Ward against deputy Riverside County counsel Joyce Reikes was by turns riveting, edgy, humorous, and choppy, as justices frequently interrupted and the lawyers struggled to stay on point.

Ward quickly told the justices exactly what the *Press-Enterprise* wanted: a constitutional right of public access to preliminary hearings. He also wanted the justices to declare that California's "reasonable likelihood" standard to close a hearing "does not conform to the standards of this Court" as set forth in *Richmond*, *Globe*, and *Press-Enterprise I*. When the incredulous chief justice wondered why the Diaz preliminary hearing had chewed up forty-one days, Ward glided into a key element of the newspaper's argument: the length reflects "the importance we attach to preliminary hearings in California. Matters are extensively litigated."

In *Press-Enterprise I* Justice Sandra Day O'Connor pressed Ward about what he was really after. "Mr. Ward, would your supposed rights (of access) extend beyond *voir dire*?" When Ward replied, "We do not make the suggestion at this time," O'Connor shot back, "You're saving that for tomorrow?" "Yes, your honor. I will be back." Now, O'Connor pressed again.

> JUSTICE O'CONNOR: Do you argue that the grand jury proceeding must be open to the press?
> WARD: No, we do not argue that at this point.
> O'CONNOR: But you'll be back next year to argue?

Ward laughed along with the courtroom audience. But Mel Opotowsky didn't laugh. He winced. "Jim was not up front by making it clear we wanted to be back for grand jury access."[4]

WARD: I think we had this exchange once before, Justice O'Connor. No, indeed . . . our position is very simply that we're dealing here with judicial proceedings . . .

O'CONNOR: Well, a grand jury proceeding can be characterized by many of the same attributes that you attribute to the preliminary hearing.

WARD: Well, I suppose that is true in certain instances but . . . our position is that we're dealing with . . . proceedings where we have . . . parties that are presenting differing views and a neutral magistrate is making decisions upon those views. That, granted, would take in most if not all of pretrial proceedings.

But grand jury hearings, he added, were "investigatory. . . . We do not seek access to the police investigatory process."

As the justices listened to Ward explain that, in California, a defendant who was indicted by a grand jury was entitled to a preliminary hearing, Justice Powell scribbled, "Wasteful duplication!"[5]

O'Connor wasn't the only justice who was curious about how far Ward and the *Press-Enterprise* wanted to push.

CHIEF JUSTICE BURGER: Could there be some preliminary hearing in which the Court could be justified . . . to close it to the public?

WARD: Yes, we believe so Justice Burger. We think our right is obviously a qualified right to access.

But suspending that right could not be done arbitrarily. Ward began to recite the conditions the court itself had laid out: any closure of a criminal trial must be "narrowly tailored to meet specific governmental or societal interests, all less restrictive alternatives must be looked to . . ."

Justice William Rehnquist had heard enough.

JUSTICE REHNQUIST: What if defendant says having an open preliminary hearing is going to prejudice my chance for a fair trial in Riverside County. Would the judge have to say, well, we could transfer it to Yolo County. Would judges have to go that far . . . have to accept that sort of an alternative rather than close the preliminary hearing?

A Stanford graduate and, later, first in his class at Stanford Law School, Rehnquist may have been familiar enough with Golden State geography to know that his hypothetical of going "that far" was probably going a little too far. The county seats of Yolo and Riverside Counties were roughly 460 miles apart—more than six hours by car and nearly twenty hours by train. But Ward played it straight.

> WARD: The use of change of venue has always been one of the alternatives available to avoid closure. Our answer is yes, that would have to be considered by the Court.
> REHNQUIST: So the defendant would have to be tried in a county in a different part of the state so that the Riverside County proceeding could be opened up to the press. That's what you're saying.
> WARD: We're dealing, of course . . .
> REHNQUIST: That's what you're saying, isn't it?
> WARD: In the end, if the only alternative to provide a fair trial is a motion for change of venue, and that contrasts with the right of access, our answer is yes.

Ward attempted to steer his argument to the historic roots of open preliminary hearings. This time it was Justice Harry Blackmun who interrupted.

> JUSTICE BLACKMUN: That history has been gone over in these other cases. I don't think we have to worry about it. I think we have it in mind.

Ward thanked, then ignored Blackmun, telling the justices about "one of the more fascinating matters of our investigation": the open preliminary hearing of Aaron Burr "during the course of which the crowd that attended . . . was so great that they had to adjourn from the courtroom and move to another chamber in order to accommodate it."

In his log of *Press-Enterprise II* Ward wrote, Blackmun "told me to quit getting into history." Blackmun, taking notes during oral argument, wrote "whine" next to Ward's name and gave him a grade of 5—the same grade he received from Blackmun in *Press-Enterprise I*.[6] Justice Powell, in his trademark blue ink, offered a more generous review of the newspaper's lawyer: "Ward (competent counsel)."[7]

If juror privacy was the elephant in the room in *Press-Enterprise I*, the same could be said for pretrial publicity in *Press-Enterprise II*. Chief Justice Burger asked Ward if a judge could close a suppression hearing, reasoning that evidence a defendant sought to toss out would just end up in the newspapers and on TV.

> WARD: We suggest, Justice Burger [Ward repeatedly demoted the chief justice to justice], that the problem of prejudicial publicity is not real . . . It is a very manageable problem . . . The statistical data available suggest that a minuscule number of cases were ever reversed on the basis of prejudicial pretrial publicity.

Wrote Justice Powell: "Publicity as to crimes & trials is *pervasive* in this country."[8]

> BURGER: If you have the transcripts a little bit later on, is there any problem about that?
> WARD: Yes, I believe so, Justice Burger, because I think this Court has held that the transcript is only a second best alternative.
> BURGER: Second best?
> WARD: The first is to be there.
> BURGER: Seriously, isn't the transcript going to be more accurate than what some person can take down in longhand when he's hearing testimony?
> WARD: Except Justice Burger to this degree, that timeliness is lost, and in so many of these instances we're dealing with the problem of timeliness of the proceedings . . .

If Ward had been a quarterback, he might have been blindsided and sacked by what happened next.

JUSTICE REHNQUIST: You want to print a picture of the defendant with his hands over his face, don't you?

WARD: I'm sorry, Justice Rehnquist.

REHNQUIST: Don't you want to print a picture of the defendant with his hands over his face, trying to prevent from being photographed?

Ward was staggered, but only for a moment. The star debater regained his footing and sought to turn the question to his advantage.

WARD: Oh, I think not, Justice Rehnquist. That isn't precisely the point. But I think that you do raise an important point . . . that I think should be made, that the process of criminal justice in this country is replete with publicity. It begins from the moment of the arrest until the final disposition of the case. All that this Court and this rule would concern itself with would be the preliminary hearing which is but a small part of it.

As Ward's thirty minutes ran down, the justices seemed to become more skeptical of the newspaper's case. Justice Byron White picked up an earlier theme and Ward's previous exchanges came back to haunt, or at least taunt, him.

JUSTICE WHITE: Something happens *after* the preliminary hearing when cases are disposed of without a trial. A plea bargain . . . I would think you'd be much more interested in that process. I suppose your next claim would be to sit in on those.

WARD: Only if a judge were hearing the matter before opposing counsel. Just for clarification, we make no claim of access to the plea bargaining—

WHITE: I know you don't now, but as Justice O'Connor says, you may be here tomorrow for that?

WARD: We, but of course we look to the logic of what we're dealing with here. We're dealing with the values of openness that this Court—

WHITE: I think the logic of your argument would say: We should get in on the real (plea) bargaining.

Ward tried to change the subject, citing the McMartin preliminary hearing in which five defendants were ordered to stand trial, only to have all charges against them dropped a few days later.

WARD: Fortunately, [it was] an open [to the public] process, because if it had not been, consider the potential outrage of the community having had a secret process going on for that length of time.

JUSTICE REHNQUIST: Well, of course, the community can remedy its outrage by requiring the proceedings open, if really the majority is outraged. Your hypothesis is really, the majority has decided otherwise so you have to put it on a constitutional basis.

Ward asked to save his remaining time for later and Chief Justice Burger summoned deputy Riverside County counsel Joyce Reikes to the lectern.

Reikes was, at times, firmly in command and off balance. Once, she corrected herself after calling Thurgood Marshall "Chief Justice Marshall." Another time, she laughed nervously and apologized—"Forgive me, Justice Blackmun"—when he corrected her on a constitutional point. In notes taken during oral argument, Blackmun jotted "medium blond, plump" beside Reikes's name. Her grade: 4, the same that he gave Deputy County Counsel Glenn Salter, the losing lawyer in *Press-Enterprise I*.[9]

Addressing the justices in her crisp Brooklyn accent, she got right down to business.

REIKES: Rather than begin with an opening statement, I would like to bring to this Court the difference between a preliminary hearing and a trial, in terms of the incentive of the parties to prevail.

In a trial, she said, the prosecution and defense are out to win. "The defendant's liberty is at stake, and in a capital case, possibly his life." But in a preliminary hearing, a judge is just deciding whether there should be a trial or whether "this is an unwarranted prosecution and should be cut off, if you will, at the pass, right here."

Reikes and the justices then probed the difference between preliminary hearings and pretrial hearings that were held to determine whether to admit or not allow evidence. Because Reikes did not always respond to justices by name, it was sometimes difficult to know who asked the questions.

UNIDENTIFIED JUSTICE: [What if a defendant says] "I don't want this hearing closed at all, any part of it, even for that witness, and I have a Sixth Amendment right to an open and public trial."

REIKES: I think there the defendant has certainly a Sixth Amendment concern if the closure will affect his right to trial.

JUSTICE O'CONNOR: But you would say the press does not have an equivalent [First Amendment] right?

REIKES: The press in a suppression of evidence hearing . . . does have that First Amendment right. . . . Because the suppression hearing unquestionably is different than the preliminary hearing itself. There, like a trial, both sides have the incentive to prevail.

JUSTICE REHNQUIST: Well, yet, the defendant surely has an incentive [in a preliminary hearing] to ask the magistrate to hold there is no probable cause to bind over.

REIKES: Unquestionably, that's true. However, this is an early stage of the proceedings where . . . the prosecutor may have taken some months in building his case . . . [and] where the defendant is newly arrested. And so, if the defendant is sitting there at a preliminary hearing and he's pretty sure, or his counsel is, that he is going to be bound over, he is not going to, as Mr. Diaz did not, put on witnesses. Mr. Diaz put on not one witness.

JUSTICE THURGOOD MARSHALL: I don't think defense counsel will agree with you at all. You are saying that they lay down on the job.

REIKES: No, your honor. I'm not saying that they lay down on the job. . . . The defendant does that . . . as a matter of defense strategy, the purpose being to save his case for trial.

MARSHALL: You mean that if he has a chance of getting his man off at the preliminary he will not do it?

REIKES: No. I would think that if any counsel has a chance of getting his client off at the preliminary hearing he would go for it. I would.

Chief Justice Burger asked Reikes if she knew of any case when a preliminary hearing "resulted in a negative for the prosecution."

REIKES: I'm not personally familiar with one, your honor.

BURGER: Then it would seem that the preliminary hearing has a limited utility.

Reikes disagreed. A preliminary hearing has "a tremendous societal interest, in being a check on the prosecutor in terms of cutting off unwarranted prosecutions." It gives the defendant a chance to see "the demeanor of the district attorney's witnesses and so forth, and some of his case."

JUSTICE BLACKMUN: But if it has a tremendous societal interest, why shouldn't it be open?

REIKES: Not every interest, Justice Blackmun . . . should be embellished or elevated to a constitutional right. . . . There are a number of interests in this country that are passionate interests in this society that have never been elevated to a federal constitutional right. This Court . . . in 1973 spoke of public education and found that it is not a right.

UNIDENTIFIED JUSTICE: We're talking about the Bill of Rights here.

REIKES: I realize we are and perhaps it was a bad analogy. But the Bill of Rights nowhere discusses the preliminary hearing. Certainly the preliminary hearing was known in the early colonies. It literally crossed the ocean, I think, with the colonists.

Several times during her presentation Reikes sighed audibly, possibly frustrated by questions that were not exactly in her wheelhouse.

UNIDENTIFIED JUSTICE: What provision is there under California law for television access to trials?

REIKES: I do know that we . . . I don't know the specific code section. I believe there is an experimental pilot program under the
Rules of Court in California.

UNIDENTIFIED JUSTICE: You mean there's no regular ongoing
procedure for televising criminal trials?

REIKES: I believe there probably is, but I . . . and I believe there
may have been that in Mr. Diaz's trial because I believe . . . and
I'm not entirely sure, I believe I remember seeing parts of it on
TV myself, but it's something that I am just not familiar with at
this point.

She was much more comfortable with the issue of pretrial publicity.
Whereas Jim Ward told the justices that the "problem of prejudicial
publicity is not real," Reikes argued that the real problem was that
its impact could not possibly be known. "Do we really know what
the effect of pretrial publicity is on anyone's mind? I submit that we
cannot really know that."

Reikes told the justices California already protected public access
to preliminary hearings. "That first sentence of Penal Code Section
868 . . . now reads, since, 1982, 'The examination shall be open and
public.'" But, she added, they should be closed if the defendant requests
it and the judge finds "a reasonable likelihood of substantial prejudice"
if the hearing is kept open. Granting a constitutional right of public
access would "dilute" the accused's right to a fair trial, said Reikes,
because it would shoulder a defendant with "the burden" of meeting
the U.S. Supreme Court's stiff standards for a closed hearing "at a very
early stage . . . when the specter of pre-trial publicity may be looming
before him but may not be concrete enough" to persuade a judge.

JUSTICE MARSHALL: Why not close them all?

REIKES: We do not stand here, Respondent Court does not stand
here today saying, "close everything." We feel that proceedings
should be open where possible.

Marshall then asked a question that seemed to expose a serious
weakness in the county's case.

MARSHALL: What was the reasonable likelihood of prejudice in this case that this Court found?

REIKES: In this particular case, the magistrate indicated, and the records . . . it was very spare, admittedly, but he said there has been national publicity."

MARSHALL: My question was . . . The defendant said close the trial. What reason did the judge give for closing the hearing?

REIKES: The defendant's fair trial rights . . . The right to a fair trial, to protect him from that publicity.

MARSHALL: And that was the only reason given?

REIKES: Yes, at that time.

Reikes's time was running out.

JUSTICE BLACKMUN: As I understand your argument, though, you are saying that there is no First Amendment right at all to access?

REIKES: We see no basis for declaring one.

Jim Ward returned to the lectern, determined to use his spare minutes to deliver his final plea. But he was interrupted just as he was getting up a head of steam. Justice White, wrote Ward, was determined to pin him down.[10]

WARD: We cannot have secret hearings. We cannot have closed proceedings. . . . Our position is—

JUSTICE WHITE: [I]f we agree with you on the applicability of the First Amendment, which one of our cases do you think most narrowly states the standard that would have to be satisfied to justify closure?

White already had an answer in mind. "How about the Waller standard? Would that satisfy you?"

Waller v. Georgia, decided just months after *Press-Enterprise I*, ruled that a defendant had a Sixth Amendment right to a public preliminary hearing unless the party that wanted it closed could show that "closure was absolutely necessary to preserve higher values and was narrowly tailored to serve those interests." Ward didn't have to think long before answering.

> WARD: The Waller standard, yes, because the Waller standard as we recall it, referred specifically to *the Press-Enterprise I* standard.

Before another justice could break in, Ward proceeded to the big finish, parts of which he "plagiarized" from the amicus brief written by his old pal Ed McIntyre, the San Diego lawyer and fellow court-access crusader. McIntyre was in the courtroom audience.[11]

> WARD: What we quarrel with is the California Supreme Court standard which did not call for reasonable alternatives, which did not call that it be narrowly tailored, which did not call that there be an overriding interest, which did not require articulated findings. The California standard has none of the constitutional underpinnings that this Court has found essential in connection with evaluating openness. . . . It is our opinion that the California Supreme Court in the standard that it has set has violated our constitutional rights and must be reversed.

With the clock ticking down to zero, Ward managed to contrast the recent Supreme Court decisions with the treatment the *Press-Enterprise* had received from the state supreme court.

> WARD: Three times this Court has called for openness of various judicial proceedings, at least three times. Twice the California Supreme Court since 1982 [voir dire and preliminary hearings] has not heeded that admonition at all but has instead found for closure of proceedings and provided an easy standard for closure which we believe will result in a denial of the rights of the citizens of the State of California . . .
>
> CHIEF JUSTICE BURGER: Thank you, counsel. The case is submitted.

A few days later, Ward received a short note from the man who stuck with him. "Dear Jim," wrote Tim Hays, "Helen and I enjoyed our whole Washington experience and we thought our White Knight was absolutely superb."[12]

21

"Safeguard against the Corrupt and Eccentric"

On Friday, February 28, 1986, two days after the oral arguments, the Supreme Court justices met in conference to state their views and cast their votes in *Press-Enterprise II*. Most justices planted their feet squarely in the "soil of openness." At the top of his tally sheet Justice Powell wrote, "Reverse 8–1." But that wouldn't be the final count.[1]

The Powell and Blackmun tally sheets show that a consensus emerged in the closed-door conference: the California-style preliminary hearing was "almost" a trial and should be "presumptively open"; the public had a near "absolute right" to the transcript, and the California Supreme Court's "reasonable likelihood" standard that enabled judges to close preliminary hearings was woefully weak.

Once again Justice Brennan composed and presumably read aloud what appears to be a conference statement that included a surprising echo from *Press-Enterprise I*.[2] "[L]ike *voir dire*, the preliminary hearing is really part of the trial." The conclusion emerged from his analysis of what the Supreme Court's recent guarantee of a First Amendment right of access really targeted. Grand juries? No. "Grand jury proceedings were closed to prevent the accused from learning he was being investigated" because he might skip town. Plea bargains and police interrogations? No. "[T]hese too must be private to work effectively." Riverside County's "parade of horribles"—warning that open preliminary hearings would lead to the invasion of these private proceedings—was, wrote Brennan, "illusory."

But the preliminary hearing was different. It was "part of the state's official proceedings for dealing with criminals, part of the public show that—like the trial—reveals how we treat criminals." Brennan went out of his way to be clear. "Note: I am not arguing that access to preliminary hearings is necessary because [it] is the only judicial proceeding that is held in a large number of cases. I would reach the same result if every case in California went to trial. Rather, my point is that the preliminary hearing is literally part of the trial, at least for the purposes of the First Amendment right recognized in *Richmond*."

But even though the conference yielded a consensus among most justices, Justice Stevens seemed to agonize out loud. "I may come around," he said, according to Blackmun's notes. Yet Stevens set himself apart from his colleagues. "I give greater concern to fair trial right of defendant. . . . Why is this unique proceeding different from a grand jury? . . . What they [presumably the California courts] have done here is constitutional." Justice Powell's notes also portray Stevens as leaning against the *Press-Enterprise*. "Here defendant requested closing & the magistrate & then trial court found that defendant's right to fair trial would be prejudiced. . . . This finding merits more consideration than other justices seem to give it. . . . Standard of California statute is OK." And even though Powell and Blackmun both had Justice Rehnquist voting to reverse, Powell's notes suggest Rehnquist was not all in: "May not go so far as majority of court in emphasizing right of access."

On the last day of its term—and almost exactly seven years after the 1979 *Gannett* ruling unwittingly launched a series of cases that opened the nation's courtrooms—the Supreme Court ruled that the public and press have a First Amendment right to attend pretrial hearings. *Press-Enterprise II* became the fourth in a quartet of decisions that pried open America's courtrooms, barring judges from arbitrarily shutting the public out of criminal trials and hearings. From now on they would have to explain themselves, specifically and on the record, so their actions could be reviewed by higher courts.

Unlike *Press-Enterprise I*, this June 30, 1986, decision was not unanimous. Justice John Paul Stevens, who had tipped his hand when the justices met to vote, dissented from the majority opinion, which, once again, Chief Justice Burger assigned to himself. Justice William Rehnquist initially voted to go along with what would have been an

8–1 majority. But he ended up joining part of the Stevens dissent, making the final tally on *Press-Enterprise II* a still-convincing 7–2.

Jim Ward had drawn the line in oral argument: preliminary hearings were judicial proceedings and should be open; grand juries were investigatory and should be closed. But he failed to sway Justice Stevens, whose dissent warned of a slippery slope. Stevens wrote that the "obvious defect" in Burger's majority opinion was that, despite its "valiant attempt to limit the logic of its holding," the newly extended constitutional right applied to preliminary hearings *and* grand juries. Stevens also argued that the Riverside County judges Howard Dabney and John Barnard were right to seal the Diaz preliminary hearing transcript—and keep it sealed until Diaz decided he didn't want a jury trial. "In this case, the risk of prejudice to the defendant's right to a fair trial is perfectly obvious. For me, that risk is far more significant than the . . . interest in publishing the transcript . . . sooner rather than later."

But Stevens's dissent was overpowered by the majority opinion, which drove a stake through the heart of *Gannett* and made new law. Unlike Burger's opinion in *Press-Enterprise I*, his early drafts weren't savaged or ridiculed. "For the most part," law clerk David Sklansky wrote to his boss, Justice Blackmun, "the Chief Justice's proposed opinion . . . is excellent . . . well written and clear." He noted that Burger adopted the standard Blackmun crafted in his *Gannett* dissent: a pretrial hearing could be closed only if there was a "substantial probability" that a defendant's fair-trial right would be damaged.

Justice Powell wanted Burger to add something to his opinion. In a brief June 6, 1986, letter he wrote, "I . . . write only to you to express the hope that you will include in your opinion—possibly in a footnote—a reference to my concurring opinion in *Gannett*. There are several portions . . . that seem to me to be fully supportive of your position." In *Gannett*, Powell had stood alone in recognizing a First Amendment right of access to preliminary hearings, and he hoped his concurring opinion would get a mention in *Press-Enterprise II*.[3] The chief obliged. When Burger circulated his second draft, Powell, in customary blue ink, wrote at the top of his copy, "The CJ added reference to my concur in *Gannett* p. 5."

The Supreme Court's ruling continued to build on its recent body of work. It noted that the 1984 *Waller v. Georgia* ruling—decided just months after *Press-Enterprise I*—held that when a defendant objects to a closed pretrial hearing, the party that's trying to close it must show that excluding the public and press "advances an overriding interest that is likely to be prejudiced." This protected the defendant's Sixth Amendment right to a public trial. In *Press-Enterprise II* the shoe was on the other foot. The public and press were asserting a First Amendment right to attend a preliminary hearing that the defendant wanted closed. Wrote Burger: "The right to an open public trial is a shared right of the accused and the public, the common concern being the assurance of fairness." But did that *shared* right extend to preliminary hearings? The majority opinion answered that question: "The considerations that led the Court to apply the First Amendment right of access to criminal trials in *Richmond Newspapers* and *Globe* and the selection of jurors in *Press-Enterprise I* lead us to conclude that the right of access applies to preliminary hearings as conducted in California."

Burger relied on "a tradition of accessibility to preliminary hearings of the type conducted in California" to make his case. Adrienne Wieand, the young Baker & Hostetler lawyer who had been dispatched to the Library of Congress on what must have seemed like a snipe hunt, found it, to put it mildly, "very exciting" when she read: "Long ago in the celebrated trial of Aaron Burr for treason, for example, with Chief Justice Marshall sitting as trial judge, the probable cause hearing was held in the Hall of the House of Delegates in Virginia, the court room being too small to accommodate the crush of interested citizens. From *Burr* until the present day, the near uniform practice of state and federal courts has been to conduct preliminary hearings in open court."

History, or experience, dictated openness. But what about logic? "The second question," wrote Burger, is whether public access to preliminary hearings as they are conducted in California plays a particularly significant positive role in the actual functioning of the process." Once again, he recalled that *Richmond*, *Globe*, and *Press-Enterprise I* had already answered this question in regard to criminal *trials*. "California preliminary hearings are sufficiently like a trial to justify the same conclusion."

The ruling said the importance of public access to preliminary hearings is "even more significant" because they are conducted without juries, which are "long recognized as [a] . . . safeguard against the corrupt or overzealous prosecutor and against the compliant, biased or eccentric judge." Denying transcripts of the forty-one-day Diaz hearing frustrated "what we have characterized as the community therapeutic value of openness." Noting that violent crimes trigger public "outrage" and "hostility," Burger addressed the benefits of openness by quoting from his opinion in *Press-Enterprise I*: "When the public is aware that the law is being enforced and the criminal justice system is functioning, an outlet is provided for these understandable reactions and emotions."

Burger drew on the *Gannett* majority opinion to acknowledge that "[p]ublicity concerning the proceedings at a pretrial hearing . . . could influence public opinion against a defendant." But the *Press-Enterprise II* opinion reflected Jim Ward's contention that pretrial publicity was a manageable problem and not an excuse for automatic closure. "[T]he preliminary hearing," declared the Supreme Court as it killed off the "reasonable likelihood" standard, "shall be closed only if specific findings are made demonstrating that first, there is a substantial probability that the defendant's right to a fair trial will be prejudiced by publicity that closure would prevent and, second, reasonable alternatives to closure cannot adequately protect the defendant's free trial rights." And even if those standards were met and closure was justified, closing "an entire 41-day proceeding would rarely be warranted. . . . [A]ny limitation [to public access] must be narrowly tailored" to protect the defendant's right.

The First Amendment right of public and press access to pretrial hearings was not absolute, and the *Press-Enterprise* had not argued that it should be. But the burden had shifted. Now that the public and the press had a constitutional right to attend pretrial hearings, judges could close them only for compelling, specific, narrow, and on-the-record reasons.

The Supreme Court victory was front-page news—below the fold—in the next day's *Press-Enterprise*. Another Supreme Court story snared page one's top billing: "Court Affirms Law Banning Homosexual Conduct." The *Los Angeles Times* also shoved *Press-Enterprise II* down below the front-page fold, giving better play to a Supreme Court ruling on gerrymandering. The *New York Times* made room for the *Press-Enterprise* decision on page fifteen. Its front page Supreme Court story informed readers that a 5–4 ruling meant "the Constitution does not protect private homosexual relations between consenting adults, even in their own homes."

Still, *Press-Enterprise II*, characterized as a "stunning victory for open government" in the Riverside paper, created a buzz—and some initial uncertainty. The executive director of the Reporters Committee for Freedom of the Press said the ruling appeared to apply only to California,[4] but that proved not to be the case. The Society of Professional Journalists called it "an important milestone" that "will bolster public confidence in the quality of justice."[5] The California Newspaper Publishers Association predicted the ruling would "enhance public support of the administration of justice because more information will be available. This is particularly a concern when such a large number of criminal cases never reach trial."[6]

Not surprisingly, Bruce Sanford, the lead writer of the national brief in support of the *Press-Enterprise*, called the ruling "an absolutely stunning victory for the American press and public."[7] Sharon Waters, lead writer of the *Press-Enterprise*'s own brief, said the decision swept away "the mythical distinction between a pretrial hearing and a trial."[8] Charles S. Rowe, editor of Virginia's *Fredericksburg Free Lance-Star* and head of the press freedom committee of the American Society of Newspaper Editors, put himself in the shoes of the man on the street. "This guy is not going to sit tonight and have an extra beer to salute the Supreme Court. But democracy is going to work better and the judicial system will improve because people have greater knowledge" of it.[9]

Joyce Reikes, who argued the case for Riverside County, called the ruling a "continuation of the whole trend of guaranteeing First Amendment access to trials that the U.S. Supreme Court established in the 1980 Richmond decision." She knew the momentum was against her and struck a philosophical note. "There is always a certain amount of disappointment when you lose. But that goes with being a lawyer. You win some and you lose some."[10] The day after the ruling, Riverside Superior Court judge Howard Dabney, who had closed Diaz's forty-one-day preliminary hearing and sealed the transcript, wrote to Ward: "Dear Jim, Congratulations. We'll probably all be the better for the recent decision."[11]

The *Press-Enterprise* editorial assumed the understated tone of the late Norman Cherniss. "We do not, to say the least, take exception to the Supreme Court decision." It expressed "no small satisfaction" that the court came through with a First Amendment right. A state law "is not enough; what one legislative body giveth, another legislative body can taketh away. It had to be grounded in the federal Constitution."[12]

If there was one man in America who, for much different reasons, was as gratified as anyone about the outcome of *Press-Enterprise II*, it had to be Robert Bernius, the losing lawyer in *Gannett v. DePasquale*. The ghost of *Gannett* had eaten away at him for seven years. He had the case won until Justice Powell flipped. But the ghost had finally been vaporized. *Press-Enterprise II* had given the public and press what Bernius had argued they *should* have been given: First Amendment protection from near-automatic and vaguely reasoned decisions to hold secret pretrial hearings.

"When those cases [*Richmond, Globe, Press-Enterprise*] kept coming down, I certainly felt vindicated. We were right. For a long time, I have been in denial and believe with all my heart that we won in DePasquale. It was a moral victory and set the stage for the rest of them. That sucker, Powell. If he hadn't flipped, I would have been a hero."[13]

Epilogue

Nearly two years had passed since the Aurora movie theater massacre in which twelve people were shot dead and seventy others were wounded during a midnight showing of *The Dark Knight Rises*. Now it was time to pick a jury for the Colorado death penalty trial of James Eagan Holmes. Lawyers for the defense and prosecution asked Arapahoe County district judge Carlos A. Samour Jr. to eject the public and press from his courtroom while a jury was selected from a pool of six thousand people. When Samour issued his ruling on June 11, 2014, he cited a familiar string of First Amendment court-access cases: *Richmond*, *Globe*, *Nebraska Press Association*. And when he explained why the defense and prosecution had failed to meet the basic standards necessary to close his courtroom, Samour turned to *Press-Enterprise I* and *Press-Enterprise II*.[1]

To overcome the "presumption of openness"—and kick out the public and press—the defense and prosecution had to pass the *Press-Enterprise I* test: show there is "an overriding interest based on findings that closure is essential to preserve higher values and is narrowly tailored to serve that interest." When a criminal defendant sought to close jury selection to protect his right to a fair trial, Judge Samour said the *Press-Enterprise II* "balancing test" came into play. Voir dire "shall be closed only if specific findings are made demonstrating . . . a substantial probability that the defendant's right to a fair trial would be prejudiced by publicity that closure would prevent" and "reasonable alternatives to closure" would not protect the defendant's rights. Samour ruled that the defense and prosecution had failed to make the case that the only way he could protect James Eagan Holmes's constitutional right to a fair trial was to shut the public and press out of jury selection.

Concerns about damaging pretrial publicity and fears that, by its mere presence, the media would intimidate prospective jurors were, Samour said, purely speculative. He faulted the lawyers for ignoring the alternatives he himself had put in place: assigning the jurors numbers and not releasing their names, contact information, or completed juror questionnaires to the press or the public. When he rejected the argument that voir dire must be closed because prospective jurors might be asked to answer sensitive, personal questions about mental illness, he again turned to *Press-Enterprise I*: "'[T]hose individuals believing public questioning will prove damaging . . . because of embarrassment' may request to speak 'to the judge *in camera* but with [the parties] and counsel present and on the record.'"

Addressing the "importance of openness in trials," Samour quoted the U.S. Supreme Court's ruling in *Press-Enterprise I*: "Criminal acts, especially violent crimes, often provoke public concern, even outrage and hostility. . . . When the public is aware that the law is being enforced and the criminal justice system is functioning, an outlet is provided for these understandable reactions and emotions. Proceedings held in secret would deny this outlet and frustrate the broad public interest." Paraphrasing the legendary Justice Louis Brandeis, Judge Samour wrote, "In the Court's view, sunshine, not darkness, is the appropriate disinfectant here."

Steven Zansberg, a Denver lawyer who represented national media that opposed closed voir dire in the Aurora shooting case, called Samour's ruling "breathtaking. . . . When you read it you could hear the music of John Philip Sousa in the background . . . the role of the free press and keeping trial participants honest and instilling confidence in the system. The *Press-Enterprise* cases are the foundation for much of why that trial was open."[2]

More than three decades have passed since the U.S. Supreme Court decided *Press-Enterprise I* and *II*, capping a seven-year stretch that saw the court give the public and press a qualified First Amendment right of access to courtrooms and court documents. In 2010 the Supreme

Court fortified *Press-Enterprise I*, ruling in *Presley v. Georgia* that even if the defense and prosecution offer no alternatives to closing voir dire, judges cannot constitutionally conduct secret jury selection unless they independently consider and reject "reasonable alternatives."[3] Said Zansberg: "It places front and center the judges' role to assure the public's right of access. You either get this right" or risk having a conviction overturned.[4] By early 2017 each *Press-Enterprise* case had been cited thousands of times in judicial opinions, trial orders such as Judge Samour's, trial and appellate court documents, law reviews, and more.[5] Like the Aurora shooting, some of those cases became immediate household names.

Boston Marathon Bombing

When Dzhokhar Tsarnaev stood trial for his role in the April 15, 2013, bombing that killed three and wounded hundreds, the defense and prosecution wanted to close jury selection. After federal district court judge George A. O'Toole Jr. refused, the lawyers agreed to what O'Toole called a "modest partial closure" that allowed two pool reporters and two sketch artists in the courtroom. There would be audio and video feeds of voir dire in two overflow courtrooms, one for the public, one for the media. Viewers would not be able to see the jurors' faces. The *Boston Globe* and other media cited *Press-Enterprise I* in an effort to obtain greater access to the courtroom. But O'Toole noted that, unlike the *Press-Enterprise* case, this was not a *total* closure. He observed that based on Twitter traffic the "arrangement has not significantly impeded media coverage of the *voir dire* process." Citing his reasons—or findings—for imposing "the relatively minor restrictions," O'Toole denied the motion.[6]

Oklahoma City Bombing

In 1997, media organizations challenged a federal judge's pretrial decision to seal or redact certain documents related to defendants Terry Nichols and Timothy McVeigh. But after applying the *Press-Enterprise II* test, the Tenth District Court of Appeals ruled the judge had "properly balanced" First Amendment rights against the defendants' fair trial rights; had made findings to support his actions; and had "narrowly tailored" his orders.[7]

U.S. v. Koubriti

In the "immediate aftermath" of the September 11, 2001, attacks, Karim Koubriti, Ahmed Hannan, Abdel-Ilah El Mardoudi, and Farouk Ali-Haimoud were arrested and charged with conspiracy to support and aid terrorists. Defense lawyers moved to close the individual voir dire. The *Detroit News* and the *Detroit Free Press* opposed the motion. On March 24, 2003, Michigan-based U.S. district judge Gerald Rosen noted that in *Press-Enterprise I* the Supreme Court had outlined ways a judge could protect juror privacy "but had no occasion to discuss the very serious, and very different concerns" about "how to protect the accuseds' right to a fair trial by avoiding inhibitions upon jurors' candor." Rosen decided to close individual jury voir dire, finding that "because of the potential for juror taint, the need for complete candor from the jurors, and the danger of chilling that candor, the interest of the media must give way to the fair trial rights of the Defendants." Unlike Riverside County's Judge Mortland, Rosen said the press would be given a transcript of the closed voir dire proceedings once the jury was seated. Demographic information about the jurors would also be provided. This, he said, "diminished" the infringement upon the newspapers' First Amendment rights.[8]

Martha Stewart

In 2004 a federal judge barred the public and press from jury selection in the perjury trial of the celebrity home-designer and lifestyle trendsetter Martha Stewart. The Second District Court of Appeals, citing *Press-Enterprise I* and *II*, reversed the lower court, finding that it "did not set a sufficient factual basis for closure" of voir dire, and the order "was not narrowly tailored" to protect Martha Stewart's right to a fair trial.[9]

On occasion the *Press-Enterprise* cases have galloped far beyond the sedate courts of law. In 2010 Laura Leigh, a photographer for *Horse-*

back magazine, tried to take pictures of a wild-horse roundup on federal land in Nevada. When the Bureau of Land Management (BLM) restricted her access, she sued and lost in federal court. But the Ninth District Court of Appeals said the judge failed to conduct a *Press-Enterprise II*–style First Amendment analysis: Were such wild-horse roundups traditionally open to the public? Did public access play a positive role in demonstrating how the government functioned? (Leigh had heard horses had been mistreated.) Had the BLM shown there was an overriding interest in restricting access to "horse gathering"? Were the restrictions "narrowly tailored" to serve that interest? These were First Amendment issues, and not even wild horses could excuse a judge's failure to address them. The appeals court ordered the judge to determine if the public had a First Amendment right of access to such wild-horse roundups and, if so, whether the BLM's restrictions were "narrowly tailored" to serve the government's overriding interests.[10]

Lawyers and journalists differ on which of the two *Press-Enterprise* cases is most significant. "It isn't until *Press-Enterprise II* that you've totally broken a barrier," said Lee Levine, who cowrote the national amicus briefs in both cases.[11] There is now a constitutional right of access to *pretrial* hearings as well as the trial itself. Bruce Sanford, the lead writer on those briefs, stresses the impact of *Press-Enterprise I*. "I can't tell you how many times we've had to go into court because some trial judge is going to close it and protect his jurors. It happens over and over again."[12]

It happened in Los Angeles on December 5, 2016, when U.S. district court judge Percy Anderson, without explanation, closed jury selection in the criminal trial of former LA County sheriff Lee Baca. But the next day's voir dire was held in public. The *Los Angeles Times* reported that its lawyer had "informed Anderson's courtroom deputy that the media organizations intended to formally object to closure." The newspaper cited a U.S. Supreme Court ruling, in "a 1984 criminal case involving the rape and murder of a teenage girl, that the questioning of jurors was presumed part of the open court proceeding," and closure "must be rare and only for cause shown that outweighs the value of openness."[13]

But despite the Supreme Court rulings and their often-soaring language, judges continue to close their courtrooms for a simple reason. "They don't realize there's this standard they're supposed to follow," said Gregg Leslie, legal defense director of the Reporters Committee for Freedom of the Press. "Media covers about one percent of all trials. This [closure] goes on all the time without us knowing it. When confronted, judges say, 'This is how I've always done it.' I'm comfortable with saying that hundreds of times a year, there's an attempt to close."[14]

Harold "Hal" Fuson, who became the vice president and general counsel for Copley Press as the Copley newspapers, the *Press-Enterprise*, and others waged these court-access battles, doubts whether the public has become more enlightened "by any great body of informative by-play" since *Press-Enterprise II*. But something perhaps more important has taken root. "If judges are going to close anything—*voir dire*, suppression hearings, the trial itself—they've got to be serious about it. This is not some one-off decision. This is an accumulation of a series of cases that makes it the law of the land. They have to have a damn good reason. Judges don't like to make reasons. It's hard. They don't want to be overturned. What's the real message [of these cases]? The Supreme Court didn't like what was happening."[15]

Yet even though these cases provide important constitutional guarantees, the rulings were, to use the court's own language, "narrowly tailored." They zeroed in on the judicial branch. Courtroom proceedings and transcripts. "There's not a recognized First Amendment right of access to the other branches" of government, noted Steven Zansberg, the Denver media lawyer. In some cases congressional committees meet behind closed doors.[16] There is no constitutional right of access to deportation hearings, a function of the executive branch. Nor is there such a right to obtain *all* government records under the Freedom of Information Act.[17] Even within the judicial branch, there is no constitutional access to grand juries or juror questionnaires. There are, said Lee Levine, "plenty of new frontiers."[18] But exploring them today seems less likely than it was three decades ago. "I've spent as much as $200,000 on access cases for Copley Press," said Fuson. "That just wouldn't happen today. We have clearly passed a period of time when Tim Hays would say, 'I might not spend as much on other things, but it's worth doing.' It is the case today that, particularly with court access cases, there's no payback. The Superior Court is not going to pay your fees for suing it."[19]

When Sharon Waters reflects on the *Press-Enterprise* cases today, she does so as a Riverside County Superior Court judge.[20] Judges closed their courtrooms not out of any fear that they'd be reversed, but out of a get-the-job-done pragmatism. Their view from the bench, as described by Waters: "The two parties here are fine with what I'm doing. Why should I do anything different? Who's going to challenge it?" Before *Press-Enterprise I*, she said, "the judges never showed any acknowledgment that there was a duty to the public at large." Then came the *Press-Enterprise* cases. "Now they were scared. Now they thought, 'We're gonna be the next judge up before the U.S. Supreme Court' because the *Press-Enterprise* showed the determination to take a case as far as they need to." Perhaps more importantly, these same judges began applying the "balancing test that had always been there." Now, they were balancing the *constitutional* rights of defendants, the public, and the press when it came to jury selection and preliminary hearings.[21]

If it was a sweet victory to see Riverside County judges finally recognize their "duty to the public at large," sweeter still was the turnaround at the California Supreme Court. Three times it had thwarted the *Press-Enterprise*'s efforts to win the public and the press access to jury selection and preliminary hearings. But in 1999, liberally citing the U.S. Supreme Court's rulings in *Press-Enterprise I* and *II*, the state's highest court extended the First Amendment right of access to civil cases. (Other state and federal courts have done the same, said Waters. Some have also extended the First Amendment access to court records.) The California Supreme Court ruling arose from the 1996 fraud trial pitting actor/director Sondra Locke against actor/director Clint Eastwood. Though the trial unfolded well before the invention of smartphones and social media, it followed the notorious televised trial of O. J. Simpson by just four years. Los Angeles County Superior

Court judge David Schacter closed his courtroom to the public and press during portions of the trial that took place outside the presence of the jury. He explained that the "very, very small intrusion on the First Amendment" would prevent jurors from being exposed to "the type of information that ends up in tabloids, that faces everybody that walks . . . into a grocery store to buy their groceries. It's on television. It's in the newspapers. It's on radio."[22]

The California Supreme Court threw out the judge's order, ruling that Schacter had failed to follow the playbook that the U.S. Supreme Court had started to write in *Richmond*, refined in *Globe*, and expanded in *Press-Enterprise I* and *II*: "The need to comply with the requirements of the First Amendment right of access may impose some burdens on trial courts. But courts can and should minimize such inconveniences by proposing to close proceedings only in the rarest of circumstances." And when they to propose to bar the public and press, judges must make "constitutionally required findings," which Schacter had failed to do. "We conclude, in light of the high court case law and its progeny, that, in general, the First Amendment provides a right of access to ordinary civil trials and proceedings, that constitutional standards governing closure of trial proceedings apply in the civil setting."[23]

If the *Press-Enterprise* cases have left a national legacy, it is a legacy rooted in the deaths of a deputy sheriff, a high school sophomore, and a dozen hospital patients who most likely thought they would soon be going home. The American criminal justice system is more open today—an openness guaranteed by the U.S. Constitution—because of what happened to them. And if the *Press-Enterprise* cases have left a national legacy, it is not without a local irony. The newspaper's briefs and the Supreme Court rulings declared that open courtrooms contribute to the public's confidence that justice is being served. But like many American newspapers, the *Press-Enterprise* has not been immune to shrinkage on almost every front, including news staff. Armed with the constitutional right of access to courts, few reporters actually show up on a day-to-day basis. "Nobody's there anymore," said District Attorney Michael Hestrin. "When I started, there were two or three covering the courts. There's just not the manpower anymore."[24] In 1997 Tim Hays sold the *Press-Enterprise* to the Dallas-based A. H. Belo Corp. The paper has been sold twice since, first to Freedom Communications in 2013 and to Digital First Media in 2016. Save for its name, the *Press-Enterprise* bears little resemblance to the Hays-Cherniss newspaper of the twentieth century.

James D. Ward, the World's Greatest Attorney, became a Riverside County Superior Court judge and, later, a justice on the California Court of Appeal—the same court that had consistently rejected the *Press-Enterprise*'s appeals of closed voir dire and preliminary hearings. John Boyd survived the intra–law firm kerfuffle over *Press-Enterprise II* and made partner in Thompson & Colegate, a position he holds to this day. Mel Opotowsky became the managing editor of the *Press-Enterprise* and, though retired, continues to be a vigorous advocate of First Amendment access in California. He also served as a Pulitzer Prize juror. Albert Greenwood Brown Jr., who was twenty-five years old when he raped and murdered Susan Jordan in 1980, remains on California's Death Row. Robert Rubane Diaz, the lidocaine serial killer, died of natural causes in 2010 after spending twenty-six years on Death Row. He was seventy-two.

Patrick Magers, who prosecuted Diaz, became a Riverside County Superior Court judge. Robert Spitzer, who prosecuted Albert Greenwood Brown Jr., also became a Riverside County judge but was removed from the bench by the California Commission on Judicial Performance in 2007 for "gross neglect" of his duties. Joseph Peter Myers, who defended Albert Greenwood Brown Jr., continues to practice law in Riverside.

Glenn Salter, the deputy county counsel who argued and lost *Press-Enterprise I*, is a superior court judge in Orange County. Joyce Reikes, the deputy county counsel who, loss aside, viewed her appearance before the U.S. Supreme Court in *Press-Enterprise II* as the highlight of her professional career, became a Riverside County Superior Court commissioner. She died in 2015.

Judge William Mortland, who closed the Albert Greenwood Brown Jr. jury selection and sealed the transcript, died in 1991. He was sixty-one. Judge Howard M. Dabney, who closed the Robert Diaz preliminary hearing and sealed the transcript, became a justice on the California Court of Appeal. He died in 1996 at sixty-nine. Judge John Barnard, who kept the Diaz transcript sealed but eventually released it, then presided over Diaz's nonjury trial and sentenced him to death, also died in 1996. He was seventy-six.

Bruce Sanford, the First Amendment lawyer who was the lead writer of both national *Press-Enterprise* briefs and arranged the moot court sessions for Jim Ward, continues practice in Washington DC. The Baker & Hostetler partner is general counsel for the Society of Professional Journalists. His clients have ranged from the *New York Times* to an editor for Breitbart, Inc. Lee Levine, also a key contributor to the national briefs, is a partner in Washington DC–based Levine Sullivan Koch & Schultz. From 1989 through 2015 he taught a "Free Press Seminar" at Georgetown University Law School. Each year one of the two-hour weekly sessions was devoted to the *Press-Enterprise* cases. Brian Harvey, the young Baker & Hostetler lawyer whose journey to the Library of Congress produced evidence that voir dire had been open to the public in Jolly Old England, practices law in Washington DC, specializing in arbitration and mediation. Adrienne Wieand (now Adrienne Danforth), whose Library of Congress excavation proved that preliminary hearings in the United States had been open to the public as early as 1807, became an adult literacy instructor and curriculum developer at the Washington Literacy Council in Washington DC.

Tim Hays shielded his eyes from the glare of publicity, but there was no way he could avoid the afterglow of the *Press-Enterprise* rulings. In 1985, following the 9-0 decision in *Press-Enterprise I*, the newspaper won the Agness Underwood Award for its support for open government and First Amendment rights. It also received the Edward Willis Scripps Award for Service to the First Amendment. A year later, the Associated Press Managing Editors Association gave the paper its Freedom of Information Award. Hays and Opotowsky helped found the California First Amendment Coalition in 1987. Among the first publishers to sign on, Hays persuaded many others to join. He later contributed more than his name: his money.[25]

Hays died in St. Louis, Missouri, on October 14, 2011. He was ninety-four. The man who inherited a newspaper, hired Norman Cherniss, won a Pulitzer, and stuck with Jim Ward, usually deferred to others—or shoved them on stage—whenever the spotlight switched on. But there was at least one time when Hays had no choice but to talk to a reporter and speak to his readers. It was June 30, 1986; Cherniss was dead, and the U.S. Supreme Court had handed the *Press-Enterprise* its second First Amendment victory in just thirty months. Twenty-two paragraphs into the next day's story, Hays briefly explained why the *Press-Enterprise* had taken up the battle. But his brevity did not conceal how strongly the newspaper reflected the character and values of the man who owned it. "We went to considerable effort and expense not only to protect our own rights and those of other newspapers but because of our belief that openness is the most important characteristic of free government. . . . That openness may be more important in the courts than anywhere else."[26]

ACKNOWLEDGMENTS

My debt to Jim Ward, the Riverside lawyer who argued both cases before the U.S. Supreme Court, cannot be repaid. He demonstrated the patience of the judge he later became as I asked, re-asked, and re-re-asked questions designed to trace the path he took to the Supreme Court and what he did once he got there. I am also indebted to Jim Ward the amateur historian, who compiled thick binders on both cases and entrusted them—along with his unpublished memoir—to me. Mel Opotowsky, a longtime senior editor at the *Press-Enterprise* and the paper's point man in preparing the Supreme Court brief for *Press-Enterprise II*, was also indispensable to this project. Like Ward, he was there. He knew the First Amendment issues as well as, sometimes even better than, the lawyers.

John Boyd and Sharon Waters, who worked for Ward at Thompson & Colegate, were genuinely excited about the book and more than generous with their time, ideas, and suggestions. I am doubly indebted to Waters, now a judge, for planting the seed of this book during a chance visit to her courtroom in May 2014.

Bruce Sanford, the Washington DC First Amendment lawyer with Baker & Hostetler, was the lead writer on both national friend-of-the-court briefs in support of the *Press-Enterprise*. I benefited immeasurably from the time he spent explaining the *Press-Enterprise* cases and placing them in proper historic perspective. Lee Levine, also at Baker & Hostetler in those days, worked on and signed the two national briefs. Lee was one of the most enthusiastic supporters of this project and helped me immensely. Brian Harvey and Adrienne Wieand (now Danforth), young Baker & Hostetler associates back in the 1980s, each struck gold in the musty stacks of the Library of Congress and told me their stories.

My search to understand the legacy of the *Press-Enterprise* cases led to Steven Zansberg, a Denver-based First Amendment lawyer who successfully opposed closed jury selection in the trial of the Aurora theater shooter. Zansberg sent me the trial judge's opinion that demonstrated why, three-plus decades later, the *Press-Enterprise* rulings remain so relevant.

I am grateful to Alan Madans, who clerked for Justice Harry Blackmun in the 1980s. Madans explained the critical role of Supreme Court clerks and helped me decipher the handwriting of his former boss. I also received decoding assistance from Jeremy Bernstein, my brother the lawyer. Our early Sunday conversations were not only helpful but fun. Robert Bernius, the First Amendment lawyer who took *Gannett v. DePasquale* through the New York courts and up to the U.S. Supreme Court, was a passionate and knowledgeable voice from the trenches and a great storyteller, too.

My debt of gratitude extends to California lawyers. In Riverside County Robert Spitzer, who prosecuted Albert Greenwood Brown Jr., spent hours discussing the case that began with the brutal rape and murder of Susan Louise Jordan. Joseph Peter Myers, the court-appointed attorney who defended Brown, was equally thorough as we discussed the case he almost didn't take. Patrick Magers, who prosecuted Robert Diaz, explained with dramatic clarity how a science had to be "invented" in order to bring this serial-killer nurse to trial. San Diego lawyers Hal Fuson and Ed McIntyre, court-access crusaders for Copley Press, explained how widespread these California courtroom closures were and the times in which they occurred: when newspapers spent money to fight for a principle. University of Southern California journalism professor Jonathan Kotler alerted me to the strict U.S. Supreme Court rules that, if violated, could sink a case before justices ever heard it. Donald Grant, one of Jim Ward's partners at Thompson & Colegate, helped me understand what made Ward such a successful courtroom lawyer and took me behind the scenes of the law firm as the *Press-Enterprise* cases wended their way upward. Charlie Field, a lawyer, judge, and tennis partner of the *Press-Enterprise* owner, painted a revealing portrait of the enigmatic Tim Hays. Jane Carney, a Riverside lawyer and community leader, knew Hays and Jim Ward well and helped me better understand both men and their relationship with one another. Katherine Lind, the former assistant Riverside County counsel, described that office in her characteristic plain-speaking manner and made me appreciate the drive and desire of the two lawyers who argued against the *Press-Enterprise* at the U.S. Supreme Court. Longtime Riverside County DA Grover Trask, an unlikely, if not always consistent, *Press-Enterprise* ally, explained how his commitment to open courtrooms was translated into office policy.

This book benefits beyond measure from the support and careful critiques of former *Press-Enterprise* colleagues. Jim Bettinger read the manuscript with his customary thoroughness and insight. Joel Blain's disarming eloquence added rich texture to this book. Chris (Packrat) Bowman provided stellar court coverage and saved his clips, many of which form the backbone of this account. Ron Gonzales, also a court reporter, supplied vivid impressions of key figures in the Brown and Diaz cases; his trial coverage made complex issues easy to understand. Bob LaBarre, a gumshoe reporter, provided a big-picture perspective and steered me away from potential potholes. Marcia McQuern rose from reporter to editor and publisher of the *Press-Enterprise*; her insights and recollections, including a story-killing episode recounted in these pages, added essential texture to the story. Jim Richardson, who covered the courts as death penalty cases piled up in California, pretty much invented the *Press-Enterprise*'s court beat; his ideas and suggestions were as precise as they were priceless. Tom Willman, a gifted reporter and, later, chief editorial writer, proved to be a helpful historian and astute skeptic who helped me maintain my focus. Tom Hays, Tim's son and a reporter for the Associated Press, assured me I was not nuts to take on this project and has been supportive at every turn. Thanks to Adriana Wilson, who sent me a copy of the late George Ringwald's unpublished history of the *Press-Enterprise*; to the family of the late Judge John Barnard for providing me with copies of newspaper clippings; and to the Southern California News Group for giving me access to *Press-Enterprise* photography archives. Thanks also to Carol Ritter, the Gannett reporter who described how she was booted out of the preliminary hearing in the case that led to *Gannett v. DePasquale*. And much gratitude to Tom Hunter, who described his experience during the closed-to-the-public jury selection in the murder trial of Albert Greenwood Brown Jr.

Thanks to Dr. Paulette Brown-Hinds, my Riverside friend who told me exactly what I didn't want to hear: write an outline; UC Riverside professor Freya Schiwy, who helped me navigate the early path to publication; Marita Ford, public information officer for Riverside County Superior Court, and Charlene Nelson, executive director of the Riverside County Bar Association, for assisting my research; John N. Jacob, archivist and special collections librarian, Washington and Lee University School of Law, for his above-and-beyond help: putting Justice Lewis Powell's *Press-Enterprise I* and *II* files online and providing a key illustration for this book; Bruce Kirby, reference librarian, and Karen King, freelance researcher, for their invaluable help at the Library of Congress; Fred Schilling, Office of the Curator, Supreme Court of the United States, for providing a photograph of the Burger court; Annie Stone, Supreme Court public information specialist, for providing me with a copy of the court's rules; Whitney A. Brown, editor-in-chief, *UCLA Law Review*, who instantly sent me an important article; Dave Cherniss for helping me learn more about his uncle, Norman Cherniss; the helpful personnel at UC Riverside's Tomas Rivera Library and the Riverside County Law Library; my Oregon friend Ron Muggerud, who asked, "But who's gonna read it?"—a question I taped to a music stand and kept in plain view as I wrote.

I thank the author Jonathan Eig for his generosity, encouragement, and advice; Gary Aagaard, a longtime friend and gifted painter, for ideas and concepts that only an artist of his caliber could conjure; Mark Reikes and Dr. Andrew Reikes for talking to me about their mother, Joyce, who argued against the *Press-Enterprise* at the U.S. Supreme Court; Yolanda DeLeon and Phyllis Crabtree, who occupied unique perches in the *Press-Enterprise* newsroom. Deepest gratitude to Alicia

Christensen of the University of Nebraska Press, who agreed to critique my book proposal and ended up passing it on to a fellow editor, Bridget Barry. The staff of the press, especially Barry and editorial assistant Emily Wendell, along with project editor Sara Springsteen and freelance copy editor Jane Curran, have been unstintingly helpful, supportive, and responsive at every stage of this project.

Finally, an entirely inadequate thank you to Candia, my wife, best pal, and voice of reason, who told me straight up that spending three-plus years writing a "term paper" was the last thing any sane person would do upon retirement. But she backed me, listened patiently, and gave me exceptionally good advice at the most critical stages. In return, I promised I would never do this again.

NOTES

Prologue

1. Woodward and Armstrong, *Brethren*, 156.
2. Woodward and Armstrong, *Brethren*, 160.
3. The Bill of Rights containing the first ten amendments to the U.S. Constitution was ratified by Congress on December 15, 1791.

1. "They Can't Do That, Can They?"

1. Dan Bernstein, Terry Colvin, Iris Hayward, Holly Kurtz, Carla Lazzareschi, and James Richardson, "Deputy, Robber Killed after Norco Bank Holdup," *Press-Enterprise*, May 10, 1980. Unless otherwise specified, accounts of the May 9, 1980, Norco bank robbery are drawn from *Press-Enterprise* articles.
2. Maura Dolan, "Ex-Chief Justice Rose Bird Dies of Cancer at 63," *Los Angeles Times*, December 5, 1999. Dolan states, "Bird lost a retention election in 1986 largely because she had voted to overturn every death penalty case she reviewed." Uelmen, in his review of death penalty judgments, reports: "From 1979 through 1986, the Supreme Court of California reviewed sixty-four judgments of death. Five of them, or 7.8 percent, were affirmed. From 1987 through March of 1989, the Supreme Court of California reviewed seventy-one judgments of death. Fifty-one of them, or 71.8 percent, were affirmed. . . . The revolution which demarcates this dramatic shift was the retention election of November 1986" (Uelmen, "Review of the Death Penalty," 237, 238).
3. Hovey's death sentence was overturned by the U.S. Ninth District Court of Appeals in 2006.
4. Hovey v. Superior Court of Alameda County, 28 Cal.3d 1 (1980). *Hovey* addressed the challenge of achieving "jury neutrality"—a jury "drawn from a pool which reasonably mirrors the diversity of experiences and relevant viewpoints of those persons in the community who can fairly

and impartially try the case." It included a thoughtful and thorough analysis of various studies about juror behavior, attitudes, demographics, and how jurors evaluate evidence.

5. Dr. Craig Haney, an assistant professor of psychology at UC Santa Cruz, conducted the 1979 study in which sixty-seven subjects were randomly divided into two groups and watched a video of a simulated jury selection in a death penalty case. Both groups were asked to imagine themselves to be "prospective jurors in this very case." One group saw the full two-hour video, including thirty minutes of death qualification. The "control" group saw the same videotape with the death-qualifying segment deleted.

6. *Hovey v. Superior Court*.

7. The Bird court's *Hovey* ruling was not the first to raise questions about juror prejudice in death penalty cases. The U.S. Supreme Court, in Witherspoon v. Illinois, 391 U.S. 510 (1968), reversed a jury-imposed death sentence, holding, "If the State had excluded only those prospective jurors who stated in advance of trial that they would not *even consider* returning a verdict of death, it could argue that the resulting jury was simply 'neutral' with respect to penalty. But when it swept from the jury all who expressed conscientious or religious scruples against capital punishment and all who opposed it in principle, the State crossed the line of neutrality. In its quest for a jury capable of imposing the death penalty, the State produced a jury uncommonly willing to condemn a man to die" (emphasis added). Some death penalty scholars say the Witherspoon ruling jump-started the successful, if short-lived, drive to end capital punishment in California and the nation in 1972.

8. Brief Amicus Curiae of California Newspaper Publishers Association, No. 82-556 in the Supreme Court of the United States (submitted on behalf of California news organizations and associations in support of *Press-Enterprise* in 1983).

9. James D. Ward, Riverside attorney who argued both *Press-Enterprise* cases before the U.S. Supreme Court, interview with author, October 6, 2014.

10. Ward, interviews with author, February 12, 2015, and March 25, 2015.

11. Less frequently Boyd appeared in court in a futile effort to keep voir dire open.

12. Chris Bowman, "Another Judge Closes Jury Selection Process," *Press-Enterprise*, December 31, 1981. The fifth closure was made by Judge Robert Garst on January 11, 1982 (Bowman, "Jury in Coach's Killing Being Picked in Secret," *Press-Enterprise*, January 12, 1982).

13. Riverside County Sheriff Association, "The Norco Bank Robbery," May 9, 1980, htttp://www.rcdsa.org/norcorobbery/robbery.html.

14. Michele McLellan, "Reign of Terror at Attorney's Home Ends in Shootout, Arrests," *Press-Enterprise*, March 16, 1977.

15. James Bettinger, former *Press-Enterprise* city editor and retired director of Stanford University's John S. Knight Journalism Fellowship program, interview with author, April 7, 2015. (Hennigan's wife, Mary Jane, did not appear to object to having her name printed in the March 16, 1977, story. "I'm over caring about the publicity," she told the *Press-Enterprise*, "and I think people ought to know what goes on in the world.")

16. Mel Opotowsky, former *Press-Enterprise* managing editor and day editor, interview with author, June 30, 2015.

17. Opotowsky, interview with author, June 30, 2015.

18. James Richardson, *Press-Enterprise* court reporter, interview with author, June 9, 2015.

19. Opotowsky, interview with author, June 30, 2015.

20. Edward J. McIntyre, San Diego attorney who represented Copley Press, interview with author, February 9, 2015.

21. Robert LaBarre, "Papers Appeal Ruling on Jury Selection," *Press-Enterprise*, December 4, 1981.

22. Richmond Newspapers, Inc. v. Virginia, 448 U.S. 555 (1980).

2. "You'll Never See Your Daughter Again"

1. Unless otherwise specified, accounts of the Susan Jordan murder are drawn from *Press-Enterprise* articles, the first of which was published on October 29, 1980: "Teen Girl's Body Found in Grove."

2. Chris Bowman, "Library Book Links Victim to Killer, Prosecutor Insists," *Press-Enterprise*, January 6, 1982.

3. Robert Spitzer, Riverside deputy district attorney who prosecuted the case against Albert Greenwood Brown Jr., interview with author, January 26, 2015.

4. Spitzer, interview with author, January 26, 2015.

3. Slamming the Door

1. Chris Bowman, "Judge Innovates to Test Jurors and Avoid Venue Change," *Press-Enterprise*, August, 28, 1981.

2. Bowman, "Judge Innovates to Test Jurors."

3. Bowman, "Judge Innovates to Test Jurors."

4. United States Census, 1980.

5. Bowman, "Judge Innovates to Test Jurors."

6. Press-Enterprise Co. v. Superior Court, 464 U.S. 501 (1984) Syllabus.

7. "In Memoriam, Judge J. William Mortland," *Riverside County Bar Association Bar Bulletin*, July/August 1991.

8. "In Memoriam."

9. Don Grant, retired attorney and former Jim Ward law partner at Thompson & Colegate, interview with author, June 7, 2016.

10. Chris Bowman, "Judge, Miffed with Press, Briefly Rejects Criminal Cases," *Press-Enterprise*, May 29, 1981.

11. Joint Appendix submitted to the U.S. Supreme Court (No. 82-556) by the *Press-Enterprise* and Riverside County includes selected transcripts of the Riverside County Superior Court proceedings, 74.

12. Joint Appendix, No. 82-556, 47.

13. Joint Appendix, No. 82-556, 48.

14. Joint Appendix, No. 82-556, 49.

15. Joint Appendix, No. 82-556, 83–84.

16. Joint Appendix, No. 82-556, 50.

17. Joseph Peter Myers, attorney representing Albert Greenwood Brown Jr., interview with author, January 19, 2015.

18. Myers, interview with author, January 19, 2015.

19. Joint Appendix, No. 82-556, 76.

20. Joint Appendix, No. 82-556, 77–78.

21. Joint Appendix, No. 82-556, 86.

22. Joint Appendix, No. 82-556, 93.

23. Spitzer, interview with author, January 26, 2015.

24. Chris Bowman, "Ex-ACLU Leader Has No Qualms in Asking for Penalty of Death," *Press-Enterprise*, October 17, 1981.

25. Spitzer, interview with author, January 26, 2015.

26. Chris Bowman, "Judge Denies Bid to Oust Rape-Murder Prosecutor," *Press-Enterprise*, October 20, 1981.

27. Joint Appendix, No. 82-556, 82.

28. Unless otherwise specified, this brief section is based on the Tom Hunter interview with the author, June 3, 2015.

29. In 1972 California voters approved Proposition 17, which called for reinstatement of capital punishment.

30. Chris Bowman, "Jury Picked in Teen Murder Case," *Press-Enterprise*, December 16, 1981.

31. Bowman, "Jury Picked."

4. The "Thrill-Killer" Nurse

1. Tim Skrove, "Anonymous Tip Launched Massive, Complex Probe," *Press-Enterprise*, November 29, 1981.

2. Skrove, "Anonymous Tip Launched."

3. Ronnie Smith, "'The Lidocaine Killer': Robert Diaz," *Crime Magazine*, November 22, 2010, http://www.crimemagazine.com/%E2%80%9Clidocaine-killer%E2%80%9D-robert-diaz.

4. Ronnie D. Smith, "Nurse Diaz's Life Full of Many Unusual Twists," *Press-Enterprise*, November 25, 1981.

5. Smith, "Nurse Diaz's life."

6. Patrick Magers, former Riverside County deputy district attorney, interview with author, May 29, 2015. Unless otherwise noted, this interview is the source of the account that follows.

7. The district attorney felt Magers had to be totally isolated from those cases. Otherwise the public defender might declare that the DA had a conflict of interest and insist that the state attorney general take over.

8. Smith, "'Lidocaine Killer.'"

9. Patrick Magers, email to author, October 26, 2016.

10. Dabney based his decision partly on the U.S. Supreme Court's ruling in Gannett v. DePasquale, 443 U.S. 368 (1979), which upheld the closure of a pretrial hearing, and partly on a section of the California Penal Code that been amended just months earlier. Both are discussed in later chapters.

11. Joint Appendix submitted to the U.S. Supreme Court (No. 84-1560) by the *Press-Enterprise* and Riverside County includes selected transcripts of the Riverside County Superior Court proceedings, 23a.

5. The Hays-Cherniss Newspaper

1. Ward, interview with author, February 12, 2015; Appendix, Press-Enterprise Petition for Writ of Certiorari, No. 82-556 in the Supreme Court of the United States.

2. Press-Enterprise Petition for Writ of Certiorari, No. 82-556.

3. Laura A. Kiernan and Phil McCombs, "Hinckley Jurors Had Relatives in Mental Hospitals," *Washington Post*, June 24, 1982.

4. Marcia McQuern, who later became editor and publisher of the *Press-Enterprise*, interview with author, April 23, 2015; Mellon, *Howard H.* [*sic*] *(Tim) Hays*, 95. (This oral history project includes interviews with McQuern and Hays's longtime secretary, Jean Wingard. The title incorrectly includes a period after Hays's middle initial.)

5. Mellon, *Howard H. (Tim) Hays*, 96.

6. Mellon, *Howard H. (Tim) Hays*, 95.

7. Mellon, *Howard H. (Tim) Hays*, 95.

8. Mellon, *Howard H. (Tim) Hays*, 95.

9. George Ringwald, "Unpublished History of the *Press-Enterprise*." Ringwald's stories exposing corrupt conservators who were bilking Native Americans helped the newspaper win a Pulitzer Prize in 1968.

10. "Riverside Publisher Succumbs at 85," *Desert Sun*, January 6, 1969.

11. Ringwald, "Unpublished History."

12. Joel Blain, former *Press-Enterprise* editorial page editor, interview with author, June 27, 2016.

13. Ringwald, "Unpublished History."

14. Blain, interview with author, June 27, 2016.

15. Ringwald, "Unpublished History."

16. Charlie Field, former judge, *Press-Enterprise* board member, and Tim Hays's longtime friend and tennis partner, interview with author, April 21, 2016.

17. Bruce Sanford, partner in Washington DC law firm Baker & Hostetler and lead writer on both national amicus briefs in support of the *Press-Enterprise*, described Hays's publishing connections in an interview with the author, December 15, 2014. Copies of 1980s Buffet-Hays correspondence were provided to the author by a source wishing to remain anonymous.

18. Lecturers included retired *Washington Post* executive editor Ben Bradlee; Gene Roberts, former managing editor of the *New York Times*; W. Thomas Johnson, president of Cable News Network; and *Washington Post* columnist George F. Will.

19. Whitley Austin, *Salinas (KS) Journal*, quoted by Tom Hays in eulogy to his father, Howard H Hays Jr., who died in 2011. Hays delivered the eulogy on February 11, 2012, at the University of California, Riverside.

20. Mellon, *Howard H. (Tim) Hays*, 139.

21. Tom Hays, eulogy, February 11, 2012.

22. Patterson retired from the *Press-Enterprise* in 1974 but continued to write a weekly local history column. His book *A Colony for California*, published in 1971, chronicles Riverside's first one hundred years.

23. Ringwald, "Unpublished History."

24. Bettinger, interview with author, April 7, 2015.

25. Ringwald, "Unpublished History."

26. Mellon, *Howard H. (Tim) Hays*, 96.

27. Joel Blain, "Tim Hays, Editor: He and His Paper Were One," *Press-Enterprise*, August 3, 1997.

28. Copy of letter provided to the author by a source who requested anonymity.

29. "Digging by the Riverside," *Newsweek*, September 12, 1966.

30. Ringwald, "Unpublished History."

31. Ringwald, "Unpublished History."

32. Blain, interview with author, June 27, 2016.

33. Bettinger, interview with author, April 7, 2015; Blain, interview with author, June 27, 2016; *Press-Enterprise* obituary, October 5, 1984.

34. Blain, interview with author, June 27, 2016.

35. Phyllis Crabtree, former secretary to Norman Cherniss, interview with author, June 16, 2016.

36. Bettinger, email to author, April 25, 2017.

37. Yolanda DeLeon, former *Press-Enterprise* newsroom administrator, interview with author, June 16, 2016.

38. Crabtree, interview with author, June 16, 2016.

39. DeLeon, interview with author, June 16, 2016.

40. "Cherniss Championed Responsible Journalism as Well as Free Press," *Press-Enterprise*, October 5, 1984.

41. Blain, interview with author, June 27, 2016.

42. Landau wrote to *Press-Enterprise* managing editor Mel Opotowsky in February 1983 after the U.S. Supreme Court agreed to hear the Albert Brown closed voir dire case.

43. Jane Carney, Riverside lawyer, community leader, and friend of Hays and Cherniss, interview with author, May 18, 2015.

6. "They Won't Laugh at You Now"

1. Graetz and Greenhouse, *Burger Court*, 9.

2. Ward, interview with author, March 25, 2015.

3. James Ward Log & Binder, *Press-Enterprise I*, October 1983.

4. Grant, interview with author, June 7, 2016.

5. Petition for Writ of Certiorari, No. 82-556.

6. Perhaps because the *Press-Enterprise* appeal arose from a death penalty case, it was not clear whether the newspaper sought open voir dire in all criminal trials until Chief Justice Warren Burger appeared to steer Ward toward that position during oral argument.

7. Brief Amicus Curiae of California Newspaper Publishers Association, No. 82-556.

8. Alan Madans, law clerk for Justice Harry Blackmun, 1982–83, interview with author, December 9, 2016.

9. Justices Harry Blackmun, William Brennan, Thurgood Marshall, and Byron White donated their papers to the U.S. Library of Congress. Justice Lewis Powell donated his papers to Washington and Lee University. Some papers, including the *Press-Enterprise* cases, are cataloged by case or docket numbers. The author has relied on and cited these papers in this book. The papers of Chief Justice Warren Burger, John Paul Stevens,

and Sandra Day O'Connor were not open to the public at this writing. Justice and later Chief Justice William Rehnquist donated his papers to Stanford University. In November 2008, Rehnquist papers from 1947 to 1974 (including his first three terms on the Supreme Court) were made available to researchers. But the rest of his papers, which may include material pertaining to the *Press-Enterprise* cases, remain closed, said Stanford, "during the lifetime of any member of the Supreme Court who served with William H. Rehnquist." At this writing Justices Stevens and O'Connor are living.

10. Justice Powell's papers, donated to Washington and Lee University, http://law2.wlu.edu/deptimages/powell%20archives/82-556_Press -Enterprise_SuperiorCourtCalifornia.pdf. Smalley's preliminary memorandum refers to Gannett v. DePasquale, 443 U.S. 368 (1979), discussed in detail in chapter 8.

11. Powell, Washington and Lee, 82-556.

12. Powell, Washington and Lee, 82-556.

13. Justice Blackmun's papers, donated to Library of Congress, Docket 82-556.

14. Brief in Opposition to Petition for Writ of Certiorari, No. 82-556 in the Supreme Court of the United States.

15. Richmond Newspapers, Inc. v. Virginia, 448 U.S. 555 (1980) and the standards for closure discussed in chapter 8.

16. Blackmun, Library of Congress, 82-556; Madans, interview with author, December 9, 2016.

17. Ward Log, *Press-Enterprise I*, 1983.

18. Powell, Washington and Lee, 82-556.

19. Powell, Washington and Lee, 82-556.

20. Ward Log, *Press-Enterprise I*, 1983.

7. "Mr. Everything"

1. Ward Log, *Press-Enterprise I*, 1983.

2. Ward, interview with author, February 12, 2015.

3. Bruce Sanford, First Amendment lawyer with Baker & Hostetler in Washington DC and lead writer of national amicus briefs in support of the *Press-Enterprise*, interview with author, December 15, 2014.

4. McIntyre, interview with author, January 22, 2016.

5. McIntyre, interview with author, January 22, 2016.

6. Carney, interview with author, May 18, 2015.

7. "Not a Memoir," an unpublished memoir written by James D. Ward, covering the first twenty-five years of his life.

8. Ward, interview with author, May 8, 2015.

9. Ward, interview with author, May 8, 2015.

10. Ward, "Not a Memoir."

11. Ward, interview with author, May 8, 2015.

12. Ward, interview with author, April 25, 2016.

13. Ward, interview with author, April 25, 2016.

14. Ward, "Not A Memoir"; extemporaneous speaking result confirmed by National Speech and Debate Association (formerly National Forensic League) in email to author, June 22, 2016.

15. Ward, interview with author, April 25, 2016.

16. Grant, interview with author, June 7, 2016.

17. Ward, "Not a Memoir."

18. In a March 23, 2017, email to author, Ward wrote that he enlisted to avoid the draft. He served six months on active duty and six years as a reservist, including annual summer camps.

19. Ward, "Not a Memoir."

20. Ward, interview with author, February 12, 2015.

21. Field, interview with author, April 21, 2016.

22. Ward, interview with author, June 30, 2016.

23. Ward, interview with author, June 30, 2016.

24. Field, interview with author, April 21, 2016.

8. The Battleground

1. The First and Sixth Amendments were included in the Bill of Rights, the first ten amendments to the Constitution. The Bill of Rights was ratified by the states and became part of the Constitution on December 15, 1791.

2. The Fourteenth Amendment, which grew out of the Civil War and granted citizenship to "all persons born or naturalized in the United States"—including former slaves—was ratified on July 28, 1868.

3. Branzburg v. Hayes, 408 U.S. 665 (1972).

4. Zurcher v. Stanford Daily, 436 U.S. 547 (1978).

5. Levine and Wermiel, *Progeny*, 185; Herbert v. Lando, 441 U.S. 15 (1979).

6. Ward, interview with author, February 12, 2015.

7. Neff, *Wrong Man*, 74.

8. Neff, *Wrong Man*, 82. (Many believe the crime inspired *The Fugitive*, a popular TV series and later a movie with the same title. But the writer who created the concept for the TV show denied he was influenced by the Sheppard case [235].)

9. Neff, *Wrong Man*, 56.

10. Neff, *Wrong Man*, 84.

11. Neff, *Wrong Man*, 85.

12. Neff, *Wrong Man*, 100.

13. Neff, *Wrong Man*, 101.

14. Neff, *Wrong Man*, 118–19.

15. Neff, *Wrong Man*, 124–25, 127.

16. Neff, *Wrong Man*, 120.

17. Neff, *Wrong Man*, 123; Sheppard v. Maxwell, 384 U.S. 333 (1966).

18. Neff, *Wrong Man*, 124.

19. The Cleveland Memory Project, Sheppard v. Maxwell (1966-490), http://www.clevelandmemory.org/legallandmarks/sheppard/index.html.

20. Neff, *Wrong Man*, 132.

21. Neff, *Wrong Man*, 230.

22. "Maxwell" was E. L. Maxwell, warden of the Ohio Penitentiary.

23. Neff, *Wrong Man*, 243.

24. Sheppard v. Maxwell, 384 U.S. 333 (1966).

25. *Sheppard v. Maxwell.*

26. Nebraska Press Association v. Stuart, 427 U.S. 539 (1976).

27. Margaret Reist, "38 Years Later, Simants Murder Case Still Raises Tough Questions," *Lincoln Journal Star*, October 21, 2013.

28. Reist, "38 Years Later."

29. *Nebraska Press Association v. Stuart.*

30. Reist, "38 Years Later." (Simants was convicted and sentenced to die, but he was found innocent by reason of insanity in a second trial.)

31. *Nebraska Press Association v. Stuart.* Unless otherwise specified, further descriptions and quotations in the *Nebraska* case are taken from the Supreme Court's ruling.

32. Gannett Co. v. DePasquale, 43 N.Y.2d 370, 372 N.E.2d 544 (1977), New York Court of Appeals ruling.

33. Gannett v. DePasquale, 443 U.S. 368 (1979).

34. Carol Ritter, former reporter for Gannett newspapers, interview with author, May 11, 2015.

35. Ritter, interview with author, May 11, 2015.

36. Robert Bernius, attorney who represented Gannett, interview with author, May 5, 2015.

37. Gannett Co., Inc. v. Hon. Daniel A. DePasquale, Brief of Petitioner, No. 77-1301 in the Supreme Court of the United States, Petition for Writ of Certiorari, Robert Bernius author.

38. *Gannett*, Brief of Petitioner.

39. Gannett Co. v. De Pasquale, 43 N.Y.2d 370, New York Court of Appeals (1977).

40. Lee Levine, a former Baker & Hostetler associate who played a key role in preparing the national briefs in support of both *Press-Enterprise* cases,

interview with author, February 23, 2015. Levine is a founding partner of Levine Sullivan Koch & Schultz law firm.

41. Sanford, interview with author, March 19, 2015.
42. Levine, interview with author, January 19, 2017.
43. *New York Times* obituary, April 19, 2013; Sanford, interview with author, March 19, 2015.
44. Sanford, interview with author, March 19, 2015.
45. Sanford, interview with author, March 19, 2015.
46. Levine, interview with author, February 23, 2015.
47. Robert Bernius, email to author, March 15, 2017. Gannett had fought and won other New York closure cases and, as a chain with more than eighty newspapers, "was seeing the closure issue a lot more than other media outlets."
48. Bernius, interview with author, May 5, 2015.
49. American Civil Liberties Union, "Gannet [*sic*] Co. v. DePasquale," ProCon.org, updated January 21, 2010, https://aclu.procon.org/view .additional-resource.php?resourceID=003325; Bernius, interview with author, May 5, 2015.
50. Bender, "Greatest First Amendment Victory."
51. Schwartz, *Ascent of Pragmatism*, 167.
52. *Gannett*, Brief of Petitioner; "In Seneca County, New York, where this case originated, 100 percent of all felony dispositions in 1976, 1975 and the latter half of 1974 took place without a trial."
53. Schwartz, *Ascent of Pragmatism*, 168.
54. Schwartz, *Ascent of Pragmatism*, 168.
55. "Secret Trials," *Washington Post*, July 3, 1979.
56. Anthony Lewis, "Decision in the Dark," *New York Times*, July 5, 1979.
57. Morton Mintz, "Brennan Assails Media Criticism of Court Decisions," *Washington Post*, October 18, 1979. *Herbert v. Lando* is discussed earlier in this chapter.
58. Morton Mintz, "Split Court Rules Criminal Trials May Be Closed," *Washington Post*, July 3, 1979.
59. Saundra Saperstein, "Judge Shuts Maryland Pretrial Hearing; Controversial Supreme Court Ruling Invoked," *Washington Post*, July 19, 1979.
60. Eric Newhouse, "Domestic News," Associated Press, September 26, 1979.
61. "Burger Suggests Some Judges Err in Closing Trials," *New York Times*, August 9, 1979.
62. Linda Greenhouse, "Stevens Says Closed Trials May Justify New Laws," *New York Times*, September 9, 1979.
63. "Appeal Court Could Clarify Justices' Stand on Closing Courts," *New York Times*, September 4, 1979.

64. Linda Greenhouse, "Powell Says Court Has No Hostility toward Press," *New York Times*, August 14, 1979.

65. Bender, "Greatest First Amendment Victory," 2009.

66. Levine, interview with author, February 23, 2015.

67. Richmond Newspapers, Inc. v. Virginia, 448 U.S. 555 (1980).

68. Levine, interview with author, February 23, 2015.

69. Except for concurring with the majority that the issue was not moot.

70. "Opening Those Closed Doors," *Washington Post*, July 3, 1980.

71. "Secrecy Is Our Enemy," *Los Angeles Times*, July 3, 1980.

72. "Wiping the Graffiti of the Courtroom," *New York Times*, July 3, 1980.

73. "A Landmark and a Watershed," *Press-Enterprise*, July 6, 1980.

74. Globe Newspaper Co. v. Superior Court 102 S.Ct. 2613 (1982).

9. Building the Case

1. Rules of the United States Supreme Court, effective June 1980 (not revised again until 1989). The briefs were essentially thin, bound 61/8 x 91/4-inch booklets.

2. Rules of the United States Supreme Court, 34.6.

3. Mary Wood, "Scalia Defends Originalism as Best Methodology for Judging Law," News & Media, University of Virginia School of Law, April 20, 2010, https://content.law.virginia.edu/news/2010_spr/scalia.htm.

4. Wood, "Scalia Defends Originalism."

5. Sanford, interview with author, December 15, 2014.

6. Jonathan Kotler, associate professor of journalism, usc Annenberg School for Communication and Journalism, Los Angeles, interview with author, December 17, 2015. From Rule 33.7 of the U.S. Supreme Court (1980): "The Clerk shall not accept for filing any document presented in a form not in compliance with this Rule, but shall return it indicating to the defaulting party wherein he has failed to comply." The court will accept a "promptly" corrected version, but "[i]f the Court shall find that the provisions of this Rule have not been adhered to, it may impose . . . appropriate sanctions including but not limited to dismissal of the action."

7. Crosby, Heafey, Roach & May.

8. Levine, interview with author, January 19, 2017.

9. Levine, interview with author, January 19, 2017.

10. John Boyd, Thompson & Colegate associate lawyer and lead writer on the newspaper's brief to the U.S. Supreme Court in *Press-Enterprise I*, interview with author, April 16, 2015.

11. Ward, interview with author, October 6, 2014.

12. Brief for Petitioner on the Merits, No. 82-556 in the Supreme Court of the United States.
13. United States v. Brooklier, 685 F.2d 1162 (9th Cir.1982).
14. "Judicial Profile: Matters of the Heart," desertbar.com, June 26, 2009 (site has been modified or deleted).
15. "Matters of the Heart."
16. John Boyd, email to author, April 19, 2017.
17. Boyd, interview with author, April 16, 2015.
18. Boyd, interview with author, April 16, 2015.
19. Boyd, interview with author, April 16, 2015.
20. Katherine Lind, former assistant Riverside County counsel, interview with author, November 2, 2016.
21. Brief of Respondent on the Merits, No. 82-556 in the Supreme Court of the United States.
22. Joint Appendix, *Press-Enterprise I* (No. 82-556); 106 (Myers) and 121 (Mortland).
23. Reply Brief of Petitioner, No. 82-556 in the Supreme Court of the United States.
24. Ward Log, *Press-Enterprise I*, 1983.
25. Cherniss's undated memo was stamped by Thompson & Colegate law firm on April 22, 1983.
26. Cherniss memo.
27. Brief of Amici Curiae in Support of Petitioner, Filed on Behalf of *USA Today* and *Oakland Tribune*, etc., No. 82-556 in the Supreme Court of the United States.
28. *Hovey* was the California version of *Gannett v. DePasquale*. In *Gannett*, just one sentence—"[W]e hold that members of the public have no constitutional right under the Sixth and Fourteenth Amendments to attend criminal trials"—led to the closure of hundreds of courtrooms. With *Hovey*, it took just one word—"sequestration"—to trigger secret voir dire in capital cases.
29. Ward, interview with author, March 25, 2015; Epstein did not respond to interview requests.
30. John Carne, email to author, January 1, 2016. A single Peoples Temple defendant, Larry Layton, was tried three times between 1981 and 1986.
31. Brief Amici Curiae of the Society of Professional Journalists, Sigma Delta Chi, etc., No. 82-556 in the Supreme Court of the United States.
32. Sanford, interview with author, March 19, 2015.
33. Sanford, interview with author, March 19, 2015.
34. Levine, interview with author, February 2, 2015.

35. The national brief said *Brooklier* "applied the teachings" of the Supreme Court's *Globe* ruling, which held that trials cannot exclude the press or public unless closure "is necessitated by a compelling governmental interest, and is narrowly tailored to serve that interest."

36. Levine, interview with author, February 2, 2015.

37. Levine, interview with author, February 23, 2015.

38. Sanford, interview with author, March 9, 2015.

39. Brian Harvey, former Baker & Hostetler associate attorney, interview with author, April 29, 2015.

40. Harvey, interview with author, April 29, 2015.

41. Harvey, interview with author, April 29, 2015.

42. Harvey, interview with author, April 29, 2015.

43. Brief of Amicus Curiae, The State of California, No. 82-556 in the Supreme Court of the United States.

44. Brief Amicus Curiae of the California State Public Defender, No. 82-556 in the Supreme Court of the United States.

45. Brief Amicus Curiae in Support of Respondent, No. 82-556 in the Supreme Court of the United States.

46. In the May 1983 hearing, wrote Myers, "Respondent Court" said voir dire was closed due to a "substantial probability of irreparable harm" to the rights of Brown and the jurors. But the U.S. Supreme Court did not have a record of that hearing.

10. The Diaz Case Advances

1. Chris Bowman, "Detective Tells of Finding Items Tying Defendant to Murdered Girl," *Press-Enterprise*, January 19, 1982. Though the author was unable to find a court order closing the preliminary hearing, Riverside County judge Ernest Lopez issued a January 14, 1981, order sealing the transcript of the Brown preliminary hearing, which occurred on December 15 and 16, 1980.

2. Bettinger, interview with author, April 7, 2015.

3. Levine, interview with author, February 2, 2015. As noted in chapter 8, the *Washington Post* reported that in the twelve months following the *Gannett* ruling, judges across the country closed their courtrooms for all or part of criminal proceedings, including preliminary hearings, 260 times.

4. *FOI/CALIFORNIA: A Quarterly Bulletin on Freedom of Information Issues in California*, Fall 1983: By the fall of 1983, three cases, in addition to the Diaz case, had reached the California Court of Appeal. In San Luis Obispo the *Telegram-Tribune* sued after a municipal court decided that only a "preponderance of evidence" was needed to close a courtroom

in order to protect a defendant's right to a fair trial. The newspaper argued this standard was too weak because "First Amendment values" were in play in preliminary hearings. In San Diego the *Union* sued after a judge wouldn't even allow the newspaper's lawyer into the courtroom to argue against closure of a preliminary hearing. The paper also argued that closure had to be based on "competent evidence," not "unsupported speculation," and that alternatives to shutting out the public and press had to be considered. The third case, brought by the *San Jose Mercury-News*, involved the alleged theft of proprietary data in a computer systems case. The courtroom had been closed after a judge determined that witnesses' reluctance to publicly reveal trade secrets might prejudice the defendant's case. Though there were closures, there was not always consistency. Less than eighteen months after Robert Diaz's secret forty-one-day preliminary hearing, a judge in the San Bernardino County city of Ontario—a mere twenty minutes west of Riverside—denied a defense motion to close the preliminary hearing for Kevin Cooper, accused of the hatchet and knife slayings of four people.

5. Joint Appendix, *Press-Enterprise II*, No. 84-1560, 36a–37a.

6. Grover Trask, former Riverside County district attorney, email to author, October 20, 2016.

7. Trask, email to author, October 20, 2016; Ron Gonzales, "Two Courts Consider Arguments; Diaz Transcripts Remain Sealed," *Press-Enterprise*, October 6, 1983.

8. Declaration of Riverside County Public Defender, by John J. Lee, People of the State of California v. Robert Rubane Diaz, Case No. CR 19889, filed in Riverside County Superior Court, February 8, 1983.

9. "Judge Howard M. Dabney" (undated profile), *Los Angeles Daily Journal*.

10. "Judge Howard M. Dabney."

11. Joint Appendix, *Press-Enterprise II*, No. 84-1560, 27a.

12. Joint Appendix, *Press-Enterprise II*, No. 84-1560, 59a–60a.

13. Declaration of *Press-Enterprise* attorney John Boyd, People of the State of California v. Robert Rubane Diaz, Case No. CR 19889, filed in Riverside County Superior Court, February 7 1983.

14. Joint Appendix, *Press-Enterprise II*, No. 84-1560, 60a–61a.

15. "Appeal to Disclose Transcript of Diaz's Preliminary Hearing Denied," *Press Enterprise*, March 19, 1983.

16. Ron Gonzales, "Diaz Waives Trial by Jury If Judge Barnard Presides," *Press-Enterprise*, October 1, 1983.

17. Supplemental Index of Respondent (No. 84-1560), A-47.

18. Ramon Coronado, "Attorneys Argue in Two Courts for 'Opening' Diaz Trial," *San Bernardino Sun*, October 6, 1983.

19. Gonzales, "Two Courts Consider Arguments."

11. Mr. Ward Goes to Washington

1. Joan Biskupic, Janet Roberts, and John Shiffman, "At America's Court of Last Resort, a Handful of Lawyers Now Dominates the Docket," Reuters Investigates, December 8, 2014, http://www.reuters.com/investigates /special-report/scotus/.

2. Ward Log, *Press-Enterprise I*, 1983.

3. Boyd and Sharon Waters, also a Thompson & Colegate associate who worked for Jim Ward and was the lead writer on the *Press-Enterprise*'s brief to the U.S. Supreme Court in *Press-Enterprise II*, joint interview with author, March 24, 2016.

4. Ward Log, *Press-Enterprise I*, 1983.

5. Sanford, interview with author, December 15, 2014.

6. Waters, interview with author, April 30, 2015.

7. Levine, interview with author, February 2, 2015.

8. Ward Log, *Press-Enterprise I*, 2013.

9. Sanford, interview with author, December 15, 2014.

10. Blackmun, Library of Congress, 82-556, Elizabeth Taylor pool memo.

11. Taylor cited U.S. Supreme Court in Craig v. Harney, 331 US 367 (1947).

12. Powell, Washington and Lee University, 82-556, David Charny bench memo.

13. Powell, Charny.

14. Powell, Charny.

15. Powell, Charny.

12. The Audience of Nine

1. Unless otherwise noted, accounts of the run-up to the oral arguments for *Press-Enterprise I* are based on Jim Ward's 1983 log or other materials collected in his *Press-Enterprise I* binder.

2. Waters, email to author, April 7, 2017.

3. Guide for Counsel in Cases to Be Argued before the Supreme Court of the United States, October Term 2015, https://www.supremecourt.gov /casehand/guideforcounsel.pdf.

4. Rules of the Supreme Court of the United States, 1980, Rule 38.

5. Guide for Counsel.

6. Boyd, interview with author, April 16, 2015.

7. See Henry, "Players and the Play," 20.

8. Graetz and Greenhouse, *Burger Court*, 349.

9. Graetz and Greenhouse, *Burger Court*, 350.

10. Henry, "Players and the Play," 21.

11. Jim Ward speech to the Citizens University Committee, UC Riverside, May 20, 1986.

12. Ward Log, *Press-Enterprise I*, 1983.

13. Henry, "Players and the Play," 22.

14. Henry, "Players and the Play," 22.

15. Woodward and Armstrong, *Brethren*, 49–50.

16. Graetz and Greenhouse, *Burger Court*, 351.

17. King, *Devil in the Grove*, 9.

18. King, *Devil in the Grove*, 216–19.

19. Henry, "Players and the Play," 23.

20. Greenhouse, *Becoming Justice Blackmun*, 123–24.

21. Henry, "Players and the Play," 23.

22. Graetz and Greenhouse, *Burger Court*, 352.

23. Graetz and Greenhouse, *Burger Court*, 353.

24. Henry, "Players and the Play," 23.

25. Henry, "Players and the Play," 24.

26. Graetz and Greenhouse, *Burger Court*, 354.

27. Henry, "Players and the Play," 24.

28. Graetz and Greenhouse, *Burger Court*, 354–55.

29. Henry, "Players and the Play," 25.

30. In June 1968, soon after President Johnson announced he would not seek reelection, Chief Justice Earl Warren, fearing Nixon would win the presidency, submitted his resignation, counting on LBJ to appoint a liberal replacement. Johnson nominated liberal justice Abe Fortas, his longtime friend, whom Johnson had appointed to the U.S. Supreme Court in 1965. But a bipartisan coalition of senators—some conservative, some concerned that Fortas had engaged in unethical conduct—mounted a filibuster that killed the nomination and cleared the way for Richard Nixon to replace Earl Warren with Warren Earl Burger. Fortas's ethical problems culminated with his resignation from the court in 1969.

31. Henry, "Players and the Play," 25.

32. Stevens, *Five Chiefs*, 154–55.

33. Henry, "Players and the Play," 26.

34. Adam Liptak, "As Justices Get Back to Business, Old Pro Reveals Tricks of the Trade," *New York Times*, October 3, 2011.

35. Woodward and Armstrong, *Brethren*, 174.

36. Stevens, *Five Chiefs*, 154–55.

13. "I Will Be Back"

1. Unless otherwise noted, the dialogue below is a transcription of the taped oral argument in Press-Enterprise Co. v. Superior Court, 464 U.S. 501 (1984), October 12, 1983, Oyez, https://www.oyez.org/cases/1983/82-556.
2. Blackmun, Library of Congress, 82-556.
3. In her Pulitzer Prize–winning book *Becoming Justice Blackmun*, Linda Greenhouse wrote that Blackmun's physical descriptions of the lawyers was "rarely flattering." Of one lawyer, Blackmun wrote, "Licks fingers." Sometimes he simply noted "balding" or "hair." Greenhouse also described Blackmun's grading system. Like the physical descriptions, the grades given to Ward and other lawyers in the *Press-Enterprise* cases are found in Blackmun's papers donated to the Library of Congress.
4. Sanford, interview with author, December 15, 2014, said the moot court "justices" had anticipated virtually every question Ward would hear three days later during oral argument.
5. Boyd, interview with author, April 16, 2015.
6. Ward, interview with author, May 8, 2015.
7. Ward, interview with author, May 8, 2015.
8. Pat Alston, "Judge Glenn R. Salter (Profile)," *Los Angeles Daily Journal*, August 3, 2011. Written after Salter became an Orange County Superior Court judge, the profile portrayed him as a "thoughtful" and "punctual" person, "a real decent human being." Others, not quoted in the story and requesting anonymity, said Salter was bright and ambitious, if somewhat imperious. The *Journal* profile traced his career from a staff lawyer in various Orange County agencies to his 2010 appointment to the Orange County bench. Nowhere did it mention that he argued a First Amendment case before the United States Supreme Court. Asked to be interviewed for this book, Salter emailed, "I need to check with those who specialize in ethical matters to be sure I have the authority to talk." He concluded his November 20, 2014, email, "I would caution you, however, that I remember my victories much better than my losses!" Subsequent efforts to contact him were unsuccessful.
9. Blackmun, Library of Congress, 82-556.
10. Blackmun, Library of Congress, 82-556.
11. Ward Log, *Press-Enterprise I*, October 1983.
12. Powell, Washington and Lee, 82-556.

14. "The Presumption of Openness"

1. James Ward Log & Binder, *Press-Enterprise II*, 1986; Ron Gonzales, "Judge Unseals Records in Diaz Murder Case," *Press-Enterprise*, October 15, 1983; story says transcript was 4,239 pages.

2. Rehnquist, *Supreme Court*, 287.

3. Dickson, *Supreme Court in Conference*, 3. (This thick volume does not include either *Press-Enterprise* case.)

4. Rehnquist, *Supreme Court*, 288–89.

5. Rehnquist, *Supreme Court*, 289.

6. Dickson, *Supreme Court in Conference*, 5.

7. Rehnquist, *Supreme Court*, 290. As a new justice, Rehnquist was "surprised and disappointed at how little interplay there was between the various justices" during the conference. "Each would state his view, and a junior justice could express agreement or disagreement . . . but the converse did not apply; a junior justice's views were seldom commented upon. . . . I thought it would be desirable to have more of a round-table discussion of the matter after each of us had expressed our views." But as he rose to number one in seniority, Rehnquist realized that "while my idea is fine in the abstract it probably would not contribute much in practice and at any rate is doomed by the seniority system to which the senior justices adhere" (291).

8. Rehnquist, *Supreme Court*, 10.

9. Blackmun and Powell, Library of Congress and Washington and Lee University, Docket 82-566, contained these "score sheets."

10. In summarizing the conference discussion and voting, the author has used his best interpretation of Powell's and Blackmun's notes. Blackmun's handwritten, heavily abbreviated notes are more difficult to read than Powell's. What could not be deciphered was omitted, hopefully without changing the context.

11. Powell, Washington and Lee, Docket 82-566, handwritten notes on Rehnquist conference remarks.

12. Justice William Brennan's papers, Library of Congress, Docket 82-556. The two-page undated and unsigned statement is identical in format to a document in Brennan's *Press-Enterprise II* papers, Docket 84-1560. In his book *The Ascent of Pragmatism: The Burger Court in Action* Bernard Schwartz quotes from the *Press-Enterprise II* document and describes it as a "conference statement." Did Brennan read these statements at the *Press-Enterprise I* and *II* conferences? It seems so. In *The Supreme Court: How It Was, How It Is* Chief Justice Rehnquist wrote, "[W]e rely entirely on oral discussion for the exposition of views at conference." Brennan, the senior associate justice, "also frequently takes more time than the other associates" if, for no other reason, "he frequently disagrees with me (and also disagreed with Chief Justice Burger) in important constitutional cases" (290).

13. Blackmun, Library of Congress, 82-556, conference notes on O'Connor remarks.

14. Justice Byron White papers, Library of Congress, Docket 82-556.

15. Blackmun, Library of Congress, 82-556, Taylor.

16. Blackmun, Library of Congress, 82-556, Taylor.

17. Brennan papers, Library of Congress, Docket 82-556.

18. Brennan, Library of Congress, 82-556.

19. Press-Enterprise Co. v. Superior Court, 464 U.S. 501 (1984).

20. In a footnote Marshall cited the brief by Brown's lawyer, Joseph Peter Myers. That this brief contained no case citations, yet was the only brief specifically cited in any of the opinions, has irritated *Press-Enterprise* lawyer Jim Ward for decades.

15. A Halt to the "Ominous Progression"?

1. Gene Blake, "Ruling a Victory for Riverside Newspaper," *Los Angeles Times*, January 19, 1984.

2. "Open Trials, Open Jury Selection," *Press-Enterprise*, January 19, 1984.

3. "Justice in Plain Sight," *Los Angeles Times*, January 20, 1984.

4. "Justice in the Open," *New York Times*, January 21, 1984.

5. "Court Opens Up Jury Selection," *San Francisco Chronicle*, January 23, 1984.

6. Linda Greenhouse, "U.S. Justices Sharply Restrict Secrecy in Selection of Juries," *New York Times*, January 19, 1984.

7. "High Court Protects Our Right to Know," *Redlands (CA) Daily Facts*, January 25 1984.

8. Ron Gonzales, "Ruling Limiting Judges' Ability to Close Jury Selection Draws Praise," *Press-Enterprise*, January 19, 1984.

9. Waters, interview with author, April 30, 2015.

10. Ron Gonzales, former *Press-Enterprise* court reporter, interview with author, April 3, 2015. Months passed, and the transcript remained sealed. Frustrated and angry, Norman Cherniss wrote a lengthy editorial—"Too Slow, the Wheels of Justice"—that ended, "Stay tuned. But don't hold your breath." Then a year passed. And well before Mortland finally released the transcript, Norman Cherniss was dead. As for attorneys' fees, it was Riverside County that received a bill. The same day it issued its 9–0 ruling, the Supreme Court ordered "that the petitioner, Press-Enterprise Company, recover from Superior Court of California, Riverside County, Three Thousand Two Hundred Thirty-six Dollars and Twelve Cents for its costs herein expended."

11. Gonzalez, "Ruling Limiting Judges' Ability."

12. Boyd, interview with author, April 16, 2015.

13. Ward Log, *Press-Enterprise I*, October 1983.
14. Sanford, interview with author, December 15, 2014.

16. Smacked Down Again

1. Ward Log, *Press-Enterprise II*, 1986.
2. Ward Log, *Press-Enterprise II*, 1986. Ward wasn't exactly a stranger to the chief justice, either. In the summer of 1981, when he was going from court to court in Riverside County asking judges to conduct jury selection in public, Ward became the first lawyer from Riverside or San Bernardino Counties to win a seat on the State Bar Board of Governors—the body that "reserves authority over all matters pertaining to the State Bar." He described his victory as a "huge political coup" since the district he represented also included neighboring Orange County, which pretty much owned that seat for years. By 1983 Ward had risen to vice president and occasionally socialized with state supreme court justices. On October 5, 1983, a week before he argued the voir dire case in Washington DC, Chief Justice Bird wrote him a short note. "Dear Jim: Thank you for your recent notes and the enclosed photographs. I appreciate you sending me the pictures. They will serve as a pleasant reminder of a very enjoyable evening at your home. It was gracious of you and your wife to have invited me. Sincerely, Rose."
3. Though Barnard released the transcript in October 1983, the court ruled anyway because other judges could be faced with the same issue.
4. Until California Penal Code Section 868 was amended, judges were required to close preliminary hearings at the request of the defendant. This had been California law since the mid-nineteenth century, when the state adopted the Field Code, named for David Dudley Field II, a lawyer and, very briefly, a New York congressman. Automatically closing a preliminary hearing at the defendant's request was rarely enforced. But in January 1982 the California Supreme Court upheld a judge's decision to do just that, ruling in San Jose Mercury News v. Municipal Court, 30 Cal.3d 498, 638 P.2d 655, 179 Cal.Rptr. 772 (1982) that the public and press had no constitutional right to attend a preliminary hearing. At the urging of California news organizations, the legislature passed emergency legislation amending the penal code to require that preliminary hearings be open unless a judge made a "finding" that the closure is "necessary" to protect the rights of the accused.
5. The 1982 ruling by the Ninth Circuit Court of Appeals in *United States v. Brooklier* concerned public access to jury selection. The U.S. Supreme Court set a similarly tough standard in *Press-Enterprise I*.

6. Ron Gonzales, "State Appeals Court Supports Judge in Sealing Transcript of Diaz Hearing," *Press-Enterprise*, January 13, 1984.

7. Ward Log, *Press-Enterprise II*, 1986. A copy of the letter in the scrapbook is accompanied by Ward's handwritten Post-It note: "Norm kept meeting with Rose despite my suggestions that he refrain."

8. "State High Court Agrees to Consider the Public's Right to Attend Hearings," *Press-Enterprise*, March 16, 1984.

9. Ward Log, *Press-Enterprise II*, 1986.

10. Ward Log, *Press-Enterprise II*, 1986. Affixed to the letter, another Ward note: "At last Norm stops & then chides me about it!"

11. Ronnie D. Smith, "Diaz Gets Death Penalty for 12 Murders," *Press-Enterprise*, April 12, 1984. On August 11, 2010, Diaz died of natural causes on California's death row. He was seventy-two.

12. Bob Pratte, "Executive Editor Norman Cherniss Dies at 58," *Press-Enterprise*, October 5, 1984.

13. Pratte, "Executive Editor."

14. "Cherniss Championed," *Press-Enterprise*, October 5, 1984.

15. Pratte, "Executive Editor."

16. Pratte, "Executive Editor."

17. "Cherniss Championed."

18. Mortland had finally done exactly what the Supreme Court instructed him to do. In the court document ordering the release, Mortland listed twenty-two exceptions to the full release of the transcript. They involved the examination of prospective jurors who had "valid privacy interests." Among them: "One prospective juror indicated that her daughter was raped by a black"; "One prospective juror indicated that the husband was arrested and prosecuted for child molestation"; "A prospective juror indicated that he had problems with blacks and mexicans [*sic*]"; "One prospective juror had had to obtain an annulment because her husband already had a wife in Europe"; "One prospective juror's spouse is an alcoholic"; "One prospective juror indicated that her son was a victim of a homosexual rape"; "One prospective juror admitted living with a boyfriend prior to marriage." People of the State of California v. Albert Greenwood Brown, Jr., Case No. CR 18104.

19. Diaz was the "real party of interest" in the case, so the Riverside Superior Court did not get involved at this stage. In a January 6, 2015, interview, Margolin said he could not recall how he became involved, but that it was one of his pro bono cases. He likely did so with the approval of the Riverside County public defender's office.

20. "Supreme Court Urged to 'Keep Courts Open,'" *Press-Enterprise* and wire reports, October 16, 1984.

21. "Supreme Court Urged."

22. "Supreme Court Urged."

23. Two years later, November 4, 1986, Rose Bird, along with Justices Cruz Reynoso and Joseph Grodin, were kicked out of office in a statewide reconfirmation election. California Supreme Court justices face such elections after they are confirmed and at regular intervals thereafter. Bird had voted against every death penalty case (the number varies between 61 and 64) that came before her. She was also viewed by some as "anti-business." "Rose Bird," Ballotpedia, https://ballotpedia.org/Rose _Bird; Brown, "Rise and Fall."

24. Ward Log, *Press-Enterprise II*, 1986.

17. "Expanding the Right of Access"

1. Ron Gonzales, "State Supreme Court Upholds Trial Judge in Closing Hearing," *Press-Enterprise*, January 1, 1985.

2. Rivian Taylor, "Court's Ruling Seen as Victory for Press," *San Diego Union*, January 19, 1984.

3. Boyd, interview with author, April 16, 2015.

4. Petition for Writ of Certiorari, No. 84-1560 in the Supreme Court of the United States.

5. Brief of Amici Curiae in Support of Petition for Writ of Certiorari, No. 84-1560 in the Supreme Court of the United States.

6. Brief of Respondent in Opposition to Petition for Writ of Certiorari, No. 84-1560 in the Supreme Court of the United States.

7. Blackmun, Library of Congress, 84-1560.

8. Powell, Washington and Lee, 84-1560.

9. Nelson wrote that most cases cited by the *Press-Enterprise* petition referred to proceedings that occurred *after* a preliminary hearing or grand jury determined that a defendant should face a trial.

10. The Nelson memo was included in the Blackmun *and* Powell papers, suggesting other justices may have seen it as well.

11. Powell, Washington and Lee, 84-1560.

12. Alan Lecker, "Supreme Court Agrees to Hear Appeal on Closing of Hearings," *Press-Enterprise*, October 16, 1985.

13. Lecker, "Supreme Court Agrees."

14. Lecker, "Supreme Court Agrees."

18. Needle in a Haystack

1. Sanford, interview with author, December 15, 2014; Levine, interview with author, March 27, 2017.

2. But as noted earlier, the national briefs in support of the *Press-Enterprise* cases were remembered and praised decades later by at least one justice—Antonin Scalia—who wasn't even on the Supreme Court when *Press-Enterprise I* and *II* were decided.

3. This occurred before DA Grover Trask took office. In the ensuing months, he took the lead (ahead of the *Press-Enterprise*) to unseal the Diaz transcript, only to reverse course as the Diaz trial neared.

4. Bettinger, interview with author, April 7, 2015.

5. Chris Bowman, former *Press-Enterprise* court reporter, interview with author, January 8, 2015.

6. Robert LaBarre, email to author, March 18, 2017.

7. Waters, interview with author, April 30, 2015.

8. Brief of Petitioner on the Merits, No. 84-1560 in the Supreme Court of the United States.

9. The brief argued the California Supreme Court standard would be unconstitutional because (a) California judges didn't have to consider alternatives to closing preliminary hearings; (b) closure didn't have to be "narrowly tailored and no broader than necessary" (the U.S. Supreme Court's own words); (c) judges didn't have to find that closure would eliminate a threat to a defendant's rights; and (d) judges didn't have to make specific, on-the-record findings that support the closure.

10. Brief of Respondent on the Merits, No. 84-1560 in the Supreme Court of the United States.

11. Johnson v. Superior Court, 15 Cal.3d 248 [S.F. No. 23168. Supreme Court of California. September 19, 1975].

12. Joint Appendix, *Press-Enterprise II*, No. 84-1560. Diaz told Barnard he might have to be sent "hundreds of miles away" and that his "umpteen" witnesses would have to travel that distance to testify (61a).

13. Brief Amici Curiae of American Newspaper Publishers Association, etc., No. 84-1560.

14. DA Ira Reiner dismissed the cases. The two remaining defendants, who spent years in jail, were eventually acquitted in a case that spanned seven years.

15. Gerald Uelmen, "Reiner's McMartin Decision Shows Need for Open Preliminary Hearings," *Los Angeles Herald Examiner*, January 26, 1986.

16. Adrienne Wieand (now Danforth), former associate attorney with Baker & Hostetler, interview with author, January 8, 2015.

17. Levine, interview with author, March 27, 2017.

18. Graetz and Greenhouse, *Rise of the Judicial Right*, 335.

19. Brief Amici Curiae of California News Organizations in Support of Petitioner, No. 84-1560 in the Supreme Court of the United States.

20. "There is something radically, flagrantly wrong in the conduct of most newspapers of the United States," Dudley Field wrote, adding that while Jefferson considered the press "putrid, it has since become putrescence putrefied." He likened newspaper coverage of a recent trial to "cormorants over a carcass." Geis, "Preliminary Hearings," 397.

21. Brief of Real Party in Interest on the Merits, No. 84-1560 in the Supreme Court of the United States.

22. Geis, "Preliminary Hearings."

23. Brief of the American Civil Liberties Union and the American Civil Liberties Union of Southern California as Amici Curiae, No. 84-1560 in the Supreme Court of the United States.

24. Amicus Curiae Brief of State of California in Support of Petitioner, No. 84-1560 in the Supreme Court of the United States.

25. Brief of Amicus Curiae in Support of Petitioner Filed on Behalf of the District Attorney, County of Riverside.

19. "The Soil of Openness"

1. Ward Log, *Press-Enterprise II*, 1986.

2. Grant, interview with author, June 7, 2016.

3. Grant, interview with author, June 7, 2016.

4. Grant, interview with author, June 7, 2016.

5. Grant, interview with author, June 7, 2016.

6. Boyd, interview with author, April 16, 2015. (In his June 7, 2016, interview with the author, Don Grant initially recalled the fee would be $35,000 and later said the $50,000 figure was "vaguely familiar.")

7. Ward, interview with author, February 15, 2015.

8. Grant, interview with author, June 7, 2016.

9. Boyd, interview with author, April 16, 2015.

10. Boyd, interview with author, April 16, 2015.

11. Ward, interview with author, March 27, 2017; Ward, email to author, March 30, 2017.

12. Ward, interview with author, February 15, 2015.

13. Ward, interview with author, March 27, 2017.

14. Ward Log, *Press-Enterprise II*, 1986.

15. Ward Log, *Press-Enterprise II*, 1986.

16. Cheryl Romo, "Commissioner Joyce Manulis Reikes (Profile)," *Los Angeles Daily Journal*, May 27, 1997.

17. Romo, "Commissioner Joyce."

18. Romo, "Commissioner Joyce."

19. Romo, "Commissioner Joyce"; Don Babwin, "No Proof of Dora Kent Decapitated Alive," *Press-Enterprise*, February 3, 1988.

20. Romo, "Commissioner Joyce."

21. Dorothy Honn, longtime attorney in Riverside County counsel's office, interview with author, November 21, 2016.

22. Dr. Andrew Reikes, son of Joyce Reikes, interview with author, November 2016.

23. Reikes, interview with author.

24. Blackmun, Library of Congress, 84-1560, Sklansky.

25. "The Court indicated that 'the presumption of openness may be overcome only by an overriding interest based on findings that closure is essential to preserve higher values and is narrowly tailored to serve that interest.'"

26. Bender, *Greatest First Amendment Victory*.

27. Powell, Washington and Lee, 84-1560.

28. "Bob" is the only Robert (or Bob) listed as a Powell clerk at the time, according to Wikipedia's List of Law Clerks of the Supreme Court of the United States. In a March 3, 2017, email to the author, Robert Allen Long Jr. cited the "confidential relationship between Supreme Court justices and their law clerks" in declining to comment (or confirm that he and "Bob" were one and the same).

29. Powell, memo by "Bob."

30. Waller v. Georgia, 104 S.Ct. 2210 (1984).

20. "Hands over His Face"

1. Ward Log, *Press-Enterprise II*, 1986.

2. Ward Log, *Press-Enterprise II*, 1986.

3. Unless otherwise noted, the dialogue below is a transcription of the taped oral argument in Press-Enterprise Co. v. Superior Court 478 US 1 (1986), February 26, 1986, Oyez, https://www.oyez.org/cases/1985/84-1560.

4. Mel Opotowsky, email to author, April 9, 2017.

5. Powell, Washington and Lee, 84-1560.

6. Blackmun, Library of Congress, 84-1560.

7. Powell, Washington and Lee, 84-1560.

8. Powell, Washington and Lee, 84-1560.

9. Blackmun, Library of Congress, 84-1560.

10. Ward Log, *Press-Enterprise II*, 1986.

11. Ward Log, *Press-Enterprise II*, 1986.
12. Ward Log, *Press-Enterprise II*, 1986.

21. "Safeguard against the Corrupt and Eccentric"

1. These are the author's best interpretations of the justices' handwritten notes, some of which are in "shorthand." Example: "petr" instead of *petitioner*; "hrg" for *hearing*; "alm" for *almost*.
2. Brennan, Library of Congress, Docket 84-1560. In his book *The Ascent of Pragmatism: The Burger Court in Action* Bernard Schwartz describes this undated, untitled, four-page document as a "conference statement" (170).
3. Powell's July 2, 1979, opinion began: "Because of the importance of the public's having accurate information concerning the operation of its criminal justice system, I would hold explicitly that [Gannett's] reporter had an interest protected by the First and Fourteenth Amendments in being present at the pretrial suppression hearing . . . because in seeking out the news the press . . . acts as an agent of the public at large."
4. John N. Maclean, "California Hearings Opened," *Chicago Tribune*, July 1, 1986.
5. Richard Carelli, "Court Opens Pretrial Criminal Proceedings to Public," Associated Press, June 30, 1986.
6. Knight-Ridder Newspapers, "Justices Support Public Access to Preliminary Hearings," *Orange County Register*, July 1, 1986.
7. Martin Salditch and Ronnie D. Smith, "Right of Access Upheld for Pretrial Hearings," *Press-Enterprise*, July 1, 1986.
8. J. M. Johnson, "Press Wins High Court Fight to Open Pretrial Hearings," *Sacramento Bee*, July 1, 1986.
9. Correction, *Press-Enterprise*, July 2, 1986. (In addition to an unrelated factual error, a line in the previous day's story was inadvertently dropped. The *Press-Enterprise* printed Mr. Rowe's full statement.)
10. Salditch and Smith, "Right of Access Upheld."
11. Ward Log, *Press-Enterprise II*, 1986.
12. "Open Trials, Open Pretrials," *Press-Enterprise*, July 1, 1986.
13. Bernius, interview with author, May 5, 2015.

Epilogue

1. People of the State of Colorado v. James Eagen Holmes, Case No. 12CR1522, Order Regarding Defendant's Request to Close Jury Selection to the Public D-154-a-2.
2. Steven Zansberg, Denver First Amendment lawyer, interview with author, November 27, 2015.

3. Presley v. Georgia 558 U.S. 209 (2010). Eric Presley, convicted of a cocaine trafficking offense in DeKalb County, Georgia, claimed his constitutional right to a fair trial was violated when the trial court excluded the public—in this case, his uncle—from voir dire. The judge said there wasn't enough space for him in the courtroom, there "was no need for the uncle to be present," and "his uncle cannot sit and intermingle with members of the jury panel." In a 7–2 decision Justices Clarence Thomas and Antonin Scalia dissenting, the U.S. Supreme Court ruled the trial court had improperly closed jury selection. "The conclusion that trial courts are required to consider alternatives to closure even when they are not offered by the parties is clear not only from this Court's precedents but also from the premise that [quoting *Press-Enterprise I*] '[t]he process of juror selection is itself a matter of importance, not simply to the adversaries but to the criminal justice system.'" In reversing the Georgia Supreme Court, the high court, again quoting *Press-Enterprise I*, said: "Even with findings adequate to support closure, the trial court's orders denying access to *voir dire* testimony failed to consider whether alternatives were available to protect the interests of the prospective jurors that the trial court's orders sought to guard. Absent consideration of alternatives to closure, the trial court could not constitutionally close the *voir dire*."

4. Zansberg, interview with author, March 24, 2017.

5. Through January 31, 2017, *Press-Enterprise I* had 4,543 "citing references"; *Press-Enterprise II*, 3,713 (Thomson Reuters Westlaw online database, http://guides.library.unr.edu/c.php?g=51173&p=331297 [subscription required]).

6. United States of America v. Dzhokhar A. Tsarnaev, United States District Court, District of Massachusetts, Civil Action No. 13-10200-GAO, Opinion and Order, February 13, 2015. Judge O'Toole's reasons, or findings, for keeping a "modest 'partial closure'" of the Tsarnaev voir dire: A "meaningful" voir dire requires juror candor about "personal history and beliefs." Voir dire in a high-profile case, in a courtroom packed with media and spectators, could discourage that candor. Even though the jurors' names were not being used, they might be identified in a larger public setting and possibly contacted by someone "outside the judicial process," resulting in "jury contamination." With restricted public and media presence, the courtroom would be much easier to manage (https://www.gpo.gov/fdsys/pkg/USCOURTS-mad-1_13-cr-10200/pdf/USCOURTS-mad-1_13-cr-10200-21.pdf).

7. U.S. v McVeigh 119 F.3d 806 (1997). The appeals court noted that the U.S. Supreme Court hadn't ruled definitively on whether there was a constitutional right of access to court documents but applied the test "assuming that the *Press-Enterprise II* right of access extends to at least some types of judicial documents."

8. United States v. Koubriti, 252 F. Supp. 2d 424 (E.D. Mich. 2003), Justia, http://law.justia.com/cases/federal/district-courts/fsupp2/252/424/2424742/.

9. ABC Inc. v. Stewart, 360 F.3d 90 (2d Cir. 2004).

10. Kristen Rasmussen, "Reporter Wins Appeal over Access to Horse Roundup," *Reporters Committee for Freedom of the Press*, February 14, 2012.

11. Levine, interview with author, February 2, 2015. Levine is a founding partner of Levine Sullivan Koch & Schulz law firm. Steven Zansberg, quoted above, is a partner in the firm's Denver, Colorado, office.

12. Sanford, interview with author, December 15, 2014.

13. Victoria Kim and Joel Rubin, "Jurors Tell of Troubles in L.A. Jails," *Los Angeles Times*, December 7, 2016. The newspaper was referring to the Supreme Court's unanimous ruling in *Press-Enterprise I*.

14. Gregg Leslie, Reporters Committee for Freedom of the Press, interview with author, April 17, 2015. The Reporters Committee, based in Washington DC, was founded in 1945. Its stated mission is: "To protect the right to gather and distribute news; to keep government accountable by ensuring access to public records, meetings and courtrooms; and to preserve the principles of free speech and unfettered press, as guaranteed by the First Amendment of the Constitution."

15. Hal Fuson, former vice president and general counsel for Copley Press, interview with author, February 16, 2015.

16. Zansberg, interview with author, November 20, 2015.

17. McBurney v. Young 569 U.S. _ (2013).

18. Levine, interview with author, February 2, 2015.

19. Fuson, interview with author, February 16, 2015.

20. Governor Pete Wilson appointed Waters to the Riverside County Municipal Court bench in 1997. When the courts were merged the following year, she became a superior court judge.

21. Waters, interview with author, April 30, 2015.

22. NBC Subsidiary (KNBC-TV), Inc. v. Superior Court (Locke), 1999 20 Cal.4th 5056924; Victoria Kim, "David M. Schacter Dies at 68; Presided over Several High-Profile Trials," *Los Angeles Times*, March 4, 2010.

23. NBC *Subsidiary (KNBC-TV), Inc. v. Superior Court (Locke)*.

24. Michael Hestrin, Riverside County district attorney, interview with author, February 29, 2016.

25. "FAC Remembers Founding Member, P-E Publisher Tim Hays," First Amendment Coalition, November 15, 2011, https://firstamendmentcoalition.org/2011/11/fac-founding-member-p-e-publisher-tim-hays-dies/.

26. Martin Salditch and Ronnie D. Smith, "Right of Access Upheld for Pretrial Hearings," *Press-Enterprise*, July 1, 1986.

BIBLIOGRAPHY

Unpublished and Archival Sources

Blackmun, Justice Harry, papers, Library of Congress, Docket 82-556, Box 393, and Docket 84-1560, Box 444.

Brennan, Justice William, papers, Library of Congress, Docket 82-556, Box I:638, and Docket 84-1560, Box I:706.

Powell, Justice Lewis, papers, Washington and Lee University, 82-556, http://law2.wlu.edu/deptimages/powell%20archives/82-556_Press-Enterprise _SuperiorCourtCalifornia.pdf; http://law2.wlu.edu/deptimages/powell %20archives/84-1560_PressEnterprise_SuperiorCourt.pdf.

Ringwald, George. "Unpublished History of the *Press-Enterprise.*"

Ward, James. Log & Binder. *Press-Enterprise I*, 1983.

———. Log & Binder. *Press-Enterprise II*, 1986.

———. "Not a Memoir." Unpublished memoir.

White, Justice Byron, papers, Library of Congress, Docket 82-556, Box I:610 and Box I:627, and Docket 84-1560, Box II:45.

Published Sources

ABC Inc. v. Stewart, 360 F.3d 90 (2d Cir. 2004).

Amicus Curiae Brief of State of California in Support of Petitioner, No. 84-1560 in the Supreme Court of the United States.

Bender, John R. "The Greatest First Amendment Victory Harry A. Blackmun Ever Lost: How the U.S. Supreme Court Decided Gannett Co. Inc. v. DePasquale." Paper presented to Law and Policy Division, Association for Education in Journalism and Mass Communications, Boston, August 7, 2009. http://citation.allacademic.com/meta/p_mla_apa_research _citation/3/7/5/0/4/pages375040/p375040-3.php.

Branzburg v. Hayes, 408 U.S. 665 (1972).

Brief Amici Curiae of American Newspaper Publishers Association, etc., No. 84-1560.

Brief Amici Curiae of California News Organizations in Support of Petitioner, No. 84-1560 in the Supreme Court of the United States.

Brief Amici Curiae of the Society of Professional Journalists, Sigma Delta Chi, etc., No. 82-556 in the Supreme Court of the United States.

Brief Amicus Curiae in Support of Respondent, No. 82-556 in the Supreme Court of the United States.

Brief Amicus Curiae of California Newspaper Publishers Association, No. 82-556 in the Supreme Court of the United States (in support of petition for Writ of Certiorari).

Brief Amicus Curiae of the California State Public Defender, No. 82-556 in the Supreme Court of the United States.

Brief for Petitioner on the Merits, No. 82-556 in the Supreme Court of the United States.

Brief in Opposition to Petition for Writ of Certiorari, No. 82-556 in the Supreme Court of the United States (Riverside County).

Brief of Amici Curiae in Support of Petitioner, Filed on Behalf of USA Today and Oakland Tribune, etc., No. 82-556 in the Supreme Court of the United States.

Brief of Amici Curiae in Support of Petition for Writ of Certiorari, No. 84-1560 in the Supreme Court of the United States.

Brief of Amicus Curiae, The State of California, No. 82-556 in the Supreme Court of the United States.

Brief of Amicus Curiae in Support of Petitioner Filed on Behalf of the District Attorney, County of Riverside.

Brief of Petitioner on the Merits, No. 84-1560 in the Supreme Court of the United States.

Brief of Real Party in Interest on the Merits, No. 84-1560 in the Supreme Court of the United States.

Brief of Respondent in Opposition to Petition for Writ of Certiorari, No. 84-1560 in the Supreme Court of the United States.

Brief of Respondent on the Merits, No. 82-556 in the Supreme Court of the United States.

Brief of Respondent on the Merits, No. 84-1560 in the Supreme Court of the United States.

Brief of the American Civil Liberties Union and the American Civil Liberties Union of Southern California as Amici Curiae, No. 84-1560 in the Supreme Court of the United States.

Brown, Patrick K. "The Rise and Fall of Rose Bird: A Career Killed by the Death Penalty." MA Program, California State University, Fullerton,

2007. https://www.cschs.org/wp-content/uploads/2014/03/CSCHS_2007
-Brown.pdf.

Craig v. Harney, 331 US 367 (1947).

Dickson, Del, ed. *The Supreme Court in Conference (1940–1985): The Private Discussions behind Nearly 300 Supreme Court Decisions*. New York: Oxford University Press, 2001.

Gannett Co., Inc. v. Hon. Daniel A. DePasquale, Brief of Petitioner, No. 77-1301 in the Supreme Court of the United States.

Gannett Co. v. DePasquale, 43 N.Y.2d 370, 372 N.E.2d 544 (1977).

Gannett v. DePasquale, 443 U.S. 368 (1979).

Geis, Gilbert. "Preliminary Hearings and the Press." UCLA *Law Review* 8 (1961).

Globe Newspaper Co. v. Superior Court, 102 S.Ct. 2613 (1982).

Graetz, Michael, and Linda Greenhouse. *The Burger Court and the Rise of the Judicial Right*. New York: Simon & Schuster, 2016.

Greenhouse, Linda. *Becoming Justice Blackmun*. New York: Times Books, 2005.

Henry, Robert. "The Players and the Play." In *The Burger Court: Counter-Revolution or Confirmation?*, edited by Bernard Schwartz, 13–54. New York: Oxford University Press, 1998.

Herbert v. Lando, 441 U.S. 15 (1979).

Hovey v. Superior Court of Alameda County, 28 Cal.3d 1 (1980).

Johnson v. Superior Court, 15 Cal.3d 248 [S.F. No. 23168. Supreme Court of California. September 19, 1975].

Joint Appendix submitted to the U.S. Supreme Court (No. 82-556) by the *Press-Enterprise* and Riverside County.

Joint Appendix submitted to the U.S. Supreme Court (No. 84-1560) by the *Press-Enterprise* and Riverside County.

King, Gilbert. *Devil in the Grove: Thurgood Marshall, the Groveland Boys, and the Dawn of a New America*. New York: HarperCollins, 2012.

Levine, Lee, and Stephen Wermiel. *The Progeny: Justice William J. Brennan's Fight to Preserve the Legacy of* New York Times v. Sullivan. Chicago: American Bar Association, 2014.

McBurney v. Young, 569 U.S. _ (2013).

Mellon, Carlotta H. *Howard H. [sic] (Tim) Hays Oral History Project, 2005–2007*. UC Riverside Public History Program. Riverside: University of California, Riverside, 2008.

NBC Subsidiary (KNBC-TV), Inc. v. Superior Court (Locke), 1999 20 Cal.4th 5056924.

Nebraska Press Association v. Stuart, 427 U.S. 539 (1976).

Neff, James. *The Wrong Man: The Final Verdict on the Dr. Sam Sheppard Murder Case*. New York: Random House, 2001.

People of the State of California v. Albert Greenwood Brown, Jr., Case No. CR 18104.

People of the State of California v. Robert Rubane Diaz, Case No. CR 19889.

People of the State of Colorado v. James Eagen Holmes, Case No. 12CR1522.

Petition for Writ of Certiorari, No. 82-556 in the Supreme Court of the United States (Press-Enterprise).

Petition for Writ of Certiorari, No. 84-1560 in the Supreme Court of the United States (Press-Enterprise).

Presley v. Georgia, 558 U.S. 209 (2010).

Press-Enterprise Co. v. Superior Court, 464 U.S. 501 (1984).

Press-Enterprise Co. v. Superior Court, 478 US 1 (1986).

Rehnquist, William H. *The Supreme Court: How It Was, How It Is.* New York: William Morrow, 1987.

Reply Brief of Petitioner, No. 82-556 in the Supreme Court of the United States.

Richmond Newspapers, Inc. v. Virginia, 448 U.S. 555 (1980).

San Jose Mercury News v. Municipal Court, 30 Cal.3d 498, 638 P.2d 655, 179 Cal.Rptr. 772 (1982).

Schwartz, Bernard. *The Ascent of Pragmatism: The Burger Court in Action.* Reading MA: Addison-Wesley, 1990.

———, ed. *The Burger Court: Counter-Revolution or Confirmation?* New York: Oxford University Press, 1998.

Sheppard v. Maxwell, 384 U.S. 333 (1966).

Stevens, John Paul. *Five Chiefs: A Supreme Court Memoir.* Boston: Little, Brown, 2011.

Uelmen, Gerald F. "Review of the Death Penalty Judgments by the Supreme Courts of California: A Tale of Two Courts." *Loyola of Los Angeles Law Review* 23 (1989).

United States of America v. Dzhokhar A. Tsarnaev, United States District Court, District of Massachusetts, Civil Action No. 13-10200-GAO.

United States v. Brooklier, 685 F.2d 1162 (9th Cir.1982).

United States v. Koubriti, 252 F. Supp. 2d 424 (E.D. Mich. 2003).

U.S. v. McVeigh, 119 F.3d 806 (1997).

Waller v. Georgia, 104 S.Ct. 2210 (1984).

Witherspoon v. Illinois, 391 U.S. 510 (1968).

Woodward, Bob, and Scott Armstrong. *The Brethren: Inside the Supreme Court.* New York: Simon & Schuster, 1979.

Zurcher v. Stanford Daily, 436 U.S. 547 (1978).

INDEX

ACLU. *See* American Civil Liberties Union (ACLU)

Adams, John, 61, 87

African Americans, 15, 17, 86, 104–5, 129

Ali, Muhammad, 2

Ali-Haimoud, Farouk, 195

alternatives to closed proceedings: circuit courts on, 145; *Gannett v. DePasquale* ruling on, 63; *Globe Newspaper Co. v. Superior Court* ruling on, 71; murder cases and, 80–81, 85, 155; *Nebraska Press Association v. Stuart* ruling on, 61–62; oral argument on, 113, 118–20, 175–76, 177; *Press-Enterprise* cases ruling on, 124, 125, 131, 189, 192, 193–94; *Richmond Newspapers, Inc. v. Virginia* ruling on, 11, 69; *San Diego Union* case and, 223n4. *See also* closure of court proceedings

American Civil Liberties Union (ACLU), 21–22, 64, 162–63

American Society of Newspaper Editors (ASNE), 36, 190

amicus briefs: California, 75, 81–83, 89, 159–61; case citations lacking in, 228n20; for county court, 75,

79–81, 100, 146, 154–56, 161–62; in *Gannett v. DePasquale*, 64; history influencing, 87, 90; importance of, 74–75; national, 75, 81, 84–89, 150–59, 222n35, 232n2; neutral, 75, 89–90; for *Press-Enterprise*, by news organizations, 44–45, 75, 142, 146, 150–51; for *Press-Enterprise*, by *Press-Enterprise*, 76–79, 151–54, 232n9; for *Press-Enterprise*, national, 84–88, 156–59, 222n35; for *Press-Enterprise*, state, 81–83, 160–61; for *Press-Enterprise*, various, 162–64; regulations on, 74–75, 220n1, 220n6

Arlington High School, 12, 15

arraignments, 160

ASNE. *See* American Society of Newspaper Editors (ASNE)

Aurora movie theater massacre, 192

awards for journalism, 38, 201

Bailey, F. Lee, 58

Baker & Hostetler, 81, 84, 87, 97, 157–58, 168, 201

Barnard, John, 92–95, 122, 138, 139, 153, 155, 187, 201, 229n3, 232n12

Been, Vicki, 147

Belli, Melvin, 37

Bentley, A. Lee, 147–48

Bernius, Robert, 63, 64, 97, 115, 191

Bettinger, James, 37, 39–40, 91, 151

Bill of Rights, 56, 70, 116, 181, 209n3, 217n1. *See also* Constitution; First Amendment; Sixth Amendment

Bird, Rose, 7, 78, 137, 138–39, 141, 143, 209n2, 229n2, 230n7, 231n23

Bird court, 78, 137, 144, 210n7

Blackmun, Harry: about, 56, 105, 110, 116, 226n3, 227n10; in cases influencing *Press-Enterprise* cases, 65–66, 68, 69, 71, 153–54, 168–69; papers of, 98, 215n9, 227n10, 231n10; in *Press-Enterprise I*, 48, 98, 123–25, 126–28; in *Press-Enterprise II*, 147, 149, 170, 176–77, 179, 183, 185–87

blacks, 15, 17, 86, 104–5, 129

Blackstone, William, 77

Blain, Joel, 35, 39, 41, 42

BLM. *See* Bureau of Land Management (BLM)

Blythin, Edward, 58, 59

Bolasky, Glyn, 5

The Book of English Law, 87

Boston Marathon bombing, 194

Bowen, Reeves, 104–5

Bowman, Chris, 21–22, 92, 151

Boyd, John: career of, 8, 200; on closing standards, 144; in Diaz murder case, 93–94; in *Press-Enterprise I*, 43, 76–79, 96–97, 101, 103, 114, 135–36; in *Press-Enterprise II*, 166, 167

Brandeis, Louis, 122, 193

Branzburg v. Hayes, 56, 64

Brennan, William: about, 103; in cases influencing *Press-Enterprise* cases, 47–48, 62, 67, 70, 72; in

Norco bank robbery case, 24; papers of, 215n9, 227n12; in *Press-Enterprise* cases, 112–13, 123–24, 127, 149, 185–86, 227n12

briefs. *See* amicus briefs; Petitions for Writ of Certiorari

Brown, Albert Greenwood, Jr., 15–18, 22, 24, 32, 90–91, 129, 131, 200, 222n46

Brown, Jerry, 7, 18

Browne, Kingsley, 125–26

Brown murder case: preliminary hearing in, 91, 222n1, 230n18; in *Press-Enterprise I*, 110, 128–29, 131, 215n42; sentencing in, 24; voir dire in, 17–21, 22–24, 90, 100, 125; voir dire transcript of, 32, 41, 44, 79–81, 124–25, 140–41. See also *Press-Enterprise I*

Brown v. Board of Education, 104, 105

Buffet, Warren, 36, 214n17

Bureau of Land Management (BLM), 196

Burger, Warren E.: Aaron Burr and, 159, 188; about, 56, 105, 107–8; in cases related to *Press-Enterprise* cases, 19, 61, 68, 69–70, 72, 86; as chief justice, 102–3, 106–8, 173–74; Harry Blackmun and, 105; historical interests of, 87–88, 157–59; papers of, 215n9; in *Press-Enterprise I*, 109–11, 120–23, 125–31, 215n6; in *Press-Enterprise II*, 175, 177, 181, 184, 186–89; reforms made by, 74, 105

Burger court, 1, 43, 55, 67, 85, 88, 102–8

Burr, Aaron, 61, 87, 88, 158–59, 176, 188

California Attorneys for Criminal Justice, 141

Neuharth, Allen, 64, 67
Newell, Mark, 46
Newspaper Enterprise Association, 38
Newsweek, 37
New York Court of Appeals, 63
New York Daily News, 58
New York Times, 55, 64, 66–67, 71,
108, 134–36, 190
Nichols, Terry, 194
Ninth Circuit Court of Appeals, 145,
229n5
Ninth District Court of Appeals, 85,
196, 209n3, 229n5
Nixon, Richard, 55, 56, 105–6, 107–8,
225n30
Norco bank robbery case, 5–6, 8–9,
11, 19, 24, 33, 41, 44–46

O'Connor, John, 107, 173
O'Connor, Sandra Day: about, 107;
as junior justice, 123; in Norco
bank robbery case, 24; papers of,
216n9; in *Press-Enterprise* cases,
47–48, 112–15, 118, 124, 174–75, 180
Oklahoma City bombing, 194–95
Old Bailey (English court), 88, 130
openness: advantages and disadvan-
tages of, 21, 77, 134–35, 142, 170,
171, 189, 193; as basic right, 85, 92,
144, 199, 202; history of, 85–90,
130, 171; oral argument on, 115,
178–79, 184; as policy consideration, 85–86; standards for overriding, 131, 155, 192, 196, 234n25
Opotowsky, Mel, 9–10, 151–52, 167,
173, 174, 200, 201
oral arguments: in *Press-Enterprise
I*, 109–21; in *Press-Enterprise II*,
173–84
Orange County CA, 226n8, 229n2

O'Toole, George A., 194, 236n6

Patterson, Tom, 36; *A Colony for
California*, 214n22
Pentagon Papers, 55, 64, 108, 118
Peoples Temple, 83, 221n30
*People v. Albert Greenwood Brown Jr.
See* Brown murder case
People v. Prairie Chicken, 160–61
People v. Robert Rubane Diaz. See
Diaz murder case
Perris CA, 25
Petitions for Writ of Certiorari, 11,
43–47, 138, 144–46, 147, 231n9
plea bargaining, 178, 185
Powell, Lewis: about, 56, 105–6; in
Gannett v. DePasquale, 66, 68, 76,
170, 187–88, 191, 235n3; papers of,
215n9, 231n10; in *Press-Enterprise
I*, 99, 118, 123–25, 130–31; in *Press-
Enterprise II*, 147–48, 149, 161, 170–
72, 175, 177, 185–86; in *Richmond
Newspapers, Inc. v. Virginia*, 70
Presley, Eric, 236n3
Presley v. Georgia, 194, 236n3
press: constitutional rights of, 91,
129, 143–44; dislike of, 19, 161,
233n20; First Amendment rights
of, 1–3, 44, 76, 85, 95, 132, 169, 186,
188, 189; proceedings closed to,
7, 8, 17, 23, 92, 160; proceedings
open to, 156–57, 193, 195; public
and, 235n3; shrinkage of, 199–
200; Sixth Amendment rights
and, 76, 169, 188; U.S. Supreme
Court favorable to, 55, 60–61, 69–
73, 108; U.S. Supreme Court unfavorable to, 56–61, 62, 64–67
press, prejudicial. *See* publicity, prejudicial

Index | 251

Ward, Jim (*cont.*)

presentation, 151, 168, 173–79, 183–84, 187; as *Press-Enterprise* lawyer, 3; Rose Bird and, 229n2; on Thurgood Marshall, 117; and Tim Hays, 53–54; voir dire work of, 10, 11, 19–21, 24, 32, 122

Ward family, 50–52, 53, 101, 173

Warren, Earl, 37, 225n30

Washington and Lee University, 215n9

Washington Literacy Council, 201

Washington Post, 32, 36, 66, 71, 134–36, 139, 222n3

Waters, Sharon: about, 77–78, 237n20; Diaz murder case and, 93; in *Press-Enterprise I*, 78, 96–97, 101, 135, 198; in *Press-Enterprise II*, 151–52, 166–67, 173, 190, 198, 224n3

Weinman, Carl A., 58

White, Byron: about, 103–4; in *Branzburg v. Hayes*, 56; opinions of, 108; papers of, 215n9; in *Press-Enterprise* cases, 115, 123–24, 149, 178, 183

White, Dan, 162

Wieand, Adrienne, 157–59, 168, 188, 201

Wilson, Pete, 237n20

Wingard, Jean, 36

Witherspoon v. Illinois, 210n7

witnesses: compared to jurors, 82, 87; in murder cases, 15–16, 28–29, 232n12; oral argument on, 180–81; press and, 59; secret testimony of, 160; swearing in of, 10–11, 21

Worthington, Mickey, 25

Zansberg, Steven, 193–94, 197, 237n11

Zurcher v. Stanford Daily, 56